WORDS LIKE ARROWS
ARROWS

A TREASURY OF YIDDISH FOLK SAYINGS

COMPILED BY
SHIRLEY KUMOVE
ILLUSTRATED BY
FRANK NEWFELD

D0870181

WARNER BOOKS

A Warner Communications Company

Warner Books Edition
Copyright © 1984 by University of Toronto Press
All rights reserved.

This Warner Books edition is published by arrangement with
Schocken Books, 62 Cooper Square, New York, NY 10003

This book was originally published in Canada by the
University of Toronto Press.

Warner Books, Inc., 666 Fifth Avenue, New York, NY 10103

W A Warner Communications Company

Printed in the United States of America
First Warner Books Printing: April 1986
10 9 8 7 6 5 4 3 2 1

Designed by William Rueter RCA

Library of Congress Cataloging-in-Publication Data
Main entry under title:

Words like arrows.

1. Proverbs, Yiddish. 2. Proverbs, Yiddish—
Translations into English. 3. Proverbs, English—
Translations from Yiddish. I. Kumove, Shirley,
1931–   II. Newfeld, Frank, 1928–
PN6519.J5W67 1986   398′.9′37   85-20232
ISBN 0-446-38193-4 (U.S.A.) (pbk.)

This book is
dedicated to my parents

רבקה לעסמאַן רעכט
Rivka Lessman Recht
and
צבי מאיר רעכט ז״ל
Tsvi Mayer Recht z''l
1904–1981

CONTENTS

LIST OF SUBJECTS

PREFACE

There has developed in recent years a growing interest in Jewish subjects, particularly in the world of one's parents and grandparents. This is based upon a sincere and genuine desire to understand the values and aspirations which sustained generations of eastern European Jewry, as well as upon romantic yearnings and a nostalgia for a world which had a special warmth and charm of its own.

This work is an attempt to offer an insight into the life of Yiddish-speaking Jews in Eastern Europe and the New World, as it reveals itself through thousands of folk sayings. These sayings reflect the experience of millions of people over a span of many generations.

For several years I have been collecting, making notes, cataloguing, and translating from the rich lore of Yiddish folk sayings. What began as a hobby has become an obsession: to make available that great storehouse of aphorisms, maxims, pithy sayings, proverbs, and witticisms of the Yiddish-speaking world of Eastern Europe and immigrant North America. It is my hope to preserve them for this and future generations. The text is based upon my collection gathered over the years with the help of relatives, friends and acquaintances, as well as on extended reading on the subject.

The sayings are classified by subject heading in order to clarify their meanings. I did not attempt to locate original sources or to place them in specific geographical, social, or economic contexts, except as indicated by the classification system. Nor have I attempted to place them within the framework of sociological or linguistic theory, although I have given some social and historical background in the introduction.

The sayings have been gathered through oral transmission or from writings identifying them as folk material. Occasionally they have been found in the writings of such eminent authors as Sholem Aleichem, Bialik, and others, who have been known to incorporate folk material in their writings, and their inclusion here is based on that belief. Some of the sayings have their origins in the Bible, Talmud, and other sacred writings; their translation into Yiddish enabled them to be incorporated into daily life. The sources from which these sayings are taken are not cited, as they range over a wide area, are often attributable to more than one source, and appear in more than one variation.

Except for correcting the most obvious errors of grammar, spelling, and pronunciation, I have not tampered with the sayings. They are rendered as received. In considering the problems of translation, liberties had to be taken with the text and literal exactness sometimes had to be sacrificed for other considerations. Throughout, I have borne in mind the following:

He falsifies who renders a verse just as it looks.

Talmud, Kiddushin

and

Sometimes one must translate not the lines themselves but what is written between them.

Chaim Nachman Bialik

I have tried to render as faithful a translation as possible, maintaining the characteristics of the original: that is, the brevity, rhyme, playfulness, contrasts, mood, and the occasional peculiarities of speech. In specific situations, it became necessary to depart somewhat from the strictly literal because the word, phrase, or thought would have little or no meaning outside the Yiddish-speaking world.

Translating from the Yiddish offers several challenges beyond those usually associated with this type of work. Translation inevitably involves distortion; one must weigh each word or turn of phrase. In the case of Yiddish, this is further complicated by the inclusion into colloquial usage of Biblical and Talmudic words, phrases, and quotations. Maurice Samuel, in his book *In Praise of Yiddish*, discusses the way Hebrew forms a canopy over the mundane world of Yiddish. He writes: 'The fusion of the secular and sacred in Yiddish makes possible a charming transition from the jocular to the solemn and back again. Well-worn colloquialisms and dignified passages jostle popular interjections without giving or taking offense.' The problem remains a difficult one: how to bring to life that world which exists beneath the layer of words and make accessible the treasure which this culture has bequeathed us.

I wish to acknowledge with appreciation several works which were frequently consulted and were especially useful in the preparation of this text.

Most of the sayings in this book were received orally and sometimes distorted and unclear, especially the Hebrew and Slavic words and phrases. In order to arrive at greater precision and clarity of the given material, I consulted a thesaurus of the Yiddish language, *Der oytser fun der yidisher shprakh* by Nokhem Shtutshkof. This volume enabled me to obtain correct spellings and to arrive at standard Yiddish pronunciation. In addition to being a source of many of the sayings and contributing valuable information and guidance, *Der oytser* provided hours of pleasurable exploration.

Two works by Uriel Weinreich, *College Yiddish* and *Modern English-Yiddish, Yiddish-English Dictionary,* were essential aids and the standard by which I was guided in questions of grammar, spelling, transliteration, and translation. *The English-Yiddish, Yiddish-English Dictionary* of Aleksander Harkavy was most useful for the definitions of localisms and words popular at the time of publication (1898). *Yidishe shprikhverter un redensarten* by Ignats Bernstein, published in 1908, is the massive work on this subject. I obtained access to this volume late in my research through the assistance of the YIVO Institute for Jewish Research in New York. This volume was most useful for supplementary notes and explanations of abstruse sayings. These scholarly works greatly facilitated my research and enabled me to proceed with greater accuracy and assurance than would otherwise have been the case.

The original Yiddish text is included so that both the serious student and the interested reader can fully appreciate the pungent flavour of the original. Transcription is provided as well as translation into English.

I have refrained from supplying lengthy explanatory notes to the text, not wishing to drown the sayings in a sea of explication. A glossary defining frequently used Hebrew and Yiddish terms appears on pages 263–6. The main form of explanation is provided by the headings, which were designed to clarify the meaning of the individual saying. There are exceptions to this general practise; some sayings require further elucidation as they refer to customs and practises with which the general reader may not be familiar. It is hoped that the additional notes will clarify otherwise obscure sayings.

This book was undertaken because of a dissatisfaction with the work that is currently available in English. In the process of completing this undertaking, I have been taught the truth of the maxim:

עס איז לײַכטער צו זײַן אַ מבקר װי אַ מחבר.

Es iz laykhter tsu zayn a mevaker vi a mekhaber.

It is easier to be a critic than an author.

My approach to this work stems from two motivations. One is my recognition of the great void in Jewish life created by the Holocaust, which destroyed an organic Yiddish culture in Eastern Europe. To imagine that void and to appreciate what was lost is one of the aims of this volume. The other motivation for this work stems from my rejection of what the eminent historian Salo Baron has called 'the lachrymose approach to Jewish history,' a recitation of one misfortune after another. Baron himself has chosen to emphasize the spiritual and social richness of Jewish communal life, which was varied and dynamic in spite of the interferences and interruptions from a hostile environment. This collection, then, is my own modest contribution to the record of a positive Jewish experience.

Such a collection can never be considered complete. New material is constantly being brought to my attention. The work must, therefore, be considered unfinished. In offering the volume to the reader at this time, I am guided by the dictum:

It is not incumbent upon you to finish the work, neither are you free to desist from it.

Pirkei avot 2:21

I wish to thank the following:

My husband Aryeh, whose knowledge and understanding of Jewish learning and culture together with his inexhaustible patience encouraged me through every stage to complete this task. His grasp of the unique problems involved was especially helpful in translating the material and editing the manuscript.

My son Aaron, for his critical evaluation of the manuscript and helpful suggestions for improvement. My son Joel, for his literary and editorial suggestions, good humour and patience through countless revisions to the text.

My parents Tsvi Mayer z''l and Rivka Recht, who reviewed the work in progress and contributed their extensive knowledge of the Yiddish language and its literature, providing insight into difficult and obscure words and phrases. It is an abiding sorrow that my father was not permitted to live to see the book in print.

Ben Kayfetz for his kind assistance and advice.

Shirley Rebecca Diamond, Shoshana Disenhouse Morag, and Anne Medres Glass z''l, for their reviews and suggestions on parts of the manuscript.

Marvin Herzog, Professor of Yiddish Language and Literature, Columbia University, for providing a number of useful suggestions. Beatrice Silverman-Weinreich and Dina Abramovitz of the YIVO Institute for Jewish Research in New York for their help in locating useful material.

Dr Ron Schoeffel, editor, University of Toronto Press, for his continued support and encouragement in preparing this manuscript for publication.

Brina Rose, whose expert knowledge of Yiddish grammar and syntax helped clarify and correct the text. It was a particular pleasure to work with her, the daughter of my Yiddish teachers, the late Esther (Stere) and Moshe Menachovsky.

I extend appreciation to my relatives and friends who supplied me with many sayings and to my teachers and the Jewish community of Toronto for providing a stimulating environment in which to carry on this work.

Toronto, Ontario
30 September 1982

EXPLANATORY NOTES

For the purposes of this work, the method of transcription used is the one established by the YIVO Institute for Jewish Research. This is the 'standard' for Yiddish speech and is consistently used in academic circles today. The only deviations from this standard are those dictated by the necessity of adhering to the rhyme which is sometimes related to regional speech.

Sound	Example in text	English equivalent
Vowels:		
a	h*a*rts	p*a*rt
e	k*e*n	p*e*n
i	d*i*	m*e*
i	v*i*sn	p*i*n*
i	v*a*yt	fire
o	h*o*t	b*o*re
u	*u*nter	h*oo*d
oy	h*oy*z	b*oy*
ey	m*ey*dl	w*ay*
Consonants:		
g	*g*ib	*g*ive
kh	no*kh*	Ba*ch*
ts	tan*ts*	gu*ts*
tsh	men*tsh*	*ch*air
dz	un*dz*er	boun*ds*
zh	gri*zh*en	sei*z*ure

*Where the i is followed by a syllable beginning with another vowel (kli'entn, mi'es, etc.) or ends the word (di, vi, etc.) the long i is used. Where the i is followed by a consonant, the short i is used (visn, tsindn, etc.).

In order to avoid confusion for the English-speaking reader, I have made slight modifications. Where two vowels occur together in the middle of a word and both are to be sounded, an apostrophe is inserted between them to so indicate. Where a 'ph' or 'sh' appear together in the middle of a word and both letters are to be separately pronounced, an apostrophe is inserted to so indicate.

Words and phrases of Hebrew-Aramaic origin are transcribed according to their pronunciation in Standard Yiddish.

( ) Words occurring within parentheses in both transcription and translation denote variations in the same saying.

[ ] Words occurring within square brackets in translation only offer clarification of the text.

" "Double quotation marks signify Biblical or Talmudic quotations.

KEY TO SOURCES

Letters in small capitals denote the source of the saying and are explained according to the following:

AC Those sayings gathered from among the author's circle of family, friends, and acquaintances.

IB Ignaz Bernstein

IF Israel Furman

LMF Lillian Mermin Feinsilver

SK Sholem Katz

SM Sholem Miller

P Popular saying frequently heard by the author.

MS Maurice Samuel

NS Nokhem Shtutshkof

MW Max Weinreich

WZ Weltman & Zukerman

Authors cited here are listed under the Bibliography.

Many sayings listed under 'AC' and 'P' are also found in *Yidishe shprikhverter un redensarten* by Ignaz Bernstein and in *Der oytser fun der yidisher shprakh* by Nokhem Shtutshkof. Their citing under these headings indicates that they are still in use or remembered by my informants, who include European Jews, as well as those from North America, Great Britain, Israel, South Africa, and South America.

In dealing with written material, I found occasional archaisms of language as well as the inevitable typographical errors. In these cases, adjustments and corrections were made.

INTRODUCTION

THE YIDDISH LANGUAGE

The Yiddish language is almost one thousand years old. Yiddish had its origins in the Rhineland when Jews, migrating from northern France, began to speak a Germanic vernacular which incorporated elements of Biblical Hebrew, Old French, and Italian. With the movement into Poland, Slavic elements were introduced and modified. The new language was written phonetically using the letters of the Hebrew alphabet. Out of these disparate elements the Yiddish language was born. Up to the end of the eighteenth century, Yiddish was spoken in Jewish communities from Holland to the Ukraine.

Historically, Yiddish and Hebrew formed an inseparable partnership: one was the language of the sacred, 'loshn koydesh' (holy tongue); the other the language of the everyday, affectionately termed 'mame loshn' (mother tongue). Hebrew was the language of liturgical concerns reserved for prayer, study, and scholarship, while Yiddish became the language of day-to-day life expressing the homely events, joys, and sorrows of the daily struggle for survival.

With the Age of Englightment in the eighteenth century and industrial development in the nineteenth, Jews for the first time found opportunities to move into the mainstream of European economic, political, and cultural life. Yiddish began to be discarded in favour of the major languages of Europe. It virtually disappeared in Western Europe; in Eastern Europe it remained alive though constantly threatened by the increasing use of Polish, Russian, and other languages. It is ironic that in the period in which Jews were discarding Yiddish, there should occur the flowering of the great achievements in Yiddish literature. In the last quarter of the nineteenth and the first quarter of the twentieth century, Yiddish literature generated and developed a rich, impressive, and fairly sophisticated body of work comprising novels, stories, poetry, plays, social criticism, and journalism. World recognition, although belated, now acknowledges the achievements of Yiddish literature with the awarding of the Nobel prize to I.B. Singer, one of its foremost luminaries.

Remarkably, despite variations in dialect and pronunciation, barriers of national boundaries, and linguistic pressures from the outside world, the language was understood by Yiddish-speaking Jews from one end of Europe to the other. The Zionist Movement promoted the use of Hebrew, instead of Yiddish, as the language of national revival. From the time of the British Mandate, Hebrew was the official language of Jewish settlements in Palestine and later of the State of Israel. Yiddish, however, was tenacious and resilient. Its literature continued to prod and stir, to remind one that the potential for human fulfillment exists even under the most adverse circumstances.

One mourns the passing of the Jewish world of Eastern Europe, but the language it created lives on. The obituary for Yiddish is premature and unseemly. True, the numbers who speak this language are greatly reduced, yet they constitute a sizeable group. In New York, London, Paris, Tel Aviv, Johannesburg, Buenos Aires, and Toronto, Yiddish is still spoken. Younger generations of students in the universities evince an interest in studying the language. While academic instruction alone does not sustain a language, one is hopeful that it will survive and someday blossom and produce new fruit. In an age which has witnessed the miracle of Jewish survival after the Holocaust and the miracle of the rebirth of the Jewish State, one remains optimistic that Yiddish will yet transcend the difficulties and that this unique distillation of the Jewish experience will be revived and regenerated.

JEWISH LIFE IN EASTERN EUROPE

Jewish life in Eastern Europe was characterized by great extremes. Periods of relative well-being and harmony with the external environment alternated with periods of direst poverty, persecution, and cultural isolation.

Although Jews lived in Poland as early as the tenth century, it was not until the fourteenth century that they were allowed entrance in large numbers. Expelled from France and fleeing the Black Death, they found a safe haven in Poland. Poland was a feudal state dependent on its peasantry; it desperately needed middlemen, skilled artisans, and financiers. Jews were received as a vital element in the population. When the Polish Kingdom expanded into Lithuania, the Ukraine, and White Russia, the Jews followed.

They organized themselves into communities with their own councils, which regulated every phase of life, from the assessment and collection of taxes to the supervision of education and the cemeteries. These local councils were, in turn, subject to a central authority known as the 'Council of Four Lands,' which dealt

with political, financial, religious, and ethical matters. This elaborate organiza-
tion of a 'state within a state' gave great impetus to Torah education. Literacy
was universal and learning highly revered. In no other country was the study
of Torah so widespread.

Jews vicariously relived the ancient Temple ritual, the agricultural cycles, and the historic events of their ancient homeland. To those in exile these practises had little immediate relevance, yet the Jews were able to transcend the present conditions of their lives and make these observances rich and meaningful, a vital element in their survival.

Until the nineteenth century, most Jews lived in shtetlekh (small towns). Life was highly organized. The social structure was hierarchical, with rabbis, scholars, and the few wealthy merchants at the top. On the bottom were the impoverished, who were sustained by the community. The tradesmen and artisans who made up the majority were found in the middle.

Industry was not yet developed; a religious way of life dominated. Boys were sent to kheyder (religious school) at an early age, while girls remained at home to help with the household chores. An emphasis on study prevailed. The family that could support a scholar merited social privileges on earth as well as the expectation of a heavenly reward in the afterlife. The class of scholars that resulted became an intellectual aristocracy wielding considerable power in the life of the community.

This golden age was of brief duration. The original welcome gradually faded and the Jewish communities began to be affected by the major upheavals in Poland and the rest of Europe. The decline of the powerful Polish state and corruption in Polish society produced anti-Jewish sentiments and reactions. Ukrainian resentment of Polish domination turned against the Jews, culminating in the uprising of 1648, led by Bogdan Chmielnitski, which ravaged and wiped out over six hundred communities. More than a hundred thousand Jews perished, a number not exceeded until World War II.

The expansion of the Russian Empire into Lithuania and the Ukraine caused further dislocation. Napoleon's sweep through Europe brought with it rising expectations of civil equality and enlightenment. But the splitting of the Polish Kingdom among Russia, Austria, and Prussia at the end of the eighteenth century brought most Jews under the domination of Russia, a country whose treatment of the Jews was not noted for tolerance. Russian bigotry culminated in the creation of the 'Pale of Settlement' which restricted and confined Jews to limited areas. These soon became impoverished and congested. By the late nineteenth century life was grim, poverty endemic, and insecurity the norm.

Concurrent with the external pressures, an internal decline began to manifest itself. The once orderly life of the Jewish communities became rent with increasingly divisive forces and the traditional social structure was steadily weakening. The rise of the various Messianic movements added to the turmoil and unrest. Hassidism challenged the prevailing traditional rabbinic structure. The Haskalah (Enlightenment) movement sought to broaden and reconstruct the economic and cultural life and attracted large numbers of young people to the idea of introducing Western European ways into the oppressed Jewish community. With industrialization there arose a Jewish working class influenced by socialist thought and secular learning. Zionism encouraged Jews to look to the ancient homeland in the Land of Israel for the solution of their problems. It urged more and more Jews to think of redemption as an act of positive Jewish will. A wealthy, assimilated class of Jews had meanwhile developed which was susceptible to cosmopolitan influences. Thousands tried to escape the narrow confines of Jewish life by conversion to Christianity.

Jews began to leave the shtetlekh for the larger towns, and by the late nineteenth century most Jews lived in the cities. Ruth Rubin in her book *Voices of a People* gives us a colorful account of the variety, congestion, and frenetic activity found in the Jewish quarters of these cities:

Their courtyards, marketplaces, streets and alleys were full of the sounds and smells, light and shadows of the various social strata rubbing shoulders: the prosperous Chassidic rebeyim in their satin coats, circular hats, white socks and slippers; the emaciated free-thinking Maskilim, clean-shaven in their top hats and short jackets; the Misnagdim in their halfway measures in short-long coats, trimmed beards, cloth caps and canes. The marketplaces were full of fishmongers and butcher stalls, millers and furniture menders, servant girls and women shoppers, porters and stallkeepers, women vendors with baskets and sacks, and children running hither and thither in this swarming beehive. Haggling went on at the stalls and booths, at the baskets and portable tables displaying fruit, vegetables, berries, baked wares, hardware, earthenware, woodenware, dry goods, barrels of herring, jars of pickles, women's aprons, men's shirts and caps, children's underwear and pants.

And from this symphony of bargaining and haggling, shouting and chanting . . . separate voices could be heard, energetically calling out their particular merchandise.

Under the canopy of devotion to religious learning and study there existed another layer of people who were ignorant, superstitious, and sometimes corrupt. Manual labor was frequently regarded as a mark of social disgrace, a badge of coarseness and ignorance. The authority of the rabbis broke down and young people, exposed to the alien influences of the non-Jewish world with which they now lived in such close proximity, became 'contaminated.' Besieged from without and divided within, Jews continued to conduct their business, arrange marriages, bear children, educate their young, and die, all within the age-old laws and customs, but the core of the family and the entire structure of the Jewish community were deeply affected.

With the restrictive legislation and the wave of pogroms of the 1880s, a large-scale exodus of Jews began to the safe havens of North and South America, South Africa, and other places. This period also brought increasing numbers to Palestine and gave impetus to the birth of a Zionist movement among the young men and women who were devotees of the Haskalah movement. Finally, the Nazi period brought about the tragic close of this chapter of Jewish life.

In spite of the decline and finally the complete destruction of this, the largest Jewish community of modern times, the Eastern European influence and the Yiddish language found a home in the new countries of settlement, and many of the institutions developed in the old home were transplanted and modified in the new setting.

THE YIDDISH FOLK SAYING

A folk saying is an expression transmitted orally from one person to another, containing a summation of spiritual, cultural, or ethical values. It usually suggests a course of action, conveys guidance for behavior, or passes judgment on people or events. It arises and is maintained by the needs and experiences of daily life. Folk sayings are often contradictory and have no unified methodology. They have no official status according to rabbinic or secular authority; their influence derives from widespread acceptance and use. To quote a popular epigram, a folk saying is 'the wisdom of many and the wit of one.'

These sayings are embedded in the character of Jewish life, in which words played so important a part. Jews are called People of the Book, but they also consider themselves people of the word. Yiddish culture, containing a world of talkers, is oriented towards speech. This being so, one is well advised to heed the warning inherent in the following maxim:

אויף דער שפיץ צונג ליגט די גאַנצע וועלט.

The entire world rests on the tip of the tongue.
Oyf der shpits tsung ligt di gantse velt.

Jews discussed, argued, and disputed the Bible, the Talmud, religious, legal, and ethical problems, as well as any other subject of interest. This was a normal part of social life. Talking was a major sport and hobby of Jews in Eastern Europe. It was the playfulness of a world without leisure refreshing itself with irrepressible wit. In this regard no distinction was made between male and female, rich and poor, young and old. Everyone was accorded equal respect for the ability to call up a terse, pithy, and well-placed saying or witticism. Jews admired people who could sum up complicated ideas in a few choice words, who could hold their own or get the better of an argument. Often the preamble *was* the point, since the manner of presentation could be more provocative, stimulating, and entertaining than the conclusions reached.

To Jews, a world without lively discourse was incomprehensible. With simple logic they concluded:

וועַן דער פֿערד וואָלט געהאַט וואָס צו זאָגן-וואָלט ער גערעדט.

If the horse had anything to say – it would speak up.

Ven der ferd volt gehat vos tsu zogn - volt er geret.

In a world where most of the senses were repressed and constrained, one faculty remained intact – speech. A sharp wit which mocked and jeered at the contradictions of life was heightened and refined to a fine art.

People talked so much they had to be reminded that:

אַ וואָרט איז ווי אַ פֿײַל-ביידע האָבן גרויסע אײַל.

A word and an arrow are the same – both deliver with speedy aim.

A vort iz vi a fayl – beyde hobn groyse ayl.

Jews so recognized in themselves their own highly developed sharpness of tongue that they offered up the prayer:

גאָט זאָל אָפהיטן פֿון גוישע הענט און ייִדישע רייד.

God protect us from Gentile hands and from Jewish tongues.

Got zol op'hitn fun goyishe hent un yidishe reyd.

Their qualms with regard to gossip and tale-bearing were wryly noted in:

פֿון ייִדישע רייד קען מען זיך ניט אָפּוואַשן אפֿילו אין צען וואַסערן.

One cannot cleanse oneself from Jewish talk even in ten waters.

Fun yidishe reyd ken men zikh nit opvashn afile in tsen vasern.

Saying such as these were admonitions that words had the potential and power to cause great harm.

Yiddish sayings range from commentary on the homeliest aspects of everyday life to the loftiest aspirations of the Jewish people. However, the greatest emphasis, as reflected in this collection, is on the daily struggle for survival: the exigencies of earning a living, bearing and raising children, educating the young, arranging marriages, growing old and dying. Jews, a loquacious people, were full of homespun counsel and folk wisdom. But for every Polonius dispensing his fatuous advice, there were dozens of jesters, punsters, and irreverent wags. Humor was the leavening agent in a life of unremitting toil, deprivation, and fear.

Irving Howe and Eliezer Greenberg in their introduction to *A Treasury of Yid-dish Stories* point out that 'This folk humor provides a means of indirect social aggression and at other times, it releases a mordant self-criticism.' Contradic-tions abound on every page of this collection. Side by side, one finds paradoxical attitudes, irony, skepticism, and downright cynicism juxtaposed with artless simplicity and charming naiveté.

Comparisons can easily be made between specific sayings in this collection and those of other cultures. Uriel Weinreich makes a significant point in describ-ing the role of Jews in the development of European folklore. He states: 'Jewish folklore is of great interest not only to people studying Jewish culture but also to students of comparative literature. That there are similarities in the folklore of distant peoples is a well-known fact. But the more the actual processes of folklore diffusion are studied, the more the active role of the Jews as agents of diffusion is brought to light. Because of their wide dispersion and their participa-tion in trade and commerce, both international and local, the Jews were for cen-turies in a position to carry popular lore from one old country to another' (*Col-lege Yiddish*, p. 153).

From their particular origins, the essence of these sayings has passed into the mainstream of more than one culture. It has found its way into contemporary English literature and idiom and into the world of entertainment. As early as 1902, the great Yiddish literary critic Ba'al Makhshoves (pen name for A. Eliashev) wrote: 'The Gentiles think highly of Jewish fish and Jewish wit. Take up any collection of their witticisms and you will soon find a joke or epithet that originated in some synagogue courtyard or bathhouse . . .' (*Collected Writings*). The world of Ba'al Makhshoves is no more and Yiddish speech is in a twilight. Nevertheless, the spirit and style of these sayings are still heard wherever Jews congregate, embodying the variety of responses to experience, the dreams, the aspirations, and the yearnings, the caustic eye turned on the pretensions of the world, the rejoicing over good news, and the grief in the face of adversity. It is the distillation of Jewish life in Eastern Europe and immigrant life in North America; a legacy for future generations attesting to an indomitability of will and an irrepressible zest for living.

WORDS LIKE ARROWS

אַ װאָרט איז װי אַ פײַל-בײַדע האָבן נרױסע אײַל

A word and an arrow are the same – both deliver with speedy aim.

A vort is vi a fayl – beyde hobn groyse ayl

ABILITY

אַז דער תלמיד איז אַ וווילער איז
דער רבי אויך אַ וווילער.

**If the pupil is good, the rabbi is
good.**
*Az der talmed iz a voyler iz der
rebe oykh a voyler.* IB

אַז מען קען ניט איז ערגער ווי מען
האָט ניט.

**Not being able is worse than not
having.**
*Az men ken nit iz erger vi men hot
nit.* AC

דעם שׂכל פֿון שווימען קען איך
אָבער שווימען איז אַן אַנדערע זאַך.

**I know all about swimming but
doing it is another matter.**
*Dem seykhl fun shvimen ken ikh
ober shvimen iz an andere zakh.* AC

געוואָרן איז ניט געבוירן.

Became so isn't born so.
Gevorn iz nit geborn. IB

קען מען - מעג מען.

If you can – do!
Ken men – meg men. NS

אַ בלינדע הון קען אויך
אַמאָל געפֿינען אַ קערנדל.

**Even a blind hen sometimes
finds a kernel.**
*A blinde hun ken oykh amol
gefinen a kerndl.* NS

4

בלינדע

אויף אַ נידעריקן טישל שפּרינגען אַלע ציגן.	All goats are able to jump onto a low table. *Oyf a niderikn tishl shpringen ale tsign.* AC
טאַטע-מאַמע איז אַ קונץ צו זײַן און אַלע נעמען עס זיך אונטער.	To be a parent takes know-how but everyone takes it on anyhow. *Tateh-mame iz a kunts tsu zayn un ale nemen es zikh unter.* NS

ABSURDITY

אַ בחור אַ שדכן , אַ מויד אַ באָבע - קען ניט זײַן.	A bachelor a match-maker, a spinster a grandmother cannot be. *A bokher a shatkhn, a moyd a bobe – ken nit zayn.* IB
אַז אַ טאָרבע פֿלעקער איז קײַלעכדיק איז די לבנה שפּיציק.	If a pack of spots is round then the moon is pointed. [Commentary on a non-sequitur] *Az a torbe fleker iz kaylekhdik iz di levone shpitsik.* NS
אַ חופּה אָן אַ כּלה ?	A wedding without the bride? *A khupe on a kale?* AC

איבער דעם בלאָזט
מען המן און מען קלאַפּט שופר.

In that case, you blow Haman,
and beat the shofar.
*Iber dem blozt men homen un men
klapt shoyfer.* NS

ADORNMENT

אַ מיידל דאַרף זיך פּוצן פֿאַר
פֿרעמדע בחורים און אַ ווײַבל פֿאַרן
אייגענעם מאַן

A girl should pretty herself for
her suitors and a young wife for
her husband.
*A meydl darf zikh putsn far fremde
bokherim un a vaybl farn eygenem
man.* NS

אַז די באָבע פּוצט זיך זעט זי
אויך אויס ווי אַ מענטש.

When grandma pretties herself,
she also looks like a somebody.
*Az di bobe putst zikh zet zi oykh
oys vi a mentsh.* NS

אַז מען טוט אָן שיין אַ בעזעם
איז ער אויך שיין.

Dress up a broom and it will
also look nice.
*Az men tut on sheyn a bezem iz er
oykh sheyn.* NS

געפּרעגלט אין האָניק איז
רעטעך אויך אַ מאכל.

Fried in honey, a radish is also a
delicacy.
*Gepreglt in honik iz retekh oykh a
maykhl.* IB

קנײַפּ דיר די באַקן און שטעל
די פֿאַרב פֿאַר לײַטן.

Pinch your cheeks for color
before you go among people.
*Knayp dir di bakn un shtel di farb
far laytn.* NS

ווען די פּאַווע וואָלט ניט געהאַט
די שיינע פֿעדערן וואָלט זיך
קיינער אויף איר ניט אומגעקוקט.

If the peacock didn't have
beautiful feathers, no one would
look at it.
*Ven di pave volt nit gehat di
sheyne federn volt zikh keyner oyf
ir nit umgekukt.* IB

ADVICE

א קליינע עצה מאכט
געזונט די פלייצע.

A little advice can heal a backache.
A kleyne eytse makht gezunt di pleytse. NS

דאָס בעסטע פֿערד דאַרף
האָבן אַ בײַטש און דער
קלינסטער מענטש אַן עצה.

The best horse needs a whip and the smartest person needs advice.
Dos beste ferd darf hobn a baytsh un der kligster mentsh an eytse. IB

פֿרעג אַן עצה בײַ יענעם און
האָב דיין שׂכל בײַ זיך.

Ask another's advice but keep your own counsel.
Freg an eytse bay yenem un hob dayn seykhl bay zikh. NS

אָדער עס העלפֿט ניט אָדער מען
דאַרף עס ניט.

Either it doesn't help or you don't need it.
Oder es helft nit oder men darf es nit. P

ווען איינער ראָט דיר–הער, נאָר
פֿאַר דיר באַקלער.

To another's advice – listen; but to your own counsel, hearken.
Ven eyner rot dir – her, nor far dir bakler. NS

AGING

אַ חזן אויף דער עלטער בילט
ווי אַ הונט און עסט ווי אַ פֿערד.

A cantor past his prime howls like a dog and eats like a horse.
A khazn oyf der elter bilt vi a hunt un est vi a ferd. NS

אַלטע הייַזער – פֿיל מייַז, אַלטע
פֿיטערס – פֿיל לייַז.

Old houses – many mice, old furs – many lice.
Alte hayzer – fil mayz, alte fiters – fil layz. AC

אַלטע לייַט זאָלן ניט געבוירן ווערן.

Old people shouldn't be born.
Alte layt zoln nit geboyrn vern. IB

אַלטע לײַט טראָגן די אױגן אין
קעשענע און די פֿים אין די הענט.

Old people carry their eyes in
their pockets and their feet in
their hands.
*Alte layt trogn di oygn in keshene un
di fis in di hent.* NS

אַן אַלטער שאַרבן לעבט איבער
אַ נײעם טאָפּ.

An old shard can survive a new pot.
*An alter sharbn lebt iber a nayem
top.* AC

אַן אַלטער זקן איז אַ בעט
מיט בײנער.

An old man is a bed full of bones.
An alter zokn iz a bet mit beyner. AC

אַן אַלטער ייִד אין הױז איז אַ ברכה,
אַן אַלטע ייִדענע איז אַ געסרחה.

An old man in the house is a
blessing, an old woman is a stench.
*An alter yid in hoyz iz a brokhe, an
alte yidene iz a gesrokhe.* NS

בעסער אַלטער װײַן אײדער אַלטע
כּוחות.

Better old wine than old strength.
Beser alter vayn eyder alte koykhes. NS

ביז דו װעסט בױען אױף דאָם נײַ
בלײַב דעם אַלטן געטרײַ.

Until you build anew, to the old
remain true.
*Biz du vest boyen oyf dos nay blayb
dem altn getray.* IB

דער װאָם װיל אַלץ װיסן װערט
גיך אַלט.

He who wants to know everything
ages early.
Der vos vil alts visn vert gikh alt. P

עם אַרט ניט װאָם װאָם מען װערט
אַלט װען די יאָרן שלעפּן ניט מיט.

Growing old wouldn't be so bad if
the years didn't drag us along.
*Es art nit vos men vert alt ven di
yorn shlepn nit mit.* AC

פֿאַרלירן צײן און האָבן קינדער
מאַכט אַלט געשװינדער.

Losing teeth and bearing children
ages one fast.
*Farlirn tseyn un hobn kinder makht
alt geshvinder.* NS

גרויע האָר זײַנען קבֿרות-בלעטער.

Grey hairs are leaves from the grave.
Groye hor zaynen kvores bleter. IB

אין דער יוגנט אַ ליגנער, אויף דער
עלטער אַ גנבֿ.

In youth a liar, in old age a thief.
*In der yugnt a ligner, oyf der elter a
ganef.* NS

אין דער יוגנט אַ זונה, אויף דער
עלטער אַ גבאיטע.

**In youth a whore, in old age a
model of propriety.**
*In der yugnt a zoyne, oyf der elder a
gabete.* AC

קינדער וואַקסן אויף,
עלטערן עלטערן זיך.

Children grow up, parents grow old.
Kinder vaksen oyf, eltern eltern zikh. AC

מען וויל זיך עלטערן
אָבער מען וויל ניט זײַן אַלט.

**Everyone wants to grow older but
nobody wants to be old.**
*Men vil zikh eltern ober men vil nit
zayn alt.* AC

מיט די יאָרן ווערן שוואַכער
די ציין און דער זכרון.

Age weakens teeth and memory.
*Mit di yorn vern shvakher di tseyn
un der zikorn.* IB

ווי צו זיבן, אַזוי צו זיבעציק.

Like seven, so at seventy.
Vi tsu zibn, azoy tsu zibetsik. P

וואָס עלטער, אַלץ קעלטער.

The older, the colder.
Vos elter, alts kelter. NS

וואָס מען כאַפט אַרײַן אין דער
יוגנט איז אויף דער עלטער ווי
געפֿונען.

**What you accomplish in youth is a
dividend in old age.**
*Vos men khapt arayn in der yugnt iz
oyf der elter vi gefunen.* NS

וואָס טויג דער גוטער קאָפּ אַז די
פֿיס קענען אים ניט טראָגן?

**What use is a good head if the feet
can't carry it?**
*Vos toyg der guter kop az di fis
kenen im nit trogn?* IB

וווייל איז דער עלטער וואָס האָט ניט
פֿאַרשעמט די יוגנט.

Happy are the aged who have not
shamed their youth.
*Voyl iz der elter vos hot nit farshemt
di yugnt.* NS

זאָל זײַן גראָ אַבי ס'איז דאָ.

Let it be grey as long as it will stay.
Zol zayn gro abi s'iz do. NS

AID

אַ ווײַטע הילף איז אַ נאָענטער
טויט.

Help from a distance is death close by.
A vayte hilf iz a no'enter toyt. NS

איין האַנט וואַשט די צווייטע
(און ביידע וואַשן דעם פּנים).

One hand washes the other (and
both wash the face).
*Eyn hant vasht di tsveyte (un beyde
vashn dem ponim).* P

קיין מת האָט זיך אַליין נאָך ניט
באַגראָבן.

No corpse has yet managed to
bury itself.
*Keyn mes hot zikh aleyn nokh nit
bagrobn.* NS

העלף דיך אַליין וועט דיך גאָט גאָט
אויך העלפֿן.

Help yourself and God will also
help you.
*Helf dikh aleyn vet dikh got oykh
helfn.* IB

פֿאַלן פֿאַלט מען אַליין אָבער
אויפֿצוהייבן זיך דאַרף מען האָבן
אַ האַנט פֿון אַ פֿרײַנד.

You can fall down by yourself but
to get up you need a friend's hand.
*Faln falt men aleyn ober oyftsuheybn
zikh darf men hobn a hant fun a
fraynd.* NS

אומעטום איז גוט הילף נאָר ניט
בײַ דער שיסל.

It's always good to have help
except when eating.
*Umetum iz gut hilf nor nit bay der
shisl.* NS

AMBITION

אַ וועלער איז בעסער ווי אַ קענער.

One who wants to know is better
than one who already knows.
A veler iz beser vi a kener. AC

אַז דו קוקסט אויף הויכע זאַכן
האַלט צו דאָס היטל.

When you look to the heights,
hold onto your hat.
*Az du kukst oyf hoykhe zakhn halt
tsu dos hitl.* NS

אַז מען זוכט אַ באָדנער געפֿינט
מען אַ גלעזער, אַז מען זוכט חלה
פֿאַרלירט מען דערווײַל דאָס ברויט.

Look for a cooper you find a
glazier, look for challah and,
meanwhile, you lose the plain
bread.
*Az men zukht a bodner gefint men a
glezer, az men zukht khale farlirt
men dervayl dos broyt.* NS

איבער אַן אײַנגעבויגענעם בוים
שפּרינגען אַלע ציגן.

Over a bent tree all the goats
jump.
*Iber an ayngeboygenem boym
shpringen ale tsign.* NS

לאָז מיך נאָר אַרײַן געפֿינען וועל
איך שוין אַן אָרט.

Just let me in and I'll find a place
for myself.
*Loz mikh nor arayn, gefinen vel ikh
shoyn an ort.* AC

וויל וועסטו זײַן אַ ווילנער.

Will it and you can become a great sage.
[Play on words]
Vil vestu zayn a vilner (ga'on). IF

ANGER

אַ חונף טאָר אין כּעם ניט ווערן.

A flatterer shouldn't lose his temper.
A khoynef tor in kas nit vern. IB

אַז אַ מענטש קומט אַרײַן אין היץ,
הערט ער ניט דעם דונער און
זעט ניט דעם בליץ.

When anger insists, neither thunder nor lightning exists.
Az a mentsh kumt arayn in hits, hert er nit dem duner un zet nit dem blits. NS

אַז מען איז ברוגז מיטן חזן
ענטפערט מען ניט אָמן?

Just because you're angry at the cantor, you don't say 'amen'?
Az men iz broyges mitn khazn entfert men nit omeyn? P

דער כּעם און דער צאָרן פֿאַרקירצען
די יאָרן.

Anger and rage will make you age.
Der kas un der tsorn farkirtsn di yorn. NS

דער צאָרן איז אין אין האַרצן אַ דאָרן.

Anger is a thorn in the heart.
Der tsorn iz in hartsn a dorn. NS

דאָס קול האָט ער פֿאַרלוירן נאָר דער
בייזער האַלדז איז אים געבליבן.

He lost his voice but his angry throat remains.
Dos kol hot er farloyrn nor der beyzer haldz iz im geblibn. AC

ער איז געוואָרן פֿלוימען און פֿלייש.

He became the color of plums and red meat.
Er iz gevorn floymen un fleysh. IB

כּעם מאַכט אַ קלוגן צו נאַר.

Anger makes a fool out of the wise.
Kas makht a klugn tsu nar. IB

ANTICIPATION

דאָס ניהנום איז ניט אַזוי שלעכט ווי
דאָס קומען צו אים.

Hell isn't so bad as the getting there.
Dos gehenem iz nit azoy shlekht vi dos kumen tsu im. IB

עס ניט די לאָקשן פאָרן שבת.

Don't eat the noodles before the Sabbath.
Es nit di lokshn farn shabes. IB

פֿון דעם בער אין וואַלד זאָל מען
דאָס פֿעל ניט פאַרקויפן.

Don't sell the hide of the bear that's still in the forest.
Fun dem ber in vald zol men dos fel nit farkoyfn. NS

מען טאָר ניט כאַפן די לאָקשן
פאַר די פֿיש.

Don't grab the noodles before the fish
Men tor nit khapn di lokshn far di fish. IB

פאַטש זיך ניט אין בײַכעלע ווען
פֿישעלע איז נאָך אין טײַכעלע.

Don't let your belly quiver while the fish is still in the river.
Patsh zikh nit in baykhele ven fishele iz nokh in taykhele. NS

זאָג ניט האָפ ביז דו שפרינגסט
ניט אַראָפ.

Don't look for applause until you have cause.
Zog nit hop biz du shpringst nit arop. LMF

APPEARANCE

א בגד וואָס האָט שוין א לאטע איז
א האַלבע שמאטע.

A garment repaired to a rag is compared.
A beged vos hot shoyn a late iz a halbe shmate. AC

א מיאוסע לאטע איז שענער ווי
א שיינע לאָך.

An ugly patch is nicer than a pretty hole.
A mi'ese late iz shener vi a sheyne lokh. AC

א שוואַרצע הון קען אויך לייגן
א ווייס איי.

A black hen can also lay a white egg.
A shvartse hun ken oykh leygn a vays ey. NS

א יפת-תואר – א פּאַס ווי א טויער
און א תּחת ווי א ריבאײַזן!

A real beauty – a hole like a gate and a rump like a grate!
A yifas to'er – a fas vi a toyer un a tokhes vi a ribayzn! WZ

אַלע מתים האָבן איין פּנים.

All corpses look alike.
Ale meysim hobn eyn ponim. IB

אַרײַן און אַרויס הייסט נאָך
ניט קיין וויזיט, א לעק און א שמעק
הייסט נאָך ניט קיין מאָלצײַט.

In and out isn't a visit, a taste and a smell isn't a meal.
Arayn un aroys heyst nokh nit keyn vizit, a lek un a shmek heyst nokh nit keyn moltsayt. NS

אז מען וויל יוצא זײַן פאַר דער
וועלט מוז קאָסטן געלט.

If you care only for show, it will cost lots of dough.
Az men vil yoytse zayn far der velt muz kostn gelt. SK

דעם ביטערסטן מזל קען מען
פאַרשטעלן מיט א שמייכל.

The bitterest misfortune can be masked by a smile.
Dem biterstn mazl ken men farshteln mit a shmeykhl. NS

די חופה פאַרדעקט אַלע עבירות.

The bridal canopy covers all sins.
Di khupe fardekt ale aveyres. WZ

דאָס אײבערשטע קלייד פֿאַרדעקט
די אונטערשטע לייד.

The outer dress hides the inner
distress.
*Dos eybershte klayd fardekt di
untershte layd.* IB

ער האָט אַ פנים ווי אַ לאָז מיך
צערו!

His face says: leave me alone!
Er hot a ponim vi a loz mikh tseru! IF

ער זעט אויס ווי אַ צעבראָכענער
לולב.

He looks like a broken-down palm
branch.
[Refers to Succoth ritual.]
Er zet oys vi a tsebrokhener lulev. IB

ער זעט אויס ווי אַן אויסגעווייקטער
הערינג.

He looks like a washed-out herring.
Er zet oys vi an oysgeveykter hering. IB

פֿיל שמייכל, ווייניק שכל.

Many smiles, few wiles.
Fil shmeykhl, veynik seykhl. IB

פֿון אויבן פוץ, פֿון אונטן שמוץ.

Finery on top, filth underneath.
Fun oybn puts, fun untn shmuts. IB

פֿון ווייטן זײַנען אַלע גוטע לייַט.

From far away everyone's okay.
Fun vaytn zaynen ale gute laytn. NS

גרויסע מענטשן האַלטן זיך קליין,
קליינע מענטשן האַלטן זיך גרויס.

Important people act humble;
humble people act important.
*Groyse mentshn haltn zikh kleyn,
kleyne mentshn haltn zikh groys.* AC

אין דער היים ווי מען וויל – צווישן
מענטשן מוז מען זיך שטעלן ווי
אַ מענטש.

At home do as you like – among
people act properly.
*In der heym vi men vil – tsvishn
mentshn muz men zikh shteln vi a
mentsh.* NS

מען באַגריסט נאָך די קליידער,
מען באַגלייט נאָכן שכל.

One is greeted according to one's
garb, bidden farewell according to
one's wisdom.
*Men bagrist nokh di kleyder, men
bagleyt nokhn seykhl.* P

קליידער באַהאַלטן דעם מום. Clothes conceal the blemish.
Kleyder bahaltn dem mum. NS

ניט אַלץ וואָס גלאַנצט איז גאָלד. All that glitters is not gold.
Nit alts vos glantst iz gold. IB

ניט פֿאַר קלוגע איז געלט, ניט The money isn't only for the
פֿאַר שיינע איז קליידער. clever nor clothes only for the
beautiful.
*Nit far kluge iz gelt, nit far sheyne
iz kleyder.* NS

אויסן ווייניק, אינען גאָרניט. Outside – little, inside – nothing.
Oysn veynik, inen gornit. IB

ס׳איז דער זעלבער מאכל נאָר אין It's the same delicacy but in
אן אַנדרער שיסל. another bowl.
*S'iz der zelber maykhl nor in an
ander shisl.* NS

ווי די מתים עסן אַזאַ פנים As the dead eat, that's how they look.
האָבן זיי. *Vi di meysim esn aza ponim hobn
zey.* AC

וויל מען פֿאַר אַלעמען יוצא זײַן If after appearances you chase,
קריכט מען ערשט אין דער בלאָטע you'll end up with mud on your face.
אַרײַן. *Vil men far alemen yoytse zayn
krikht men ersht in der blote arayn.* IB

AUTHORITY

אַ מענטש דאַרף איבער זיך קיין A person needs nothing worse over
ערגערס ניט האָבן ווי אַ מענטשן. him than another person.
*A mentsh darf iber zikh keyn ergers
nit hobn vi a mentshn.* AC

דער רבי איז גרויס ווען ער האָט The rabbi is a giant when
אַ סך קליינע ייִדעלעך. surrounded by small people.
*Der rebe iz groys ven er hot a sakh
kleyne yidelekh.* NS

יעדער הונט איז אַ בעל־הבית אויף
זײַן שוועל.

Every dog is boss on his doorstep.
Yeder hunt iz a balebos oyf zayn shvel. NS

בוקן זאָל מען זיך נאָר צום קאָפּ.

Bow only to the head.
Bukn zol men zikh nor tsum kop. IB

די חסידימלעך זאָלן פֿרײַלעך זײַן
טרינקט דער רבינו אויס דעם ווײַן.

In order for his followers to be cheerful, the rabbi drinks up all the wine.
Di khsidimlekh zoln freylekh zayn trinkt der rebenyu oys dem vayn. NS

אײַדער ווי, אײַדער וואָס,
אַ בעל־הבית בלײַבט בעל־הבית.

Whatever you will, the boss is boss still.
Eyder vi, eyder vos, a balebos blaybt balebos. IB

איטלעכער פּריץ מיט זײַן תירוץ.

Every nobleman has his own justification.
Itlekher porets mit zahn terets. NS

צו האָבן געלט איז אַ גוטע זאַך,
צו האָבן אַ דעה איבער דעם געלט
איז נאָך בעסער.

Having money is a good thing, having power over money is even better.
Tsu hobn gelt iz a gute zakh, tsu hobn a deye iber dem gelt iz nokh beser. IB

BARGAINS

אַן אָקס פֿאַר אַ גראָשן–אַז דער
גראָשן איז ניטאָ?

An ox for a penny – but if you
don't have the penny?
*An oks far a groshn – az der groshn
iz nito?* NS

ער האָט אויסגעביטן אַ שוך אויף
אַ לאַפּטשע!

He traded a shoe for a slipper!
*Er hot oysgebitn a shukh oyf a
laptshe!* SK

ער וועט באַקומען פֿיר װאָכן פֿאַר
אַ חודש!

He'll get four weeks for a month!
*Er vet bakumen fir vokhn far a
khoydesh!* IB

זוך ניט קיין מציאות וועסטו ניט
ווערן אַנטוישט.

Don't look for bargains and you
won't be disappointed.
*Zukh nit keyn metsi'es vestu nit vern
antoysht.* AC

BEAUTY

אַ מאַן אַז ער איז שענער פֿון
טײַװל איז ער שוין שיין.

A man, if he's better looking than
the devil, is already handsome.
*A man az er iz shener fun tayvl iz er
shoyn sheyn.* NS

אַ שיינע פֿרוי איז אַ האַלבע
פּרנסה.

A pretty wife is half a livelihood.
A sheyne froy iz a halbe parnose. NS

מען דאַרף ניט זײַן שײן נאָר
חנעוודיק.

You don't have to be pretty, just
charming.

*Men darf nit zayn sheyn nor
kheynevdik.* IB

ניט פֿון אַ שײנער צורקע ווערט אַ
גוטע ווײַב.

A pretty face alone doesn't
guarantee a good wife.

*Nit fun a sheyner tsurke vert a gute
vayb.* NS

BEGINNINGS

אַ גוטע התחלה איז שױן אַ האַלבע
אַרבעט.

A good beginning is the job half
done.

*A gute haskhole iz shoyn a halbe
arbet.* NS

אַ שלעכטע התחלה
ברענגט צו אַ מפּלה.

A bad onset leads to a big upset.

*A shlekhte haskhole brengt tsu a
mapole.* IB

די ערשטע פֿלױמען זײַנען
ווערעמדיק.

The first plums are wormy.

Di ershte floymen zaynen veremdik. NS

יעדער אָנפֿאַנג איז שווער און
גרינג נאָכער.

Every beginning is hard, but
easier afterward.

*Yeder onfang iz shver un gring
nakher.* NS

BELIEF

אַ ייִד האָט אמונה.

A Jew has faith.

A yid hot emune. AC

אַלע סימנים זײַנען נאַראָנים.

All signs are misleading.

Ale simonim zaynen naronim. NS

צו װאָס גלױבן אַז עס זײַנען דאָ
אױגן?

Why believe when you've got eyes
to perceive?

*Tsu vos gloybn az es zaynen do
oygn?* AC

אַז מען מיינט גענאַרט מען זיך.

Believe and you'll be disappointed.
Az men meynt genart men zikh. AC

ווילסטו ניט וויסן–גלייב, ווילסטו
ניט גלייבן–וויים!

If you don't want to know – have faith; if you don't have faith – seek knowledge!
Vilstu nit visn – gleyb; vilstu nit gleybn - veys! AC

BETTER AND WORSE

אַ שלעכטע ראָד סקריפעט
אַמערגסטן.

The worst wheel squeaks the loudest.
[The squeaky hinge gets the oil.]
A shlekhte rod skripet amergstn. AC

אַרויף קלעטערט מען פּאַוואָליע,
אַראָפּ קאַלערט מען זיך שנעל.

Uphill, it's a slow climb, downhill, it's a fast tumble.
Aroyf kletert men pavolye arop kolert men zikh shnel. NS

אַז מען אַנטלויפֿט פֿון פֿײַער
באַגעגנט מען דאָם וואַסער.

When you flee fire, you meet flood.
Az men antloyft fun fayer bagegnt men dos vaser. NS

בעסער אַ הונט אין פֿרידן איידער
אַ זעלנער אין קריג.

Better to be a dog in peacetime than a soldier in war.
Beser a hunt in fridn eyder a zelner in krig. NS

בעסער האָט קיין שעור ניט.

Better has no measure.
Beser hot keyn shir nit. P

ער אַנטלױפֿט פֿון די בערן און פֿאַלט
צװישן די װעלף.

He flees the bears only to fall
among wolves.
*Er antloyft fun di bern un falt tsvishn
di velf.* AC

עס זײַנען פֿאַראַן זאַכן װאָס אַז
זײ זײַנען דאָ איז גוט שלעכט און אַז
זײ זײַנען ניטאָ איז אױך רעכט.

Some things, if present, are sad,
and if missing, it's too bad.
*Es zaynen faran zakhn vos az zey
zaynen do iz gut shlekht un az zey
zaynen nito iz oykh rekht.* IB

װען מען זאָל גאָט דאַנקען פֿאַר גוטס
װאָלט ניט געװען קײן צײַט צו
באַקלאָגן זיך אױף שלעכטס.

If we thanked God for the good
there wouldn't be enough time to
lament the bad.
*Ven men zol got danken far guts volt
nit geven keyn tsayt tsu baklogn zikh
oyf shlekhts.* AC

BOASTING

אַ באַרימער איז גוט צו שלאָגן.

It's good to whallop a braggart.
A barimer iz gut tsu shlogn. AC

אַ גרױסער אױװן – אַ קלײנע חלה!

A big oven – a small loaf!
A groyser oyvn – a kleyne khale! IB

אַ פּוסטע פֿאַס הילכט אַ סך.

An empty barrel makes a lot of
noise.
A puste fas hilkht a sakh. NS

אַלײן זיך צו לױבן פּאַסט ניט
אָבער עס שאַט ניט.

Praising oneself isn't fitting but it
does no harm either.
*Aleyn zikh tsu loybn past nit ober is
shat nit.* AC

דער באַרימער בלײַבט שטעקן
אין בלאָטע.

The boaster remains mired in the
mud.
Der barimer blaybt shtekn in blote. IB

פֿאַראַן מער רױך װי געבראָטנס!

There's more smoke than roast!
Faran mer roykh vi gebrotens! P

פֿאַרוואָס פֿאַרמאַכט דער האָן די
אויגן בשעת ער קרייט? זאָל די
וועלט וויסן אַז ער קען אויך פֿון
אויסנווייניק.

Why does the rooster close his
eyes while crowing? So everyone
will know that he can also crow
from memory.
*Farvos farmakht der hon di oygn
beshas er kreyt? zol di velt visn az
er ken oykh fun oysnveynik.* NS

גאָט האָט מיר געגעבן אַזאַ גרויסן
שכל אַז איך קען מער אויסזאָרגן
אין איין מינוט ווי אַנדערע אין אַ
גאַנץ יאָר.

God gave me such a brain that I
can worry more in one minute
than others can in an entire year.
*Got hot mir gegebn aza groysn
seykhl az ikh ken mer oyszorgn in
eyn minut vi andere in a gants yor.* AC

מיט געלט טאָר מען ניט
שטאָלצירן ווייל מען קען עס
גלייך פֿאַרלירן.

Don't boast about your money,
you could easily lose it.
*Mit gelt tor men nit shtoltsirn vayl
men ken es glaykh farlirn.* NS

יעדער אייזל האָט ליב צו הערן ווי
ער אַליין שרייט.

Every ass likes to hear himself
bray.
*Yeder ayzl hot lib tsu hern vi er
aleyn shrayt.* AC

BODY AND SOUL

אַ גוטער מאָגן קען פֿיל פֿאַרטראָגן.

A healthy gut can endure a lot.
A guter mogn ken fil fartrogn. NS

דער האַלדז האָט אַ קליין לעכל און פֿאַרשלינגט אַ הויז מיט אַ דעכל.

The throat has a small hole and can swallow up an entire household.
Der haldz hot a kleyn lekhl un farshlingt a hoyz mit a dekhl. NS

די נשמה קען מען ניט אויסשפּייַען.

The soul can't be spat out.
Di neshome ken men nit oys'shpayen. NS

די אויערן הערן ניט וואָס דאָס מויל רעדט.

The ears don't hear what the mouth utters.
Di oyern hern nit vos dos moyl ret. AC

דער מאָגן האַלט אַ סוד בעסער ווי דאָס האַרץ.

The stomach keeps a secret better than the heart.
Der mogn halt a sod beser vi dos harts. NS

די אויגן זייַנען דער שפּיגל פֿון דער נשמה.

The eyes are the mirror of the soul.
Di oygn zaynen der shpigl fun der neshome. NS

די אויגן זייַנען קליין און נעמען אַלץ אַרייַן.

The eyes are small but absorb all.
Di oygn zaynen klayn un nemen alts arayn. NS

קאָדעגעס קלעבן זיך צו קליידער ווי קרענק צום גוף.

Thistles stick to clothes like illness to the body.
Kadeges klebn zikh tsu kleyder vi krenk tsum guf. NS

ס'איז נאָך אַ נס וואָס דער מאָגן
איז ניט פֿון גלאָז.

It's a miracle the stomach isn't
made of glass.
*S'iz nokh a nes vos der mogn iz nit
fun gloz.* AC

BOREDOM

אַ מויד װי אַ צימעס קען אױך
װערן נימאָס.

Even a beautiful girl can become
tedious.
*A moyd vi a tsimes ken oykh vern
nimes.* IB

ברויט װערט ניט נימאָס.

Bread doesn't get boring.
Broyt vert nit nimes. AC

לאָז זיַין אַן ערגערער אַבי אַן
אַנדערער.

Let it be worse, as long as it's
different.
Loz zayn an ergerer abi an anderer. NS

BORROWING AND LENDING

באָרגן מאַכט זאָרגן.

Borrowing causes sorrowing.
Borgn makht zorgn. P

דער וואָס װיל באָרגן זאָל קומען
מאָרגן.

Who wants to borrow can come
tomorrow.
Der vos vil borgn zol kumen morgn. NS

לײַען און באָרגן מאַכט גרױסע
זאָרגן.

Lend and borrow creates much
sorrow.
Layen un borgn makht groyse zorgn. IB

אויף 'וואָלט איך' און 'זאָלט איך'
באָרגט מען ניט קיין געלט.

Don't lend money on 'I would
have' or 'I should have.'
*Oyf 'volt ikh' un 'zolt ikh' borgt
men nit keyn gelt.* NS

ווער עס האָט אַליין ניט צו קיַיען
דער זאָל יענעם ניט לײַען.

If you don't have enough for
yourself, don't lend to others.
*Ver es hot aleyn nit tsu kayen der
zol yenem nit layen.* NS

אַ ווײַב און אַ פֿערד באָרגט מען
ניט אַוועק.

A wife and a horse you don't lend
out.

*A vayb un a ferd borgt men nit
avek.* AC

BRAINS

אַ קאָפּ אָן שׂכל איז ווי אַ לאָמפּ אָן
פֿײַער.

A head without a brain is like a
lamp without a flame.

*A kop on seykhl iz vi a lomp on
fayer.* NS

אַ ייִד אַ חכם מאַכט זיך ניט
תּמעוואַטע.

A Jew with brains doesn't act
stupidly.

*A yid a khokhem makht zikh nit
tamevate.* P

אַלע קינדער זײַנען קלײנערהײט
קלוג נאָר דאָס רוב בלײַבן זיי
בײַם קינדערשן שׂכל.

Everyone is clever when young but
the majority remain childish.

*Ale kinder zaynen kleynerheyt klug,
nor dos rov blaybn zey baym
kindershn seykhl.* NS

אַז מען האָט ניט אין קאָפּ האָט
מען אין די פֿים.

If it's not in the head, it's in the feet.

*Az men hot nit in kop hot men in di
fis.* AC

אז מען זוכט מיט שׂכל געפֿינען
שוין די הענט.

If one seeks with brains, the hands
will soon find.
*Az men zukht mit seykhl gefinen
shoyn di hent.* P

די נויט שאַרפֿט דעם שׂכל.

Necessity sharpens the mind.
Di noyt sharft dem seykhl. P

געבאָרגטער שׂכל טויג ניט.

Borrowed brains are useless.
Geborgter seykhl toyg nit. AC

איטלעכער איז צופֿרידן מיט
זײַן פּנים און מיט זײַן שׂכל אויך.

Everyone is satisfied with his looks
and his brains.
*Itlekher iz tsufridn mit zayn ponim
un mit zayn seykhl oykh.* IB

BUSINESS

אז מען פֿאַרקויפֿט בחינם האָט
מען אַ סך קונים.

Charge nothing and you get a lot
of customers.
*Az men farkoyft bekhinem hot men a
sakh koynim.* AC

אז מען האַנדלט ניט מיט לינקס
האָט מען ניט קיין רעכטס.

If you don't do business askew,
you won't get what is your due.
*Az men handlt nit mit links hot men
nit keyn rekhts.* AC

אז מען לייגט אַרײַן נעמט מען
אַרויס.

If you put in, you can take out.
Az men leygt arayn nemt men aroys. P

אז ס'איז דאָ אויף פֿיש איז דאָ
אויף פֿעפֿער אויך.

If there's enough for fish, there's
enough for pepper.
*Az s'iz do oyf fish iz do oyf fefer
oykh.* NS

בחינם קריגט מען נאָר כּנים.

For 'no price' all you get is lice.
Bekhinem krigt men nor kinem. IB

האַנדלשאַפֿט איז ניט קיין
ברודערשאַפֿט.

Livelihood isn't brotherhood.
Handlshaft iz nit keyn brudershaft. NS

דאָם לעבעדיקע לייגט מען ניט
אויפֿן טויטן.

Don't put the living on top of the
dead.

[Don't throw good money after bad.]

*Dos lebedike leygt men nit oyfn
toytn.* P

ער האָט געמאַכט אַ געשעפֿט ווי
פֿעטער עשׂו.

He did business like Uncle Esau.

[Refers to Biblical passage in which Esau
sells his birthright to Jacob for a mess of
pottage.]

*Er hot gemakht a gesheft vi feter
eysev.* IB

ער איז אויס קאַפעלוש-מאַכער!

He's no longer a cap-maker!

[He's no longer in business.]

Er iz oys kapelush-makher! IB

פֿון אַ יורש און אַ גנבֿ איז שלעכט
צו קויפֿן.

Don't buy from an heir or from a
thief.

*Fun a yoyresh un a ganef iz shlekht
tsu koyfn.* IB

מעגסט דערנאָך קדיש זאָגן!

You can recite mourning prayers
over it!

[You can kiss it good-bye.]

Megst dernokh kadesh zogn! IF

מיט חכמה אַליין גייט מען ניט
אין מאַרק.

With wisdom alone you don't go
to market.

*Mit khokhme aleyn geyt men nit in
mark.* P

אָדער רויט אָדער טויט!

Either red or dead! [success or failure]

Oder royt oder toyt! IB

שכנה, דרײ זיך, וועט מען מיינען
אַז דו האַנדלסט.

Shakhneh, keep moving, so they'll
think you're busy.

*Shakhne, drey zikh, vet men meynen
az du handlst.* P

CANTORS

אַ חזן דאַרף זײַן אַ באַװײַבטער, ער
זאָל קענען דאַװענען מיט אַ
צעבראָכן האַרץ.

A cantor should be married so
that he can pray with a broken
heart.
*A khazn darf zayn a bavaybter, er
zol kenen davenen mit a tsebrokhn
harts.* NS

אַ חזן אָן אַ קול איז װי אַ שאָף אָן
װאָל.

A cantor without a voice is like a
sheep without wool.
A khazn on a kol iz vi a shof on vol. IB

אַלע חזנים זײַנען נאַראָנים
אָבער ניט יעדער נאַר קען זינגען.

All cantors are fools but not every
fool can sing.
*Ale khazonim zaynen naronim ober
nit yeder nar ken zingen.* P

אַז דער חזן קען קײן עברי ניט
הײסט ער אַ קענטאָר.

If the hazzan doesn't know any
Hebrew he's called a cantor.
*Az ker khazn ken keyn ivre nit heyst
er a kentor.* AC

אַז מען װיל ניט דעם חזן הײסט
ער זיך נאָך געבן אַ הוספה.

Just when you'd like to fire the
cantor, he asks for a raise.
*Az men vil nit dem khazn heyst er
zikh nokh gebn a hesofe.* NS

אוי איז דאָס אַ חזן! ער בעט זיך
דאָך ביי גאָט ווי ביי אַ גזלן.

He's some cantor! He implores God
like he would plead with a criminal.
*Oy iz dos a khazn! er bet zikh dokh
bay got vi bay a gazlen.* AC

איינער איז אַ מבין אויף אַ פּשטל,
דער צווייטער איז אַ מבין אויף
חזיר האָר אָבער אַלע זיינען מבינים
אויף אַ חזן.

One is an expert in scholarly
discourse, another is an expert on
pig's bristles, but everyone is an
expert on the merit of cantors.
*Eyner iz a meyvn oyf a p'shetl, der
tsveyter iz a meyvn oyf khazer hor
ober ale zaynen meyvinim oyf a
khazn.* NS

ווי אַזוי דער חזן זאָל ניט זינגען
קריגט ער אַלץ אין טאַטן אַריין.

No matter how well the cantor
sings, he'll still be criticized.
*Vi azoy der khazn zol nit zingen
krigt er alts in tatn arayn.* IB

CAUTION

אַלץ איז ניט פּוטער וואָס קומט
אַרויס פֿון דער קו.

All is not butter that comes from a co'
*Alts iz nit puter vos kumt aroys fun
der ku.* NS

אַז מען פֿרעגנט בלאָנדזשעט מען
נישט.

Ask and you won't get lost.
Az men fregt blondzhet men nisht. P

אַז דו נייסט אויפֿן לייטער צייל די
טרעפּלעך.

When you climb a ladder, count the rungs.
Az du geyst oyfn leyter tseyl di treplekh. NS

אַז מען בריט זיך אָפּ מיט הייסן
בלאָזט מען אויפֿן קאַלטן.

Burnt with the hot, you blow on the cold.
Az men brit zikh op mit heysn blozt men oyfn kaltn. AC

אַז מען ישובֿט זיך צו פֿיל נעמט
דער אַנדערער דערווייַל די פּרנסה
אַוועק.

Hesitate too long and someone will meanwhile take your livelihood away.
Az men yishuft zikh tsu fil nemt der anderer dervayl di parnose avek. IB

אַז מען זיצט אין דער היים
צערייַסט מען ניט קיין שיך.

If you stay at home you don't wear out your shoes.
Az men zitst in der heym tserayst men nit keyn shikh. P

בעסער צען מאָל מעסטן און איין
מאָל אָפּשנייַדן איידער פֿאַרקערט.

Better to measure ten times and cut once, than do the reverse.
Beser tsen mol mestn un eyn mol opshnaydn, eyder farkert. NS

דער וואָלף האָט ניט מורא פֿאַרן
הונט אָבער עס געפֿעלט אים ניט
זייַן בילן.

The wolf doesn't fear the dog but he doesn't like his bark.
Der volf hot nit moyre farn hunt ober es gefelt im nit zayn biln. NS

עס איז קוק מיך אָן און ריר מיך ניט
אָן!

It's look but don't touch!
Es iz kuk mikh on un rir mikh nit on! P

האַלט מיך פֿאַר אַ מלאך און
געטרויי מיך ווי אַ גלח.

Treat me like an angel and trust me like a priest.
Halt mikh far a malekh un getroy mikh vi a galekh. NS

האַלט מיך ערלעך און זיי מיך חושד.

Treat me honorably but with suspicion.
Halt mikh erlekh un zay mikh khoyshed. NS

קריך ניט צו הויך וועסטו ניט
דארפֿן פֿאַלן צו נידעריק.

Don't climb too high and you won't sink too low.
Krikh nit tsu hoykh vestu nit darfn faln tsu niderik. NS

אָפֿגעצאָלט איז אָפֿגעלייגט.

Money paid, work delayed.
Opgetsolt iz opgeleygt. NS

טו ניט אַלץ וואָס דו קענסט,
ווייַז ניט אַלץ וואָס דו האָסט.

Don't do everything you can, don't show everything you have.
Tu nit alts vos du kenst, vayz nit alts vos du host. P

וועט משיח געבוירן ווערן מיט אַ
טאָג שפּעטער!

So the Messiah will be born a day later
Vet meshi'ekh geboyrn vern mit a tog shpeter! LMF

זייַ ניט צו זיס מען זאָל דיך ניט
אויפֿעסן, זייַ ניט צו ביטער
מען זאָל דיך ניט אויסשפּייַען.

Don't be too sweet or you'll be eaten up, too bitter or you'll be spat out.
Zay nit tsu zis men zol dikh nit oyfesn, zay nit tsu biter men zol dikh nit oys'shpayen. AC

CERTAINTY

אַ שבֿועה און אַן איי ווערן באַלד
צעבראָכן.

An oath and an egg are soon broken.
A shvu'e un an ey vern bald tsebrokhn. IB

אַלץ בייַ איינעם איז ניטאָ בייַ קיינעם.

Virtues alone are not found in anyone.
Alts bay eynem iz nito bay keynem. NS

אַז מען זוכט קעץ געפֿינט מען מייַז.

Look for cats and you find mice.
Az men zukht kets gefint men mayz. NS

בעסער איין קו אין שטאַל איידער
צען אין פֿעלד.

Better one cow in the stall than ten in the field.
Beser eyn ku in shtal eyder tsen in feld.

,אפֿשר' און ,טאָמער' ברענגען
קלאָג און יאָמער.

'Maybe' and 'perhaps' bring lament and mishaps.
'Efsher' un 'tomer' brengen klog un yomer. AC

פֿאָר דעם טויט און פֿאָר דעם
דלות קען מען זיך ניט באַוואָרענען.

There's no insurance against death and poverty.
Far dem toyt un far dem dales ken men zikh nit bavorenen. IB

„האָוחז ביד" איז די בעסטע תּפֿילה.

"What's in the hand" is the best prayer.
[A bird in the hand is worth two in the bush.]
"Ha'oykhez b'yad" iz di beste tfile. IF

װוּ דער שטריק איז דין, דאָרט
רײַסט זיך.

Where the rope is worn, it will break.
Vu der shtrik iz din dort rayst zikh. IB

זיכער איז מען נאָר מיטן טויט.

Death is the only certainty.
Zikher iz men nor mitn toyt. P

CHARACTER

אַ בײַטל אָן געלט איז נאָר אַ שטיק
לעדער.

An empty wallet is just a piece of leather.
A baytl on gelt iz nor a shtik leder. IB

אַ געלעכערטן זאַק קען מען
ניט אָנפֿילן.

A torn sack can't be filled.
A gelekhertn zak ken men nit onfiln. NS

אַ גוטער װילן איז דער בעסטער טאַט.

Good will is the best deed.
A guter viln iz der bester tat. AC

אַ הערינג איז גוט פֿאָר צען פאַרשוין,
אַ הון קוים אויף צוויי.

A herring can serve ten persons, a chicken barely two.
[Herring is salty, limiting individual consumption.]
A hering iz gut far tsen parshoyn, a hun koym oyf tsvey. NS

אַ הונט אָן ציין וואַרפֿט זיך אויך
אויף אַ ביין.

A dog without teeth will also
attack a bone.
*A hunt on tseyn varft zikh oykh oyf a
beyn.* NS

אַ חזיר בלײַבט אַ חזיר.

A swine remains a swine.
A khazer blaybt a khazer. P

אַ מענטש איז נעבעך פֿאָרט אַ
מענטש – און אַמאָל דאָס אויך ניט

A person is, after all, only a
human being – and sometimes, not
even that.
*A mentsh iz nebekh fort a mentsh –
un amol dos oykh nit.* P

אַ מענטש איז ווי דער שאָטן וואָס
פֿאַרגייט.

A human being is like a shadow
that passes.
A mentsh iz vi der shotn vos fargeyt. IB

אַ שטעקן האָט צוויי עקן.

A stick has two ends.
A shtekn hot tsvey ekn. IF

אַ ייִדישע נשמה קען מען ניט
אָפּשאַצן.

A Jewish soul is priceless.
A yidishe neshome ken men nit opshatsn.

אַן אָקס גייט קיין אָלמוץ און
קומט פֿאָרט צוריק אַן אָקס.

Even though an ox goes to town it
still comes back an ox.
*An oks geyt keyn olmuts un kumt
fort tsurik an oks.* AC

אַז די בעל-הביתטע איז ברייט באַקט
זי ברייטע ברויט.

If the housewife is stout, she bakes stout loaves.
Az di baleboste iz breyt bakt zi breyte broyt. NS

אַז עס וואָלטן געווען וויניקער חזירים
וואָלטן געווען וויניקער ממזרים.

If there were fewer swine, there would be fewer bastards.
Az es voltn geven veyniker khazeyrim voltn geven veyniker mamzeyrim. NS

אַז מען איז ביז צוואַנציק יאָר אַ קינד
איז מען צו איין-און-צוואַנציק אַ
בהמה.

If you're a child until twenty, you're an ass at twenty-one.
Az men iz biz tsvantsik yor a kind, iz men tsu eyn-un-tsvantsik a beheyme. IB

ביסטו אַ בהמה? קײַ שטרוי!

Are you a cow? - eat straw!
Bistu a beheyme? kay shtroy! P

דעם בעסטן עפל כאַפט אויס דער
חזיר.

The pig grabs the best apple.
Dem bestn epl khapt oys der khazer. NS

דער קלוגער באַהאַלט דעם שכל,
דער נאַר באַווײַזט זײַן
נאַרישקייט.

The wise conceals his intelligence, the fool displays his ignorance.
Der kluger bahalt dem seykhl, der nar bavayst zayn narishkeyt. P

די אייגענע זון מאַכט לײַוונט ווײַס
און דעם ציגײַנער שוואַרץ.

The same sun bleaches linen and darkens gypsies.
Di eygene zun makht layvnt vays un dem tsigayner shvarts. NS

דרײַ זאַכן וואַקסן איבערנאַכט:
פּראָצענט, דירה-געלט און
מיידן.

Three things grow overnight: interest, rent money, and girls.
Dray zakhn vaksn ibernakht: protsent, dire-gelt un meydn. NS

דרײַ זאַכן זעט מען קיינמאָל ניט: אַ
קליינעם טודרוסל, אַ ווײַסן
זשעבטשיק און אַ ייִדן פון
יאַכאָוויץ.

Three things one never sees: a small dwarf, a white crow, and a Jew from Yakhovitz.
Dray zakhn zet men keynmol nit: a kleynem tudrusl, a vaysn zhebtshik un a yidn fun yakhovits. NS

פֿון אַ קאַרגן גבֿיר און אַ פֿעטן באָק
געניסט מען ערשט נאָכן טויט.

A miser and a fatted calf are
useful only after death.
*Fun a kargn gvir un a fetn bok
genist men ersht nokhn toyt.* IB

פֿון אַן עק פֿון אַ חזיר קען מען קיין
שטרײַמל ניט מאַכן.

You can't make a fur hat out of a
pig's tail.
*Fun an ek fun a khazer ken men
keyn shtrayml nit makhn.* MD

האָדעווע אַ וואָלף ווי לאַנג קוקט ער
אַלץ אין וואַלד אַרײַן.

No matter how long you
domesticate a wolf, he still longs
for the forest.
*Hodeve a volf vi lang kukt er alts in
vald arayn.* NS

אין דרײַ זאַכן דערקענט מען אַ
מענטשן: בכּיסו, בכּעסו,
בכּוסו.

A person is revealed by three
things: by his treasure, by his
temper, and by his tippling.
*In dray zakhn derkent men a
mentshn: b'kise, b'kase, b'koyse.* AC

מען שמירט אים מיט האָניק און ער
שמעקט נאָך אַלץ פֿון סמאָלע.

Smear him with honey and he still
smells of tar.
*Men shmirt im mit honik un er
shmekt nokh alts fun smole.* NS

אויף אַ ניסנבוים וואָקסן ניט קיין עפּל.

A nut tree won't grow apples.
Oyf a nisnboym vaksn nit keyn epl. AC

צײנער בלײַבן צײנער אַפֿילו אַז
מען עסט מיט זיי בלויז קאַשע.

Teeth remain teeth even if all you
eat with them is porridge.
*Tseyner blaybn tseyner afile az men
est mit zey bloyz kashe.* NS

ווען די ליכט איז קרום איז דער
שאָטן קרום.

When the light is crooked, the
shadow is crooked.
*Ven di likht iz krum iz der shotn
krum.* IB

וואָס טויג אַ גוטער וויין אין אַ
פֿאַרפֿוילטער פֿאָס?

What use is a good wine in a
rotten barrel?
Vos toyg a guter vayn in a farfoylter fas? IB

וואָס קען ווערן פֿון אַ שמײַסער?
ניט מער ווי אַ בעל-עגלה.

What can you expect from a
whipper? He'll become a wagoneer.
*Vos ken vern fun a shmayser? nit
mer vi a balegole.* AC

וווּ האָניק, דאָרט פֿלינן.

Where there's honey, there are flies.
Vu honik, dort flign. P

CHARITY

אַ קאַליעקן גיט מען ניכער אַ נדבה
ווי אַ תּלמיד חכם.

Alms are sooner given to a cripple
than to a scholar.
*A kalyekn git men gikher a nedove
vi a talmed khokhem.* IB

אַז גאָט האָט פּרנסה געגעבן זאָל
מען לאָזן אַנדערע אויך לעבן.

If God blessed you with livelihood,
let others also live good.
*Az got hot parnose gegebn zol men
lozn andere oykh lebn.* NS

אַז מען גיט ניט מיט גוטן, גיט מען
מיט בּייזן.

If you don't give willingly, you
will be made to give unwillingly.
*Az men git nit mit gutn, git men mit
beyzn.* P

ער איז אַ פֿילאַנטראָפּ:
ער רעדט פֿיל און גיט אַ טראָפּ!

He's a philanthrop: he talks his fill
and gives a drop!
*Er iz a filantrop: er ret fil un git a
trop!* AC

פֿון ווינטשן ווערט מען ניט רײַך.

From good wishes you don't get rich.
Fun vinshn vert men nit raykh. P

לײַען דאַרף מען מיט עדות, געבן זאָל
מען אָן עדות.

Lending should be done with
witnesses, giving without.
*Layen darf men mit eydes, gebn zol
men on eydes.* NS

אויף אַ מיצווה געפֿינען זיך אַ סך
בעלנים.

To accept charity there are lots of
volunteers.

Oyf a mitsve gefinen zikh a sakh balonim

אויף יענעמס קעשענע איז
יעדערער אַ בעל-צדקה.

Out of someone else's pocket it's
easy to be charitable.

*Oyf yenems keshene iz yederer a
baltsedoke.* P

צדקה זאָל קיין געלט ניט קאָסטן און
גמילות-חסדים זאָל קיין עגמת-נפֿש
ניט פֿאַרשאַפֿן וואָלטן
געווען אַ סך צדיקים.

If charity cost no money and good
deeds caused no aggravation, there
would be a lot of righteous people
around.

*Tsedoke zol keyn gelt nit kostn un
gmiles-khsodim zol keyn agmes-
nefesh nit farshafn voltn geven a
sakh tsadikim.* NS

ווינטשן און שייַסן איז אַלץ איין
פֿאַרבייַסן.

Well-wishing and shitting is the
same dessert.

Vinshn un shaysn iz alts eyn farbaysn. A

CHARM

אַ ביסעלע חן איז שוין ניט געמיין.

A little charm is not vile.

A bisele kheyn iz shoyn nit gemeyn. NS

איטלעכע בת-יחידה האָט זיך איר
חנדל.

Each only daughter has her
charms.

Itlekhe bas-yekhide hot zikh ir kheyndl.

חן איז די נשמה פֿון שיין.

Charm is the soul of beauty.

Kheyn iz di neshome fun sheyn. NS

מען דאַרף ניט זייַן שיין נאָר
חנעוודיק.

You don't have to be pretty, just
charming.

*Men darf nit zayn sheyn nor
kheynevdik.* NS

ייִדישער חן איז אומעטום שיין.

Jewish charm is everywhere beautiful

Yidisher kheyn iz umetum sheyn. AC

CHILDREN

אַ קינדס טרערן רייַסן הימלען.

A child's tears rend the heavens.
A kinds trern raysn himlen. NS

אַ שלעכטע נאַם איז פֿאַרן קינד סם.

A poor wet-nurse poisons the child.
A shlekhte nam iz farn kind sam. IB

בעסער דאָס קינד זאָל וויינען איידער
דער פֿאָטער.

Better the child should cry than
the father.
*Beser dos kind zol veynen eyder der
foter.* NS

עס שטאַרבט קיין דור ניט אויס.

A whole generation doesn't die out.
Es shtarbt keyn dor nit oys. NS

איינס איז קיינס, צוויי איז קוים
איינס.

One is none, two are barely one.
Eyns iz keyns, tsvey iz koym eyns. AC

פֿינף פֿינגער אין איין האַנט און
זייַנען אויך ניט גלייַך.

Five fingers on one hand and each
one is different.
*Finf finger in eyn hant un zaynen
oykh nit glaykh.* NS

קינדער ברענגען גליק, קינדער
ברענגען אומגליק.

Children bring luck, children
bring misfortune.
*Kinder brengen glik, kinder brengen
umglik.* NS

לאָז עס זייַן פֿון קאָזאַק אַבי צו
לאַנגע יאָר.

Even if it's sired by a Cossack, as
long as it has long years.
*Loz es zayn fun kozak abi tsu lange
yor.* NS

לאָז דאָס קאַלב לויפֿן, עס וועט זיך
אויסהונגערן וועט עס אַליין
אַהיימקומען.

Let the calf run, it will come home
when it's hungry.
*Loz dos kalb loyfn, es vet zikh
oys'hungern vet es aleyn
aheymkumen.* NS

יעדעס קינד ברענגט זיך מיט זייַן
מזל.

Every child brings its own luck.
Yedes kind brengt zikh mit zayn mazl. P

אויב די וועלט וועט ווערן
אויסגעלייזט איז עס נאָר אין זכות פֿון
קינדער.

If the world is to be redeemed, it
will only be through the merit of
children.
*Oyb di velt vet vern oysgeleyzt iz es
nor in skhus fun kinder.* NS

BIG AND LITTLE CHILDREN

קליינע קינדער האָבן גרויסע אויערן

Little children have big ears.
Kleyne kinder hobn groyse oyern. P

קליינע קינדער – קאָפּווייטיק, גרויסע
קינדער – האַרצווייטיק.

Little children – headaches; big
children – heartaches.
*Kleyne kinder – kopveytik, groyse
kinder – hartsveytik.* NS

קליינע לאָזן ניט קײַען, גרויסע לאָזן
ניט באַנײַען.

Little ones don't let you chew, big
ones don't let you renew.
*Kleyne lozn nit kayen, groyse lozn
nit banayen.* NS

CLEVER CHILDREN

קלוגע קינדער האָבן קורצע יאָרן.

Clever children have few years.
Kluge kinder hobn kurtse yorn. IB

אויף אייגענע קינדער איז יעדערער
אַ בלינדער.

To the faults of his children
everyone is blind.
*Oyf eygene kinder iz yederer a
blinder.* P

וואָס אַ קינד זאָגט איז אַלץ אַ חכמה.

Whatever a child says is
considered clever.
Vos a kind zogt iz alts a khokhme. P

ORPHANS

אַ בן-זקנים איז אַ פֿאַרטיקער יתום.

A child of aged parents is a ready-
made orphan.
A benskeynim iz a fartiker yosem. NS

אַ קינד אָן אַ פֿאָטער איז אַ האַלבער
יתום, אָן אַ מאַמע אַ גאַנצער יתום.

A child without a father is half an
orphan, without a mother, a
complete one.
*A kind on a foter iz a halber yosem,
on a mame a gantser yosem.* NS

REARING CHILDREN

אַ קינד אָן אַ מאַמקע איז ווי אַ
טיר אָן אַ קליאַמקע.

A child without a pacifier is like a
door without a latch.
*A kind on a mamke iz vi a tir on a
kli'amke.* NS

אַמאָל פֿלעגן די עלטערן לערנען
די קינדער רעדן, הײַנט לערנען
די קינדער די עלטערן שווײַגן.

Once, parents taught their
children to speak; nowadays,
children teach their parents to
keep silent.
*Amol flegn di eltern lernen di kinder
redn, haynt lernen di kinder di
eltern shvaygn.* NS

אַ קונץ איז צו קויפֿן סחורה און צו
האָבן קינדער, נאָך אַ גרעסערע
קונץ איז סחורה צו פֿאַרקויפֿן און
קינדער מגדל צו זײַן.

It's an art to buy merchandise and
to bear children, it's an even
greater art to sell off merchandise
and to rear children.
*A kunts iz tsu koyfn skhoyre un tsu
hobn kinder, nokh a gresere kunts iz
skhoyre tsu farkoyfn un kinder
megadl tsu zayn.* IB

די אייער ווילן זײַן קליגער פֿאַר
די הינער.

The eggs want to be smarter than
the hens.
Di eyer viln zayn kliger far di hiner. IB

די אייער זײַנען טאַקע קלינער פֿאַר
די הינער אָבער זיי ווערן באַלד
פֿאַרשטונקען.

Eggs may really be smarter than
the hens but they rot sooner.
*Di eyer zaynen take kliger far di
hiner ober zey vern bald
farshtunken.* AC

אַזױ װי מען װיגט אײַן אַזױ װיגט
מען אױס.

**As children are raised, so they
become.**

*Azoy vi men vigt ayn azoy vigt men
oys.* P

פֿון אַ געמײנער בולבע קומט אַרױס
די פֿײַנסטע לאַטקע.

**From the lowly potato you get the
choicest latke.**

*Fun a gemeyner bulbe kumt aroys di
faynste latke.* AC

קינדער האָבן איז לײַכטער װי קינדער
דערציִען.

**Bearing children is easier than
raising them.**

*Kinder hobn iz laykhter vi kinder
dertsi'en.* P

קינדער מגדל צו זײַן מוז מען האָבן
קורחם עשירות און שמשון הגבורס
גבֿורה.

**For raising children you need
Korakh's wealth and Samson's
strength.**

*Kinder megadl tsu zayn muz men
hobn korakhs ashires un shimshon
hagibors gvure.* NS

Some of the following sayings show a marked preference for sons over
daughters. Traditionally, only sons could recite memorial prayers for
deceased parents, making them especially desirable. Daughters, on the other
hand, required dowries to make them marriageable and this placed a strain
on many families.

SONS AND DAUGHTERS

א בן-יחיד איז אַ האַלבער משומד
(איז אַן עקשן).

A one-and-only son is half an
apostate (is stubborn).
*A ben-yokhed iz a halber meshumed
(iz an akshn).* NS

אַ בן-יחיד מוז ניט זײַן קיין למדן.

A one-and-only son doesn't have to
be a scholar.
[He would likely be required to augment the
family income.]
*A ben-yokhed muz nit zayn keyn
lamdn.* NS

אַ בן-יחיד זאָל מען אויסמײַדן.

A one-and-only son should be avoided.
[He would probably be spoiled and arrogant.]
A ben-yokhed zol men oysmaydn. NS

אַ שיינע טאָכטער איז אַ האַלבע
פרנסה.

A pretty daughter is half a
livelihood.
A sheyne tokhter iz a halbe parnose. IB

אַן אויסגעגעבענע טאָכטער איז
ווי אַן אָפּגעשניטן שטיקל ברויט.

A daughter married off is like a
loaf of bread cut off.
*An oysgegebene tokhter iz vi an
opgeshnitn shtikl broyt.* NS

אַז די מיידן שלאָפֿן – וואַקסן זיי, אַז
זיי וואַכן – עסן זיי.

When the girls are asleep – they grow;
when they are awake – they eat.
*Az di meydn shlofn – vaksn zey, az
zey vakhn – esn zey.* IB

אַז עס ווערט געבוירן אַ זון איז ליכטיק
אין אַלע ווינקעלעך, אַ טאָכטער
איז חושך.

When a son is born, it's bright in
the house; when a daughter is
born, it's dark.
*Az es vert geboyrn a zun iz likhtik in
ale vinkelekh, a tokhter iz
khoyshekh.* NS

בנים איז אויך אַ גוטע מכּה.

Sons are also a good affliction.
Bonim iz oykh a gute make. AC

אַז מען האָט אַ סך טעכטער –
פֿאַרגייט דאָס געלעכטער.

If one has a lot of daughters –
good-bye laughter.
*Az men hot a sakh tekhter - fargeyt
dos gelekhter.* NS

גאָט זאָל אָפּהיטן צו האָבן איין קינד,
איין אויג און איין העמד.

God save us from having one
child, one eye, and one shirt.
*Got zol op'hitn tsu hobn eyn kind,
eyn oyg un eyn hemd.* NS

מיט אַ טאָכטער האָט מען אַ
גאַנץ לעבן צו טאָן.

With a daughter you're busy all
your life.
*Mit a tokhter hot men a gants lebn
tsu ton.* NS

CHOICE

אַז מען האָט ניט קיין ברירה מוז
מען אַפֿילו טאָן אַן עבֿירה.

If there is no other way, then
commit a sin you may.
*Az men hot nit keyn breyre muz men
afile ton an aveyre.* IB

אַז מען קען ניט ווי מען וויל מוז מען
ווילן ווי מען קען.

If you can't do as you choose you
must choose what you can.
*Az men ken nit vi men vil muz men
viln vi men ken.* NS

אַז מען קען ניט אַריבער מוז מען
אַרונטער.

If you can't go over, go under.
*Az men ken nit ariber muz men
arunter.* P

אַז נישט מיטן שעפֿל איז כאָטש מיטן
לעפֿל.

If not a pailful, at least a spoonful.
*Az nisht mitn shefl iz khotsh mitn
lefl.* AC

באַדאַרף מען האָניק ווען צוקער
איז זיס?

Who needs honey when sugar is
sweet?
Badarf men honik ven tsuker iz zis? P

בעסער איך אין שטוב און די לײַכטער
איבער דער וועלט אײדער פֿאַרקערט.

Better I should be in my house
and the candelabrum light the
world, than the reverse.
*Beser ikh in shtub un di laykhter
iber der velt eyder farkert.* IB

בעסער מיט אַ קלונג צו פֿאַרלירן
אײדער מיט אַ נאַר צו געווינען.

Better to lose with a wise man
than to win with a fool.
*Beser mit a klugn tsu farlirn eyder
mit a nar tsu gevinen.* P

'אײן ברירה' איז אַ גרױסע גזירה.

'No choice' is to be caught in a
great decree.
'Eyn breyre' iz a groyse gezeyre. IB

עס איז שווער צו טראָגן און
אַוועקוואַרפֿן טוט באַנג.

It's hard to bear but you'll regret
getting rid of it.
*Es iz shver tsu trogn un avekvarfn
tut bang.* P

אין אַ טײַך זײַנען דאָ
פֿאַרשידענע פֿיש.

In a lake there is a variety of fish.
[There are lots of good fish in the sea.]
In a taykh zaynen do farshidene fish. IF

איז דאָ אַ ברירה דאַרף ניט זײַן קײן
מורא.

When there's more than one way,
have no dismay.
Iz do a breyre darf nit zayn keyn meyre. NS

מען קען ניט פֿאָרן אױף אַלע
ירידן מיט אײן מאָל.

You can't attend more than one
fair at a time.
*Men ken nit forn oyf ale yaridn mit
eyn mol.* P

מיט אײן הינטן זיצט מען ניט אױף
צװײ פֿערד.

You can't sit on two horses with
one behind.
*Mit eyn hintn zitst men nit oyf tsvey
ferd.* IB

יעדער לױט זײַן געשמאַק.

Each to his taste.
Yeder loyt zayn geshmak. AC

CHUTSPEH

אַ ייִד האָט אַכט-און-צװאַנציק
פּראָצענט פּחד, צװײ
פּראָצענט צוקער און זיבעציק
פּראָצענט חוצפּה.

A Jew is composed of twenty-eight
per cent fear, two per cent sugar,
and seventy per cent nerve.
*A yid hot akht un tsvantsik protsent
pakhed, tsvey protsent tsuker un
zibetsik protsent khutspe.* NS

אַז דער רבֿ טוט אַ שידוך מיטן בעדער,
האַלט זיך דער בעדער פֿאַר אַ רבֿ.

If the rabbi enters into
matchmaking with the bath-house
attendant, the latter begins to
think he's a rabbi.
*Az der rov tut a shidekh mitn beder,
halt zikh der beder far a rov.* NS

אַז מען װיל ניט דעם חזן הײסט ער
זיך נאָך געבן אַ הוספֿה.

Just when you'd like to fire the
cantor he asks for a raise.
*Az men vil nit dem khazn, heyst er
zikh nokh gebn a hesofe.* NS

גאָט זאָל אָפּהיטן פֿון ייִדישער חוצפּה,
ייִדישע מײַלער און ייִדישע קעפּ.

God protect us from Jewish
chutspeh, Jewish mouths, and
Jewish brains.
*Got zol op'hitn fun yidisher khutspe,
yidishe mayler un yidishe kep.* IB

ער וויל מיר אײַנרעדן אַ קינד אין
בויך!

He wants to convince me I'm
pregnant!
Er vil mir aynredn a kind in boykh! P

נעם אַ ייִדן אונטערצופירן וואַרפֿט
ער דיך אַרויס פֿון וואָגן.

Offer a Jew a ride and he throws
you out of your own wagon.
Nem a yidn untertsufirn varft er dikh
aroys fun vogn. IB

CLEANLINESS

אַז די בעל-הביתטע איז אַ שטינקערן
איז די קאַץ אַ פֿרעסערן.

If the housewife is a slob, the cat
is a glutton.
Az di baleboste iz a shtinkern iz di
kats a fresern. NS

אַז איטלעכער קערט פֿאַר זײַן אייגן
שטוב איז די גאַנצע גאַס רייַן.

If everyone swept his own doorstep,
the whole street would be clean.
Az itlekher kert far zayn eygen shtub
iz di gantse gas reyn. NS

בײַם אויסקערן די שטוב
געפֿינט מען אַלץ.

When you sweep the house you
find everything.
Baym oyskern di shtub gefint men
alts. IB

רייַנקייט היט אָפּ דאָס געזונט.

Cleanliness is good for the health.
Reynkeyt hit op dos gezunt.

CLEVERNESS

אַ קלוגער קאָפּ האַלט זיך ניט לאַנג.

A clever head doesn't last long.
A kluger kop halt zikh nit lang. NS

אַז דער קלוגער באַנאַרישט זיך
בלײַבט ער אויך אַ נאַר.

When a clever person does something silly, he's also considered a fool.
Az der kluger banarisht zikh blaybt er oykh a nar. NS

אַז מען וויל זײַן קלוג
באַנאַרישט מען זיך גאָר (ליגט מען
גאָר אין דר׳ערד).

He who wants to be clever makes an ass out of himself (ends up going to the devil).
Az men vil zayn klug banarisht men zikh gor (ligt men gor in drerd). P

דער חכם שאָקלט זיך אַפֿילו ׳פֿון
דער תליה אַראָפּ.

A clever person can outwit even the gallows.
Der khokhem shoklt zikh afile fun der tli'e arop. IB

צוויי קלוגע קענען ניט שטימען.

Two clever people can't agree.
Tsvey kluge kenen nit shtimen. AC

ווער עס איז שיין – איך בין קלוג.

Let them be handsome as long as I'm clever.
Ver es iz sheyn – ikh bin klug. P

וואָס טויג מיר די חכמה אַז
נאַרישקייט גילט?

What's the use of being clever when folly reigns?
Vos toyg mir di khokhme az narishkeyt gilt? IF

COMMUNITY

אַז עס קומט אויף קהל אַ מכּה
קומט אויפֿן יחיד אַ בלאָטערל.

When the community gets an abscess, individual gets a blister.
Az es kumt oyf ko'ol a make kumt oyfn yokhed a bloterl. IB

גאַנץ אשכּנז איז איין שטאָט.

All Eastern European Jewry is one town.
Gants ashkenaz iz eyn shtot. IB

גאַנץ קהל איז ניט קיין גזלן.

The entire community isn't a robber.
[Not everyone in town is a crook.]
Gants ko'ol iz nit keyn gazlen. IB

קהלישע געלט האָט אין זיך אַ מאַגנעט.

Community funds are a magnet.
Kehilishe gelt hot in zikh a magnet. IB

מיט קהל איז זיך שלעכט צו משפּטן.

It's not a good idea to sue the community.
Mit ko'ol iz zikh shlekht tsu mishpetn. IB

אָן אַ קהלישע קליאַמקע איז זיך גוט אָנצוהאַלטן.

It's good to fasten yourself onto the community handle.
On a kehilishe kli'amke iz zikh gut ontsuhaltn. IB

וואָס טוט קהל אָן אַן אתרוג? מען בענטשט ניט.

What does the community do without a citron? It doesn't make the blessing.
[Refers to Succoth ritual.]
Vos tut ko'ol on an esreg? Men bentsht nit. IB

COMPARISON

אַ פֿאַרשפּאָרער איז בעסער ווי אַ פֿאַרדינער.

A saver is better than an earner.
A farshporer iz beser vi a fardiner. AC

אַן אַלטער איז גלײַך צו אַ קינד און אַ קינד צו אַ חזיר.

An old person can be compared to a child and a child to a pig.
An alter iz glaykh tsu a kind un a kind tsu a khazer. IB

אז קרופּניק איז אַן אַכילה איז איישישעק אַ קהילה.

If bean soup is a delicacy then Eyshishek is a community.
Az krupnik iz an akhile iz eyshishek a kehile. NS

צוויי פֿירער: יאָסל משה פֿירט
וואַסער־און גאָט פֿירט די וועלט.

Two managers: Yosel Moyshe
manages to carry water and God
manages the world.
*Tsvey firer: yosl moyshe firt vaser
un got firt di velt.* NS

אַז שקצים מיט מאָן איז אַ מאכל
איז פּיפּיווקע אַ טײַכל.

If noodles with poppy seeds is a tasty
dish, then Pipivkeh is a lake with fish.
['Shkotsim' has two meanings; in this
instance, it refers to a local delicacy.]
*Az shkotzim mit mon iz a maykhl iz
pipivke a taykhl.* IB

בעסער אַן אויפֿגעקומענער גביר
איידער אַן אָפּגעקומענער עושר.

Better a new millionaire than a
once bankrupt one.
*Beser an oyfgekumener gvir eyder an
opgekumener oysher.* IB

דער מלמד אַרבעט מיטן טײַטל און
דער גבֿיר מיטן בײַטל.

The teacher flogs with his stick
and the rich man with his wallet.
*Der melamed arbet mitn taytl un der
gvir mitn baytl.* IB

איינער האָט הנאה פֿון האַרטן קעז, אַ
צווייטער פֿון לאַנג והוא רחום און
אַ דריטער פֿון אַ טיר צו דער גאַס.

One person enjoys a piece of hard
cheese, a second a spun-out prayer
chant, and a third a door to the street.
*Eyner hot hano'e fun hartn kez, a
tsveyter fun lang vehu rakhum un a
driter fun a tir tsu der gas.* AC

CONCEIT

אַ צדיק וואָס ווייסט אַז ער איז אַ
צדיק איז קיין צדיק ניט.

A saint who knows he's saint is no
saint.
*A tsadik vos veyst az er iz a tsadik iz
keyn tsadik nit.* AC

ער האָט די ווערט פֿון אַ פּאים און
פֿאַרריַיסט דעם קאָפּ ווי אַ בוים.

He has as much worth as a
conscriptee yet he holds his head
high like a tree.
*Er hot di vert fun a poym un
far'rayst dem kop vi a boym.* NS

פֿאַר לויב איז קיינער ניט טויב.

No one is deaf to praise.
Far loyb iz keyner nit toyb. AC

אַז מען איז צו קלוג ליגט מען גאָר
אין דר'ערד.

Too smart outsmarts itself.
*Az men iz tsu klug ligt men gor in
drerd.* P

קיינער זעט ניט זַיַן אייגענעם
הויקער.

No one sees the hump on his own
back.
Keyner zet nit zayn eygenem hoyker. P

צו פֿיל עניוות איז אַ האַלבער שטאָלץ.

Too modest is half conceited.
Tsu fil anives iz a halber shtolts. IB

זיי האָבן זיך ביידע ליב – ער זיך און
זי זיך.

They are both in love – he with
himself, she with herself.
*Zey hobn zikh beyde lib – er zikh un
zi zikh.* P

CONFUSION

ער מישט אוים קאַשע מיט באָרשט.

He lumps together porridge with
soup.
Er misht oys kashe mit borsht. P

אין אָן אָפֿן טעפּל שטעקט
איטלעכע מויז אַרַיַן איר קעפּל.

An uncovered pot in the house
attracts every mouse.
*In an ofn tepl shtekt itlekhe moyz
arayn ir kepl.* IB

מען הערט די מגילה ווי דעם רב, דעם
רב ווי די מגילה, און זיי ביידע ווי
דעם פֿאַראיאָריקן שניי!

People pay attention to the megillah
like to the rabbi, to the rabbi
like to the megillah and to both
of them like to last year's snow!
*Men hert di megile vi dem rov, dem
rov vi di megile un zey beyde vi dem
farayorikn shney!* NS

צוליב די הייליקע קרעפלעך קען מען
די זינדיקע שול פֿאַרשפּעטיקן.

Because of the 'holy' dumplings we
could be late for the 'sinning'
synagogue.
*Tsulib di heylike kreplekh ke men di
zindike shul farshpetiken.* AC

CONSEQUENCE

אַ גוט מאָרגן ברענגט אַ גוט יאָר.

A 'good morning' is answered by
'good year.'
A gut morgn brengt a gut yor. IB

אַמאָל איז געווען און הײַנט איז ניטאָ,
מוז מען עסן וואָס איז דאָ.

Once there was and now there's
not, we have to eat what we've
got.
*Amol iz geven un haynt iz nito, muz
men esn vos iz do.* IF

אַלע קוימענס שמעקן מיט רויך.

All chimneys smell of smoke.
Ale koymens shmekn mit roykh. IB

אַז דער מלמד קריגט זיך מיט דער
ווײַב איז אָך און וויי צו די תלמידים.

When the teacher quarrels with
his wife, the pupils suffer.
*Az der melamed krigt zikh mit der
vayb iz okh un vey tsu di talmidim.* IB

אַז די באָרד ברענט איז הייס אין
מויל.

When the beard burns, the mouth
gets hot.
As di bord brent iz heys in moyl. IB

אַז עס דאַכט זיך באַפּישט מען זיך.

If you're uncertain, you wet your
pants.
Az es dakht zikh bapisht men zikh. IF

אַז מען בלאָזט ווערט קאַלט.

When you blow, it cools off.
Az men blozt vert kalt. NS

אַז מען עסט אָפּ די בייגל בלײַבט אין קעשענע דער לאָך.

If you eat the bagel only the hole remains in your pocket.
Az men est op di beygl blaybt in keshene der lokh. NS

אַז מען קלאַפּט אָן, ענטפֿערט מען.

If you knock, they answer.
Az men klapt on enfert men. IB

אַז מען הייצט אין באָד ווערט וואַרעם אין דער גאַנצער שטאָט.

If you heat the bath-house, the whole town warms up.
Az men heytst in bod vert varem in der gantser shtot. NS

אַז מען קאָכט אויף שטרוי איז דאָס עסן רוי.

If you cook with straw, the food remains raw.
Az men kokht oyf shtroy iz dos esn roy. NS

אַז מען לייגט אַרײַן, נעמט מען אַרויס.

If you put in, you can take out.
Az men leygt arayn, nemt men aroys. P

אַז מען לייגט זיך אין קלייען שלעפּן די חזירים.

If you lie in the pen, you'll be mauled by the pigs.
Az men leygt zikh in kleyen shlepn di khazeyrim. NS

אַז מען זייט אינדיקעס וואַקסן נאַראָנים.

If you sow turkeys, fools grow.
Az men zeyt indikes vaksn naronim. IB

אַזוי ווי מען בעט זיך אויס אַזוי שלאָפֿט מען.

The way you make your bed, that's how you will sleep.
Azoy vi men bet zikh oys azoy shloft men. AC

ברעכט זיך אַ רינג צעפֿאַלט די גאַנצע קייט.

One link snaps and the whole chain falls apart.
Brekht zikh a ring tsefalt di gantse keyt. NS

פֿון וואַנען קען זײַן חלה אַז ס'איז
ניטאָ קיין מעל?

How can you have challah without
any flour?
*Fun vanen ken zayn khale az s'iz
nito keyn mel?* AC

פֿון יענער זײַט פּלאַנקען האָט
מען אַנדערע געדאַנקען.

When you cross the fence, other
thoughts commence.
*Fun yener zayt planken hot men
andere gedanken.* NS

קיינער קען קיין הינדל ניט שעכטן
אַז ס'זאָל ניט גיין קיין בלוט.

A hen can't be slaughtered without
blood being shed.
*Keyner ken keyn hindl nit shekhtn az
s'zol nit geyn keyn blut.* NS

נאָך אַ חתונה קומט אַ ברית.

After the wedding comes the bris.
Nokh a khasene kumt a bris. IB

צי דער שטיין פֿאַלט אויפֿן טאָפּ
אָדער דער טאָפּ פֿאַלט אויפֿן שטיין
איז ווי צו דעם טאָפּ.

Whether the stone falls on the pot
or the pot on the stone, woe to the
pot!
*Tsi der shteyn falt oyfn top oder der
top falt oyfn shteyn iz vey tsu dem
top!* IB

ווער עם פּאָרעט זיך מיט סמאָלע
שמירט זיך אײַן די הענט.

If you deal in tar, your hands will
be smeared.
*Ver es poret zikh mit smole shmirt
zikh ayn di hent.* NS

ווילסטו קנײַדלעך? זאָג די הגדה.

If you want the dumplings, first
recite the Haggadah.
Vilstu k'neyklekh? zog di hagode. P

וווּ הינט בילן דאָרט וווינען מענטשן.

Where dogs bark, people live.
Vu hint biln dort voynen mentshn. NS

וווּהין די נאָדל, אַהין דער פֿאָדעם.

Where the needle, there the
thread.
Vuhin di nodl, ahin der fodem. NS

יעדער וואָרום האָט אַ דאָרום. Every wherefore has a therefore.
Yeder varum hot a darum. NS

CORRUPTION

אַ קרומער קאָפּ פירט די פֿים אין
קרומע וועגן.
A corrupt head leads the feet in
corrupt ways.
*A krumer kop firt di fis in krume
vegn.* NS

אַז דער גבאי גייט ניט אין שול אַריַין
איז אַ סימן אַז די שול גייט אין
גבאי אַריַין.
If the trustee doesn't go into the
synagogue, it's a sign that the
synagogue goes into the trustee.
*Az der gabay geyt nit in shul arayn
iz a simen az di shul geyt in gabay
arayn.* IB

דער פֿיש שטינקט פֿון קאָפּ. The fish stinks from the head.
Der fish shtinkt fun kop. AC

דער פּאַרך האָט ניט ליב דעם קאַם. A scabby head doesn't like the comb.
Der parekh hot nit lib dem kam. IB

אײן פֿאַרפֿוילטער עפּל פֿאַרפֿוילט
אַלע אַנדערע.
One rotten apple spoils all the others.
*Eyn farfoylter epl farfoylt ale
andere.* NS

CRITICISM

אַ חסרון די כּלה איז צו שײן. It's too bad the bride is so pretty.
A khisorn di kale iz tsu sheyn. P

אַז דאָס מײדל קען ניט טאַנצן, זאָגט זי
אַז די כּלי־זמרים קענען ניט שפּילן.
If the girl can't dance, she says
the musicians can't play.
*Az dos meydl ken nit tantsn, zogt zi
az di klezmorim kenen nit shpiln.* NS

עם איז לײַכטער צו זיַין אַ מבֿקר
ווי אַ מחבר.
It's easier to be a critic than an
author.
*Es iz laykhter tsu zayn a mevaker vi
a mekhaber.* AC

אײנע קלאָגט װאָס די פּערל זײַנען
שיטער, די צװײיטע קלאָגט װאָס
דאָס לעבן איז ביטער.

One complains that her pearls are
too few, another complains that
life is a bitter brew.
Eyne klogt vos di perl zaynen shiter,
di tsveyte klogt vos dos lebn iz biter. IB

מע גיט ניט אַ פּתחון פּה לשטן.

Don't leave your mouth open for
Satan to enter.
Me git nit a piskhon pe l'sotn. LMF

װעמען עס איז צו ענג זאָל אָפּטרעטן.

Whoever finds it too crowded can
leave.
Vemen es iz tsu eng zol optretn. IB

װען ניט די צוהערערם װאָלט ניט
געװען קיין באַקלאָגערם.

If not for the listeners, there
would be no complainers.
Ven nit di tsuherers volt nit geven
keyn baklogers. IB

יענעמם תחת איז גוט צו שמײַסן.

It's good to flog someone else's
behind.
Yenems tokhes iz gut tsu shmaysn. P

CURIOSITY

אַ מענטש זאָל לעבן נאָר פֿון
נײַגעריקײַט װעגן.

A person should live if only for
curiosity's sake.
A mentsh zol lebn nor fun
naygerikeyt vegn. NS

דער װאָס װיל אַלץ װיסן װערט גיך אַלט.

He who wants to know everything
ages early.
Der vos vil alts visn vert gikh alt. P

ער װיל װיסן פֿון װאַנען די פֿים װאַקסן.

He wants to know where a
person's legs grow from.
[what makes him tick]
Er vil visn fun vanen di fis vaksn. P

| זי איז טשיקאַװע װי די מוטער חװה. | She's as curious as Mother Eve.
Zi iz tshikave vi di muter khave. IB |

CURSES

| אַ קללה איז ניט אַ טעלעגראַמע
– זי קומט ניט אָן אַזױ גיך. | A curse isn't a telegram – it
doesn't arrive as fast.
*A klole iz nit a telegrame - zi kumt
nit on azoy gikh.* NS |

| בעסער הערן קללות איידער הערן
נעבעך. | Better to be cursed than pitied.
Beser hern kloles eyder hern nebekh. IB |

| די מאַמע שעלט אָבער עס טוט איר
װײ דאָס האַרץ. | A mother may curse but it hurts
her heart.
*Di mame shelt ober es tut ir vey dos
harts.* NS |

| אין דער תּורה זײַנען דאָ מער קללות
װי ברכות. | The Bible contains more curses
than blessings.
*In der toyre zaynen do mer kloles vi
brokhes.* AC |

| װען דער מאַן איז אַ בעל-עגלה האָט ער
ניט מורא פֿאַר דער װײַבס קללה. | When the husband is a wagoneer,
he's not afraid of his wife's jeer.
*Ven der man iz a balegole hot er nit
moyre far der vaybs klole.* NS |

EXAMPLES

אַ בייז באַגעגעניש זאָל אים טרעפֿן!

May an evil encounter befall him!
A beyz bagegenish zol im trefn! P

אַ גרויס געשעפֿט זאָל ער האָבן מיט
סחורה: וואָס ער האָט זאָל מען ניט
וועלן און וואָס מען וויל זאָל ער ניט
האָבן!

May he own a large shop stocked
with merchandise: what he has,
may no one want and what they
want may he not have!
*A groys gesheft zol er hobn mit
skhoyre: vos er hot zol men nit veln
un vos men vil zol er nit hobn!* IB

אַ רוח אין זײַן טאַטנס טאַטן אַרײַן!

Damn him right into his father's
father!
A ru'ekh in zayn tatns tatn arayn! P

אַלע מײַנע צרות זאָלן אויסגניין צו
זײַן קאָפּ!

May all my troubles be heaped on
his head!
*Ale mayne tsores zoln oysgeyn tsu
zayn kop!* P

אַלע ציין זאָלן אים אַרויספֿאַלן, נאָר
איינער זאָל אים בלײַבן אויף
צאָנווייטיק!

May all his teeth fall out and only
one remain for toothache!
*Ale tseyn zoln im aroysfaln, nor
eyner zol im blaybn oyf tsonveytik!* AC

אײַננעמען זאָל ער אַ מיתה משונה!

May a violent death overtake him!
Ayn'nemen zol er a mise meshune! P

דער פֿאָדעם זאָל בײַ אים אויסגניין!

May his thread run out!
Der fodem zol bay im oysgeyn! NS

די נשמה זאָל בײַ אים אויסגניין!

May his soul depart from him!
Di neshome zol bay im oysgeyn! P

ער וואָלט שוין געמעגט זײַן מיט
אַ קאָפּ קלענער!

It's time he were a head shorter
already!
*Er volt shoyn gemegt zayn mit a kop
klener!* AC

ער זאָל זײַן װי אַ לאָמפּ: העננגען בײַ
טאָג, ברענען בײַ נאַכט און אויסגיין
זאָל ער אין דער פֿרי!

May he be like a lamp: hang by
day, burn all night, and be
extinguished in the morning!
*Er zol zayn vi a lomp: hengen bay
tog, brenen bay nakht un oysgeyn
zol er in der fri!* P

עס זאָל דיר דונערן אין די ציין
װעסטו מיינען אַז דו קנאַקסט נים!

May it thunder in your teeth so
that you'll think you're cracking
nuts!
*Es zol dir dunern in di tseyn vestu
meynen az du k'nakst nis!* NS

עסן זאָלסטו געהאַקטע לעבער מיט
ציבעלעס, שמאַלץ הערינג, יויך מיט
קנײדלעך, קאַרפּ מיט כריין, אײַנגע-
דעמפֿס מיט צימעס, לאַטקעס, טיי
מיט ציטרין, יעדן טאָג – און זאָלסט
זיך מיט יעדן ביס בים דערשטיקן!

May you eat chopped liver with
onions, shmaltz herring, chicken
soup with dumplings, baked carp
with horseradish, braised meat
with vegetable stew, latkes, tea
with lemon, every day – and may
you choke on every mouthful!
*Esn zolstu gehakte leber mit tsibeles,
shmalts hering, yoykh mit
k'neydlekh, karp mit khreyn,
ayngedemfs mit tsimes, latkes, tey mit
tsitrin, yedn tog – un zolst zikh mit
yedn bis dershtikn!* AC

פֿאַרגעלט און פֿאַרגרינט זאָל ער װערן!

May he turn yellow and green!
Fargelt un fargrint zol er vern! P

גלח צאָפּ, אַ מכּה דיר אין קאָפּ, מיר
אַ װאָגן, דיך באַגראָבן, מיר אַ
שליטן, דיך באַשיטן, מיר ברויט, דיר
טויט!

Priestly braid, on your head a
plague, me a cart, you apart, me
a sleigh, you away, me bread, you
dead!
[children's curse on sight of an Orthodox priest]
*Galekh tsop, a make dir in kop, mir
a vogn, dikh bagrobn, mir a shlitn,
dikh bashitn, mir broyt, dir toyt!* AC

געשוואָלן און געדראָלן זאָל ער ווערן
ווי אַ באַרג!

May he become swollen and veined
like a mountain!
*Geshvoln un gedroln zol er vern vi a
barg!* IB

גיין זאָל ער ווו דער ליבער שבת
קודש גייט אַוועק!

May he go where the beloved Holy
Sabbath disappears to!
*Geyn zol er vu der liber shabes
koydesh geyt avek!* AC

געזונט און שטײַף זאָלסטו זײַן!

Healthy and stiff may you become!
[a play on a traditional greeting]
Gezunt un shtayf zolstu zayn! AC

גאָט זאָל אים געבן אַלצדינג וואָס
זײַן האַרץ גלוסט, נאָר ער זאָל זײַן
געליימט אויף אַלע אבֿרים און ניט
קענען רירן מיט דער צונג!

May God bless him with all his
heart desires but he should be
crippled in all his limbs and not
be able to move his tongue!
*Got zol im gebn altsding vos zayn
harts glust, nor er zol zayn geleymt
oyf ale eyvrim un nit kenen rirn mit
der tsung!* NS

גאָט זאָל אים העלפֿן ער זאָל שטענדיק
זײַן געזונט און שטאַרק און
שטענדיק פֿרעגן וואָס פֿאַר אַ
וועטער ס'איז אין דרויסן!

May God keep him hale and
hearty so that he may always have
the strength to ask what the
weather is like outdoors!
*Got zol im helfn er zol shtendik zayn
gezunt un shtark un shtendik fregn
vos far a veter s'iz in droysn!* IB

גאָט זאָל אויף אים אָנשיקן אַ נאַר!

May God assign a fool to him!
Got zol oyf im onshikn a nar! AC

העענג דיר אויף אַ צוקער שטריקל
וועסטו האָבן אַ זיסן טויט!

Hang yourself with the rope from
a sugar bag and you will have a
sweet death!
*Heng dir oyf a tsuker shtrikl vestu
hobn a zisn toyt!* NS

המנס גדולה און קורחס נס זאָל
אים טרעפֿן!

May Haman's glory and Korakh's
miracle befall him!
*Homens gdule un korakhs nes zol im
trefn!* NS

איך צו אים אויף שׂימחות, ער צו
מיר אויף קוליעם!

May I visit him in celebration,
may he visit me on crutches!
*Ikh tsu im oyf simkhes, er tsu mir
oyf kulyes!* AC

קיין עין-הרע זאָל אים ניט אויסמײַדן!

May no evil eye avoid him!
Keyn eyn-hore zol im nit oysmaydn! NS

חתונה האָבן זאָל ער מיטן
מלאך-המוות טאָכטער!

May he marry the angel of death's
daughter!
*Khasene hobn zol er mitn
malekhamoves tokhter!* NS

קריגן זאָל ער דעם לעמבערגנער בראָך!

May the Lemberg disaster befall
him!
Krign zol er dem lemberger brokh! NS

מײַנע שׂונאים זאָלן אַזוי לעבן!

May my enemies live like this!
Mayne sonim zoln azoy lebn! P

מען זאָל איר שוין אָנגיסן מיט
טהרה וואַסער!

May the burial waters be spilled
over her already!
*Men zol ir shoyn ongisn mit ta'are
vaser!* AC

משוגע זאָל ער ווערן און אַרומלויפֿן
איבער די גאַסן!

May he go crazy and run around
in the streets!
*Meshuge zol er vern un arumloyfn
iber di gasn!* NS

נייען זאָל מען אים תכריכים!

It's high time they sewed his
shrouds.
Neyen zol men im takhrikhim! IB

אָפּקױפֿן זאָל מען בײַם טאַטן זײַנע
מלבושים!

May his father sell off all his clothes!
Opkoyfn zol men baym tatn zayne malbushim! IB

אויף דאָקטוירים זאָל ער עס
אַװעקגעבן!

May he spend it all on doctors!
Oyf doktoyrim zol er es avekgebn! IB

פּלאַצן זאָל ער פֿון נחת!

May he burst from pleasure!
Platsn zol er fun nakhes! AC

שפּילן זאָל ער מיטן לעבן און געװינען
זאָל ער דעם טױט!

May he gamble with life and win death!
Shpiln zol er mitn lebn un gevinen zol er dem toyt! NS

צען שיפֿן מיט גאָלד זאָל ער פֿאַרמאָגן
און דאָס גאַנצע געלט זאָל ער
אױסקרענקען!

May he own ten ships laden with gold and he should sicken away the entire worth of it!
Tsen shifn mit gold zol er farmogn un dos gantse gelt zol er oyskrenken! IB

אונדז אין דער הײם, זײ אין דער
נידער, מאָרגן שלעפּן צװאַנציק
װידער!

We at home, they underground, tomorrow twenty more laid in the ground!
[said on witnessing the passing of a Gentile funeral procession]
Undz in der heym, zey in der nider, morgn shlepn tsvantsik vider! NS

װערן זאָל פֿון איר אַ בלינץ און פֿון אים
אַ קאַץ, ער זאָל זי אױפֿעסן און זיך
דערשטיקן, װאָלט מען פֿון זײ בײדע
פּטור געװאָרן!

May she become a blintz and he a cat; he should eat her and choke so that we could be rid of both of them!
Vern zol fun ir a blints un fun im a kats, er zol zi oyfesn un zikh dershtikn, volt men fun zey beyde poter gevorn! AC

וואָס עס האָט זיך מיר געחלומט די
נאַכט און יענע נאַכט און אַלע נעכט
זאָל אויסגיין צו זיַין קאָפּ, צו זיַינע
הענט און פֿיס, צו זיַין ליַיב און
צו זיַין לעבן!

May what I dreamt last night and
the night before and every night
descend on his head, on his hands
and feet, on his body and his life!
*Vos es hot zikh mir gekholemt di
nakht un yene nakht un ale nekht zol
oysgeyn tsu zayn kop, tsu zayne hent
un fis, tsu zayn layb un tsu zayn
lebn!* IB

זאַלץ אים אין די אויגן און פֿעפֿער
אים אין נאָז!

Salt his eyes and pepper his nose!
Zalts im in di oygn un fefer im in noz! NS

זיַין טאַטע אין זיַינע יאָרן האָט שוין
עטלעכע פּאָר תכריכים צעריסן.

His father at the same age had
already worn out several shrouds!
*Zayn tate in zayne yorn hot shoyn
etlekhe por takhrikhim tserisn!* AC

זאָל דיך אַ קאָטער באַקאַקן
און אַ קאַץ באַלעקן!

May a tomcat shit on you and a
pussycat lick you!
*Zol dikh a koter bakakn un a kats
balekn!* AC

זאָל ער גיין מיטן קאָפּ אין קעסטל,
קעסטל אין דר'ערד.

May he go head in the casket,
casket in the earth!
*Zol er geyn mitn kop in kestl, kestl
in dr'erd!* NS

זאָל ער וואַקסן ווי אַ ציבעלע: מיטן קאָפּ
אין דר'ערד און די פֿים פֿאַרקערט!

May he grow like an onion: with
his head in the ground and his feet
in the air!
*Zol er vaksn vi a tsibele: mitn kop in
dr'erd un di fis farkert!* P

זאָל שוין זיַין אַ גרויסער יריד אין גן-עדן
און זאָל ער דאָרטן מצליח זיַין!

There should be a great fair in
paradise and may he prosper there!
*Zol shoyn zayn a groyser yarid in
gan-eydn un zol er dortn matsli'ekh
zayn.* NS

זאָל ער קרענקען און געדענקען!

May he sicken and remember!
Zol er krenken un gedenken! AC

זאָלסטו דערצויגן ווערן לחופה ולתליה!

May you be reared to the bridal canopy and to the gallows!
[play on words on a traditional greeting]
Zolstu dertsoygn vern lekhupe uletli'e! AC

CUSTOM

אַ געוווינהייט איז אַ צווייטע נאַטור.

A custom is second nature.
A gevoynheyt iz a tsveyte natur. NS

אַזוי ווי די צייטן, אַזוי די לייטן.

Like the times, so the people.
Azoy vi di tsaytn, azoy di laytn. AC

דאָס הינדל ווערט מיטן שעכטן געוווינט!

The chicken is accustomed to the slaughter.
Dos hindl vert mitn shekhtn gevoynt. NS

עס שטייט ניט אין מאַמעס סידורל.

It doesn't say so in mother's prayerbook.
Es shteyt nit in mames siderl. AC

"עולם כמינהגו נוהג" – דעריבער זעט טאַקע די וועלט אויס אַזוי.

"The world goes its usual way" – that's why it looks the way it does.
"Oylem keminhogoy noyheg" – deriber zet take di velt oys azoy. NS

פורים איז ניט קיין יום-טוב און יעדער מענטש האָט זיין פעקל.

If Purim is no holiday, then fever is no sickness.
Purim iz nit keyn yontev un kadokhes iz nit keyn krenk. P

צו וואָס מען געוווינט זיך אין דער יוגנט ביי דעם בלייבט מען אויף דער עלטער.

Whatever you become accustomed to in youth remains into old age.
Tsu vos men gevoynt zikh in der yugnt bay dem blaybt men oyf der elter. NS

ווען מען קומט צווישן קראָען מוז
מען קראַקן ווי זיי.

When you come among crows, you
must caw like them.
*Ven men kumt tsvishn kro'en muz
men kraken vi zey.* NS

CYNICISM

אַ גוטער מענטש נאָר דער בייזער
הונט לאָזט ניט צו.

He's a good person but his vicious
dog won't let you near him!
*A guter mentsh nor der beyzer hunt
lozt nit tsu.* IB

אַז דער אָקס פאַלט שאַרפֿן אַלע
די מעסערם.

When the ox falls everyone
sharpens his knife.
Az der oks falt sharfn ale di mesers. AC

דער שענקער האָט ליב דעם שיכּור
אָבער די טאָכטער וועט ער אים
ניט געבן.

The innkeeper loves the drunkard
but he won't let him marry his
daughter.
*Der shenker hot lib dem shiker ober
di tokhter vet er im nit gebn.* NS

מען זאָל זיך קענען אויסקויפֿן פֿון
טויט וואָלטן אַלע אָרעמעלייט
שיין פּרנסה געהאַט.

If everyone could hire others to
die for them, the poor could make
a very nice living.
*Men zol zikh kenen oyskoyfn fun toyt
voltn ale oremelayt sheyn parnose
gehat.* NS

ווען מענטשן זאָלן האָבן אַ דעה איבער
דער זון וואָלט זי לאַנג שוין
פֿינסטער געוואָרן.

If people could control the sun it
would long ago have gotten dark.
*Ven mentshn zoln hobn a deye iber
der zun volt zi lang shoyn finster
gevorn.* AC

DANGER

אַלע רויזן שמעקן אָבער זיי שטעכן. | All roses are fragrant but they have thorns.
Ale royzn shmekn ober zey shtekhn. IB

אַז עס ברענט ביַים שכן ביסטו אויך אין סכּנה. | If there's a fire at your neighbor's, you are also in danger.
Az es brent baym shokhn bistu oykh in sakone. IB

דער וואָס קען גיבן אַ לעק קען אויך גיבן אַ ביס. | He who can lick can also bite.
Der vos ken gibn a lek ken oykh gibn a bis. IB

ווי זאָל דאָס שעפעלע רויִק עסן, אַז דער וואָלף שטייט דערביַי? | How can the lamb quietly graze when the wolf is in its gaze?
Vi zol dos shefele ru'ik esn az der volf shteyt derbay? NS

DEATH

אַ קינד ווערט געבוירן מיט קוליאַקן און אַ מאַן שטאַרבט מיט אָפֿענע הענט. | A child is born with clenched fists and a man dies with open hands.
A kind vert geboyrn mit kulyakn un a man shtarbt mit ofene hent. NS

א יונגער קען שטאַרבן, אַן אַלטער
מוז שטאַרבן.

A young person can die, an old one must die.
A yunger ken shtarbn, an alter muz shtarbn. AC

אַלצדינג לאָזט זיך אויס מיט אַ געוויין.

Everything ends in weeping.
Altsding lozt zikh oys mit a geveyn. P

אַ טויטן באַוויינט מען זיבן טעג – אַ
נאַר דאָס גאַנצן לעבן.

A death is mourned seven days – a fool is mourned a whole life long.
A toytn baveynt men zibn teg – a nar dos gantsn lebn. P

אַז מען פֿאַלט צום טויט כּורעים
העלפֿן שוין ניט קיין דאָקטוירים.

When you fall dead on your face, a doctor's help is out of place.
Az men falt tsum toyt koyrim helfn shoyn nit keyn doktoyrim. NS

אַז אַ קעכן שטאַרבט באַגראָבט
מען איר אונטערן קוימען.

When a cook dies, she's buried under the hearth.
[at the seat of her crimes]
Az a kekhn shtarbt bagrobt men ir untern koymen. IB

בעסער צען מאָל פֿאַרדאָרבן איידער
איין מאָל געשטאָרבן.

Better ten times corrupted than once dead.
Beser tsen mol fardorbn eyder eyn mol geshtorbn. NS

דער מלאך-המוות געפֿינט
שטענדיק אַ תירוץ.

The angel of death always finds an excuse.
Der malekhamoves gefint shtendik a terets. NS

דער מלאך-המוות קוקט ניט אין לוח.

The angel of death doesn't look at the calendar.
Der malekhamoves kukt nit in lu'ekh. IB

די גאַנצע וועלט איז אַ חלום און דער
טויט אַ פתרון.

The whole world is a dream and
death the interpreter.
*Di gantse velt iz a kholem un der
toyt a pisorn.* AC

דרײַ זאַכן זײַנען נאָכן טויט שענער
ווי בײַם לעבן: אַ בוריק, אַ ראַק
און אַ ליטוואַק.

Three things are better dead than
alive: a beet, a cancer, and a Litvak.
*Dray zakhn zaynen nokhn toyt
shener vi baym lebn: a burik, a rak
un a litvak.* NS

אײדער אַזוי צו פאָרן איז שוין בעסער
צו פֿוס צו גיין.

Rather than ride like that [in a
hearse], it's better to walk.
*Eyder azoy tsu forn iz shoyn beser
tsu fus tsu geyn.* P

פאַר דער צײַט שטאַרבט קיינער ניט.

No one dies before his time.
Far der tsayt shtarbt keyner nit. P

פון צוויי טויטן קען מען ניט לײַדן
און איינעם קען מען ניט
אויסמײַדן.

Two deaths cannot be suffered and
one cannot be avoided.
*Fun tsvey toytn ken men nit laydn un
eynem ken men nit oysmaydn.* NS

געשטאָרבן, באַגראָבן און אַראָפ פון
מאַרק!

Dead, buried, and off the market!
Geshtorbn, bagrobn un arop fun mark!

יעדער טאָג וואָס פאַרגייט צום קבר
באַלײַט.

Every day that passes brings you
closer to the grave.
*Yeder tog vos fargeyt tsum keyver
baleyt.* NS

זינט עס איז אויפֿגעקומען דאָס
שטאַרבן איז מען ניט זיכער
מיטן לעבן.

Since dying became fashionable,
living isn't safe.
*Zint es iz oyfgekumen dos shtarbn iz
men nit zikher mitn lebn.* AC

BURIAL

אַ גרוב איז ניט קיין שטוב.

A grave is not a home.
A grub iz nit keyn shtub. NS

אַ שטוב אָן פֿענסטער איז קיין
דירה ניט און אַ קאָפּאָטע
אָן קנעפּלעך איז קיין בגד ניט.

A house without windows is no
home and a garment without
buttons is no coat.
*A shtub on fenster iz keyn dire nit
un a kapote on k'neplekh iz keyn
beged nit.* NS

אַז מען שטאַרבט זאָלצט מען ניט
איַין נאָר מען באַגראָבט.

When you die you don't get
preserved but buried.
*Az men shtarbt zaltst men nit ayn
nor men bagrobt.* AC

כל-זמן דער מענטש לעבט איז אים די
גאַנצע וועלט צו קליין, נאָכן טויט
איז דער קבֿר גענוג.

As long as one lives, the whole
world is too small; after death, the
grave is big enough.
*Kolzman der mentsh lebt iz im di
gantse velt tsu kleyn, nokhn toyt iz
der keyver genug.* AC

בעסער אין וויַיטן לאַנד איידער אין
טיפֿן זאַמד.

Better in a far land than in the
deep sand.
Beser in vaytn land eyder in tifn zamd. NS

חבֿרה-קדישה טרינקט – וויַיל דער
טויטער שטינקט!

Burial Society, drink – because the
corpse stinks!
*Khevre-kedishe trinkt – vayl der
toyter shtinkt!* NS

מיט שטאַרבן באַגראָבט מען זיך נאָר.

All you accomplish by death is burial.
Mit shtarbn bagrobt men zikh nor. NS

וואָס די ערד דעקט צו מוז פֿאַרגעסן
ווערן.

What the earth covers must be
forgotten.
Vos di erd dekt tsu muz fargesn vern. IB

DEBT

באָרגן מאַכט זאָרגן.

Borrowing causes sorrowing.
Borgn makht zorgn. P

אַז מען באַצאָלט אַ חוב מעג מען
מאַכן אַ יום-טוב.

When you've repaid a debt, make
a banquet.
*Az men batsolt a khoyv meg men
makhn a yontev.* NS

עס באַצאָלט ניט דער רײַכער נאָר
דער וואָס איז שולדיק.

The rich man doesn't pay, the
debtor does.
*Es batsolt nit der raykher nor der
vos iz shuldik.* NS

פֿאַר מאָרגן וועט גאָט זאָרגן – און
הײַנט ווער וועט מיר באָרגן?

Let God worry for tomorrow –
but now, where can I borrow?
*Far morgn vet got zorgn – un haynt
ver vet mir borgn?* AC

קראַצן און באָרגן איז נאָר גוט אויף
אַ ווײַל.

Scratching and borrowing is only
good for a time.
*Kratsn un borgn iz nor gut oyf a
vayl.* NS

מיט זכות-אָבות באַצאָלט מען ניט
קיין חובות.

With noble relations you don't pay
obligations.
*Mit skhus-oves batsolt men nit keyn
khoyves.* NS

נײַע חובות האַלט מען ביז זיי ווערן
אַלט און אַלטע צאָלט מען אין גאַנצן
ניט.

New debts are kept until they get
old and old ones don't get paid at all.
*Naye khoyves halt men biz zey vern
alt un alte tsolt men in gantsn nit.* AC

אונטערגענונומען הייסט זיך פֿאַרקויפֿט.

Take on a debt and you are
obligated.
Untergenumen heyst zikh farkoyft. NS

DECEPTION

אַ שפּיגל קען אויך זײַן דער גרעסטער
פֿאַרפֿירער.

A mirror can also be the greatest
deceiver.
*A shpigl ken oykh zayn der grester
farfirer.* NS

דער מענטש איז אין זיך אַליין
פֿאַרנאַרט.

A person is deceived by himself.
Der mentsh iz in zikh aleyn farnart. P

פֿון װײַטן נאַרט מען לײַטן, פֿון דער
נאָענט זיך אַליין.

From afar you fool others; from
close up, only yourself.
*Fun vaytn nart men laytn, fun der
no'ent zikh aleyn.* AC

גאָט האָט אים געגעבן אַ צונג ער
זאָל מיט איר דרייען.

God gave him a tongue so that he
could cheat with it.
*Got hot im gegebn a tsung er zol mit
ir dreyen.* AC

מען נעמט אויס „ברחל בתך הקטנה"
מיט אַ שטיקל ליכט און מען קריגט
פֿאָרט די אַלטע בלינדע לאה.

We specifically agreed upon ''the
younger daughter Rachel,'' and I
nevertheless end up with the old
blind Leah.
[Refers to Biblical story of Jacob, Rachel, and
Leah.]
*Men nemt oys ''b'rokhl bitkhe
haktone'' mit a shtikl likht un men
krigt fort di alte blinde leye.* AC

אָפּנאַרן איז קיין קונץ ניט.

Deceiving others is no big trick.
Opnarn iz keyn kunts nit. P

DEFECT

אַ געלער איז אַ שטעלער, איז ער
ניט קיין שטעלער האָט ער אַן
אַנדערן פֿעלער.

A redhead can't be trusted; if he's
not a liar then he has some other
defect.
*A geler iz a shteler, iz er nit keyn
shteler hot er an andern feler.* NS

אַ שוחט טאָר קיין פּנימה ניט האָבן.

A slaughterer should have no defects.
A shoykhet tor keyn p'gime nit hobn. NS

דער בלינדער האָט די אויגן אין
שפּיץ פֿינגער.

A blind person has his eyes in his
fingertips.
*Der blinder hot di oygn in shpits
finger.* IB

אויף איין אויג נאָר איז די קו בלינד. | The cow is blind only in one eye.
Oyf eyn oyg nor iz di ku blind. NS

עס וועט זיך אויסהיילן ביז צו דער חתונה. | It will heal in time for the wedding.
Es vet zikh oys'heyln biz tsu der khasene. P

אין אַ שיינעם עפל געפֿינט מען אויך אַ וואָרעם. | In a perfect apple you can also find a worm.
In a sheynem epl gefint men oykh a vorem. P

קוק אַריַין אין עפל וועסטו געפֿינען דעם וואָרעם. | Examine the apple and you'll find the worm.
Kuk arayn in epl vestu gefinen dem vorem. NS

DESTINY

אַ מענטש ווערט מיט קיין זאַך ניט געבוירן. | A person comes into this world with nothing.
A mentsh vert mit keyn zakh nit geboyrn. NS

אַז עס איז באַשערט דעם טויט העלפֿט ניט קיין רייד. | If you're destined to die, talking won't help.
Az es iz bashert dem toyt helft nit keyn reyd. P

אַ גוטער פֿאַל קומט במילא.

A good event comes by itself.
A guter fal kumt bemeyle. NS

אַז עם איז איינעם באַשערט
דערטרונקען צו ווערן ווערט ער
דערטרונקען אין אַ לעפֿל
וואַסער.

If one is fated to drown, a spoonful of water will do.
Az es iz eynem bashert dertrunken tsu vern vert er dertrunken in a lefl vaser. P

דער קרוג גייט אַזוי לאַנג צום וואַסער
ביז דאָס אויער ברעכט זיך אָפּ.

The pitcher goes to the well so often until its ear breaks off.
Der krug geyt azoy lang tsum vaser biz dos oyer brekht zikh op. P

דער אָקס איז געוווינט צום חלף.

The ox is destined for the knife.
Der oks iz gevoynt tsum khalef. NS

דאָס רעדל דרייט זיך.

The wheel turns round.
Dos redl dreyt zikh. P

איינעם וואַרפֿט מען אַרײַן, דעם
אַנדערן וואַרפֿט מען אַרויס.

One gets thrown in, another thrown out.
Eynem varft men arayn, dem andern varft men aroys. AC

גייט עם, גייט עם, קוועטשן דאַרף
מען ניט.

If it goes, it goes, don't force it.
Geyt es, geyt es, kvetshn darf men nit AC

מען איז טאַקע ניט ווערט אָבער
ס'איז אַזוי באַשערט.

One may be low-rated but that's how it's fated.
Men iz take nit vert ober s'iz azoy bashert. P

„מי בחרב ומי ברעב" – ווער עם זאָל
ניכשל ווערן דורך דער שווערד
און ווער דורכן רב.

"Who through the sword and who through hunger" – some will be knocked off by the sword and some by the rabbi.
[Play on words: 'rav' has two meanings, 'hunger' and 'rabbi.']
"Mi b'kherev umi b'rav" – ver es zol nikhshl vern durkh der shverd un ver durkhn rov. AC

קיינער וייסט ניט וועמענס מאָרגן
עס וועט זײַן.

No one knows whose tomorrow it
will be.
*Keyner veyst nit vemens morgn es
vet zayn.* P

וועמען צו ברויט, וועמען צו טויט.

Some get bread, some get dead.
Vemen tsu broyt, vemen tsu toyt. NS

וויל מען הגבה קריגט מען גלילה.

Seek one honor and you get
another instead.
Vil men hagbe krigt men gelile. AC

וואָס עס וועט ווערן מיט כל ישראל
וועט ווערן מיט רב ישראל.

Whatever befalls the People of
Israel will befall Mr Israel.
*Vos es vet vern mit kol yisro'el vet
vern mit reb yisro'el.* IB

וואָס גאָט טוט באַשערן קען קיין
מענטש ניט פֿאַרווערן.

What God has sent, no one can
prevent.
*Vos got tut bashern ken keyn mentsh
nit farvern.* NS

וואָס וועט זײַן, וועט זײַן.

What will be, will be.
Vos vet zayn, vet zayn. P

DISBELIEF

עס האָט זיך געטראָפֿן א מילכיקער
נס!

A wishy-washy miracle happened!
Es hot zikh getrofn a milkhiker nes! IB

א גאַנצער שטאָט פֿאַרשיקט
מען ניט קיין סיביר!

A whole city doesn't get exiled to
Siberia!
*A gantser shtot farshikt men nit keyn
sibir!* NS

דעמאָלט ווען דרײַ טעג ראָש חודש
וועט זײַן!

Not until there will be three first
days of the month!
*Demolt ven dray teg resh khoydesh
vet zayn!* IB

דו וועסט עס שוין זען ווי דײַנע אויערן!

You'll as soon see it as your own
ears!
Du vest es shoyn zen vi dayne oyern! IB

ער איז אַ בחור ווי די נאַם איז אַ מויד!

He's a bachelor like the wet-nurse
is a maiden!
Er iz a bokher vi di nam iz a moyd! IB

עס איז אין הימל אַ יריד!

In heaven there's a great fair!
Es iz in himl a yarid! P

עס איז נישט געפֿלויגן, נישט
געשטויגן!

It didn't rise, it didn't fly!
Es iz nisht gefloygn, nisht geshtoygn! P

עס קען זײַן אַן ערלעכער שענקער
און אַ שעפֿער אַ גנבֿ?

Can there be an honest innkeeper
and a dishonest shepherd?
*Es ken zayn an erlekher shenker un
a shefer a ganef?* NS

עס קלעבט זיך ווי אַרבעס צו
דער וואַנט.

It sticks like (dried) beans to the wall.
Es klebt zikh vi arbes tsu der vant. P

פֿאַראַן דאָרע גבֿירים און פֿעטע
אָרעמעלײַט?

Are there scrawny rich people and
fat paupers?
*Faran dare gvirim un fete
oremelayt?* NS

גאָטס נסים – פֿון אַן איי לאָקשן!

God's miracles – from an egg,
noodles!
Gots nisim – fun an ey lokshn! IB

אין תּוך איז אַ לאָך. | At the core is a hole.
In tokh iz a lokh. NS

כאַפּ איך מיך אויף – טאָגט עס! | I wake up – it's morning!
Khap ikh mikh oyf – togt es! P

אויב אַזוי איז מיטװאָך דער ברית! | If that's the case, Wednesday is the bris!
Oyb azoy iz mitvokh der bris! IF

שפּילן די גרילן, טאַנצן די װאַנצן. | When the crickets play, the roaches dance.
Shpiln di griln, tantsn di vantsn. IB

DIVORCE

אַ גרוש איז אַ שלעכטער פּרוש, אַ גרושה איז אַ שלעכטע ירושה. | A divorced man is a poor example and a divorced woman is a poor inheritance.
A goresh iz a shlekhter poresh, a gerushe iz a shlekhte yerushe. AC

אַז מען טוט אַ שידוך מוז מען זען מיט װעמען מען װעט זיך שפּעטער צעגײין. | Before you marry, make sure you know whom you will later divorce.
Az men tut a shidekh muz men zen mit vemen men vet zikh shpeter tsegeyn. AC

אָן אַ חטא, ניטאָ קײן גט. | Without a misdeed, no divorce can proceed.
On a khet nito keyn get. NS

װײ איז דעם װײַבל װאָס קומט אַהײם צו איר פֿאָטער אין הײַבל. | Woe to the wife who must return to her father's house!
Vey iz dem vaybl vos kumt aheym tsu ir foter in hayvl! IB

DOCTORS

בעסער דעם בעקער װי דעם דאָקטער. | Rather the baker than the doctor.
Beser dem beker vi dem dokter. IB

נוט איז די דאָקטױרים: זייערע מעלות פֿאַרקלינגען די װעלט, זייערע פֿעלערן פֿאַרדעקט די ערד.

Doctors have it good: their successes are applauded, their failures are buried.
Gut iz di doktoyrim: zeyere mayles farklingen di velt, zeyere felern fardekt di erd. NS

אַ דאָקטער און אַ רופֿא װינשט מען ניט אַ גוט יאָר.

You don't wish a doctor or a surgeon 'a good year.'
A dokter un a royfe vinsht men nit a gut yor. IB

אַ לעבעדיקער חולה װייסט מער װי אַ טױטער דאָקטער.

A living invalid knows more than a dead doctor.
A lebediker khoyle veyst mer vi a toyter dokter. AC

אַז דער קראַנקער גייט צום דאָקטער װערט דער ערשטער געהאָלפֿן דער דאָקטער.

When a patient visits the doctor, the first one helped is the doctor.
Az der kranker geyt tsum dokter vert der ershter geholfn der dokter. AC

אַז עס איז דאָ אַ דאָקטער אין שטוב זײַנען אַלע געזונט.

With a doctor in the house, everyone is healthy.
Az es iz do a dokter in shtub zaynen ale gezunt. NS

מען שטאַרבט אָן אַ דאָקטער אױך.

One dies even without a doctor.
Men shtarbt on a dokter oykh. P

דער דאָקטער און דער מלאך-המוות
ביידע הרגענען דעם מענטשן אַוועק
– נאָר דער דאָקטער קריגט באַצאָלט.

Both the doctor and the angel of
death kill – only the doctor collects
a fee.
Der dokter un der malekhamoves
beyde hargenen dem mentshn avek –
nor der dokter krigt batsolt. AC

פאַר דער צייַט קען אפֿילו אַ
דאָקטער אַ מענטשן ניט
אַוועקהרגענען.

If your time hasn't come yet, even
a doctor can't kill you.
Far der tsayt ken afile a dokter a
mentshn nit avek'hargenen. AC

DREAMS

דער חלום איז אַ נאַר און שלאָף איז
דער האר.

The dream is a fool and sleep is
the master.
Der kholem iz a nar un shlof iz der
har. NS

אין חלום זינדיקט ניט דער מענטש
נאָר זייַנע חלומות.

In dreams it is not the dreamer
who sins but his dreams.
In kholem zindikt nit der mentsh nor
zayne khaloymes. NS

מען קען מאַכן דעם חלום גרעסער
ווי די נאַכט.

It's possible to make the dream
longer than the entire night.
Men ken makhn dem kholem greser
vi di nakht. IB

וואָס מען רעדט בייַ טאָג חלומט זיך
בייַ נאַכט.

What we talk of by day, we dream
of at night.
Vos men ret bay tog kholemt zikh
bay nakht. NS

EFFORT

אַז עס גייט ניט, גייט מען װײַטער.   If it doesn't work, try harder.
Az es geyt nit, geyt men vayter. AC

ער רײַסט פֿון טויט און פֿון לעבעדיק.   He tears from the dead and from the living.
[He spares no effort.]
Er rayst fun toyt un fun lebedik. IB

מע דאַרף זיך נעמען אין די הענט אַרײַן.   One must take oneself in hand.
Men darf zikh nemen in di hent arayn. P

װאָס מען רײַסט ניט אָפּ מיט גװאַלד, דאָס האָט מען ניט.   If you're not forceful, you won't have anything.
Vos men rayst nit op mit gvald, dos hot men nit. IB

EMISSARIES

אַ הונט שיקט מען ניט אין יאַטקע אַרײַן.   You don't send a dog to the butchers.
A hunt shikt men nit in yatke arayn. IB

מיט קיין קאַץ שיקט מען ניט קיין שלח-מנות.   Don't send gifts with the cat.
Mit keyn kats shikt men nit keyn shalekh-mones. IB

א שלעכטער שליח איז א
האלבער נביא.

An unwilling messenger is half a prophet.
[He knows beforehand that it's pointless.]
A shlekhter sheli'ekh iz a halber novi. IB

„לך-לך" איז בעסער ווי „שלח-לך".

"Get-ye" is better than "send-ye."
[It's better to go yourself than to send someone.]
"Lekh-lekhah" iz beser vi "shalekh-lekhah." AC

EMOTIONS

א נאר פֿילט ניט.

A fool feels nothing.
A nar filt nit. P

אז מען וויינט זיך אויס ווערט
גרינגער אויפֿן האַרצן.

A good cry lightens the heart.
Az men veynt zikh oys vert gringer oyfn hartsn. IB

עס איז בעסער א שאנדע אין פּנים
איידער א וווייטיק אין האַרצן.

It is better to be embarrassed than heartbroken.
Es iz beser a shande in ponim eyder a veytik in hartsn. IB

עס איז ניט וואַרעם פֿון דאָברע
ריידעלע ווי פֿון דאָברע מיינעלע.

Warmer than a sweet statement is the sweet intent.
Es iz nit varem fun dobre reydele vi fun dobre meynele. NS

מען מוז זיך אַמאָל מאכן דאָס האַרץ
פֿון אַ שטיין.

Sometimes, it's necessary to harden one's heart.
Men muz zikh amol makhn dos harts fun a shteyn. P

אויס די אויגן, אויס דעם האַרצן.

Out of sight, out of mind.
Oys di oygn, oys dem hartsn. IB

ווער עם ווערט אומזיסט ברוגז ווערט
אומזיסט ווידער גוט.

**Whoever gets angry for no reason
becomes friendly again for no reason.**
*Ver es vert umzist broyges vert
umzist vider gut.* AC

ENDS

אַ נאַר ווייזט מען ניט קיין האַלבע
אַרבעט.

**You don't show a fool unfinished
work.**
A nar vayzt men nit keyn halbe arbet. P

דער לעצטער מאַכט די טיר צו.

Last one in shuts the door.
Der letster makht di tir tsu. NS

לאַך ווען דו וועסט זיך לייגן שלאָפֿן.

Laugh when you go to sleep.
[when your day's work is done]
Lakh ven du vest zikh leygn shlofn. IB

צום לעצטן קומט דאָס בעסטע.

The best comes last.
Tsum letstn kumt dos beste. P

ENDURANCE

אַ גוטער זיצער איז בעסער ווי אַ
גוטער קאָפּ.

**A good seat is better than a good
head.**
A guter zitser iz beser vi a guter kop. NS

אַז מען לעבט, דערלעבט מען.

If you live long enough, you live to see everything.

Az men lebt, derlebt men. P

דער ווינט פֿליט אַוועק און די קערפעס
בלײַבן.

The storm blows over and the driftwood remains.

Der vind flit avek un di kerpes blaybn. N

די שטילע וואַסערלעך רײַסן אײַן
די ברעגן.

Quiet streams erode the shore.

Di shtile vaserlekh raysn ayn di bregn. N

אײן מענטש קען מער לײַדן ווי צען
אָקסן קענען ציען.

One person can bear more than ten oxen can haul.

Eyn mentsh ken mer laydn vi tsen oksen kenen tsi'en. NS

מען זאָל ניט געפּרוּווט ווערן צו וואָס
מען קען געוווינט ווערן.

Pray that you may never have to suffer all that you are able to endure.

Men zol nit gepruft vern tsu vos men ken gevoynt vern. P

מיר האָבן איבערגעלעבט המנען וועלן
מיר איבערלעבן משיחן אויך.

We have survived Haman and we'll survive the Messiah too.

Mir hobn ibergelebt homenen veln mir iberlebn meshi'ekhn oykh. AC

מיט געדולד בּוירט מען דורך
אַפֿילו אַ קיזלשטיין.

With patience you can even bore through granite.

Mit gedult boyert men durkh afile a kizlshteyn. NS

שײנקייט פֿאַרגייט, חכמה
באַשטייט.

Beauty subsides, wisdom abides.

Sheynkeyt fargeyt, khokhme bashteyt. IB

ENEMIES

אַ שוואַרצע קאַץ איז צווישן זיי
אַדורכגעגאַנגען.

A black cat passed between them.

A shvartse kats iz tsvishn zey adurkhgegangen. P

אַז דער שׂונא פֿאַלט טאָר מען זיך
ניט פֿרייען אָבער מען הייבט
אים ניט אויף.

When the enemy falls, don't
rejoice, but don't pick him up
either.
*Az der soyne falt tor men zikh nit
freyen ober men heybt im nit oyf.* AC

אַז מען גיט ניט יעקבֿן גיט מען עשׂון.

If you fail Jacob, you aid Esau.
*Az men git nit yankevn git men
eysovn.* P

בעסער מיטן טײַוול וואָס מ׳קען
אײדער מיטן טײַוול וואָס מ׳קען
אים ניט.

Better the devil you know than the
devil you don't.
*Beser mitn tayvl vos m'ken eyder
mitn tayvl vos m'ken im nit.* AC

דאָס יאָר איז גרוים און דער גוי
וואַקסט.

The year lengthens and the enemy
strengthens.
Dos yor iz groys un der goy vakst. NS

די קאַץ שפּילט זיך מיט דער
מויז אָבער אָפּלאָזן לאָזט זי ניט אָפּ.

The cat plays with the mouse but
won't release it.
*Di kats shpilt zikh mit der moyz ober
oplozn lozt zi nit op.* NS

עם איז ניט אַזוי „מאהבת-מרדכי"
ווי „משׂינאת המן".

It's not so much "love of Mordechai"
as "hatred of Haman."
*Es iz nit azoy "meyhaves-
mordekhay" vi "mesines-homen."* AC

איין גאָט און אַזוי פֿיל שׂונאים!

One God and so many enemies!
Eyn got un azoy fil sonim! P

פֿון בייזע לײַט זאָל מען גיין אויף אַ
זײַט.

From people in heat beat a retreat.
*Fun beyze layt zol men geyn oyf a
zayt.* NS

קיין אומזיסטער שׂונא איז ניטאָ,
מען באַצאָלט פֿאַר אים.

You don't get enemies for free,
you pay for them.
*Keyn umzister soyne iz nito, men
batsolt far im.* NS

מען זאָל אים ניט ווינטשן אַפֿילו
אויף די שונאים.

One wouldn't even wish him on
his enemies.
*Men zol im nit vinshn afile oyf di
sonim.* AC

רבֿ אָדער בעדער, אַלע האָבן שונאים.

Rabbi or bath-house attendant, all
have enemies.
Rov oder beder, ale hobn sonim. NS

וואָס אַ גראָבער בויך קאָסט וואָלט איך
געוואָלט פֿאַרמאָגן, וואָס ער האָט
די ווערט זאָלן מײַנע שונאים
פֿאַרמאָגן:

What a fat belly costs, I wish I
owned; what it's worth, I wish on
my enemies.
*Vos a grober boykh kost volt ikh
gevolt farmogn, vos er hot di vert
zoln mayne sonim farmogn.* AC

ENVY

אַ פֿרעמדער פּעלץ וואַרעמט ניט.

Someone else's fur won't warm
you.
A fremder pelts varemt nit. NS

אַז מען וויל נאָכטאָן לײַטן וואַרפֿט
מען זיך פֿון אַלע זײַטן.

If you copy another's stride, you'll
end up spending on every side.
*Az men vil nokhton laytn varft men
zikh fun ale zaytn.* NS

פֿרעמדס איז געשמאַק.

Another's is tastier.
Fremds iz geshmak. AC

געשמאַק איז דער פֿיש אויף
יענעמס טיש.

Tasty is the fish on someone else's
dish.
Geshmak iz der fish oyf yenems tish. NS

אויף גוטע קינדער מעג מען יענעם
מקנא זײַן.

It's permissible to envy others
their well-brought-up children.
*Oyf gute kinder meg men yenem
mekane zayn.* AC

EQUALITY

אַ קאַץ מעג אויך קוקן אויפֿן קייסער.

Even a cat can look at a king.
A kats meg oykh kukn oyfn keyser. P

אַ נגיד קומט אָפּ און אַן אָרעמאַן
קומט אויף איז נאָך ניט גלייך.

There's no comparison between an impoverished millionaire and a newly-rich pauper.
A noged kumt op un an oreman kumt oyf iz nokh nit glaykh. IB

דעם גרעסטן מלך לייגט מען צום
סוף אַוועק מיט אַ לאָפּעטע.

The mightiest king is at last laid to rest with a shovel.
Dem grestn meylekh leygt men tsum sof avek mit a lopete. AC

אין באָד זייַנען אַלע גלייַך.

At the baths all are equal.
In bod zaynen ale glaykh. P

ניט אָרעם, ניט רייַך, אַבי מיט
לייַטן גלייַך.

Rich or poor, as long as no one's less or more.
Nit orem, nit raykh, abi mit laytn glaykh. NS

זעקס אייַלן טיף גלייַכט אַלעמען אויס.

Six feet deep makes everyone equal.
Zeks eyln tif glaykht alemen oys. AC

ETHICS

אַז די טיר איז אָפֿן דאַרף מען ניט
קריכן דורכן פֿענסטער.

If the door is open you don't have to crawl through the window.
Az di tir iz ofn darf men nit krikhn durkhn fenster. IB

אַז מען גראָבט אַ גרוב פֿאַר יענעם
פֿאַלט מען אַליין אַרייַן.

If you dig a pit for someone else, you'll fall into it yourself.
Az men grobt a grub far yenem falt men aleyn arayn. P

אַמאָל דאַרף מען די אויגן צומאַכן.

Sometimes one should turn a blind eye.
Amol darf men di oygn tsumakhn. AC

בעסער אַ קרומער פֿוס איידער אַ
קרומער קאָפּ.

Better a crooked foot than a
crooked mind.
*Beser a krumer fus eyder a krumer
kop.* NS

בעסער גאָרנישט צו מאַכן איידער צו
מאַכן גאָרנישט.

Better to make nothing than to
make something out of nothing.
*Beser gornisht tsu makhn eyder tsu
makhn gornisht.* AC

דעם רשע גייט אויף דער וועלט, דעם
צדיק אויף יענער וועלט

Villains fare well in this world,
saints in the next world.
*Dem roshe geyt oyf der velt, dem
tsadik oyf yener velt.* NS

דער מענטש זאָל ניט זאָרגן וואָס וועט
זײַן מאָרגן – זאָל ער בעסער
פֿאַרריכטן וואָס ער האָט קאַליע
געמאַכט נעכטן.

A person should not sorrow for
what will be tomorrow – rather let
him redress yesterday's mess.
*Der mentsh zol nit zorgn vos vet
zayn morgn – zol er beser far'rikhtn
vos er hot kalye gemakht nekhtn.* NS

דורכלערנען גאַנץ ש״ס איז אַ
גרויסע זאַך, דורכלערנען איין מידה
איז אַ גרעסערע זאַך.

To learn the whole Talmud is a
great accomplishment: to learn one
virtue is even greater.
*Durkhlernen gantz shas iz a groyse
zakh, durkhlernen eyn mide iz a
gresere zakh.* IB

ערלעך איז שווערלעך, גנבֿיש איז
געפֿערלעך.

Straight is a weight but stealthy is
unhealthy.
*Erlekh iz shverlekh, ganeyvish iz
geferlekh.* AC

אויף אַ מענטשן איז ניט קיין רחמנות,
אַ רחמנות איז אויף ניט אַ מענטשן.

A human being is not to be pitied;
pitiable is one who is not even a
human being.
*Oyf a mentshn iz nit keyn
rakhmones, a rakhmones iz oyf nit a
mentshn.* NS

מיט האָניק קען מען כאפן מער
פלינן ווי מיט עסיק.

You catch more flies with honey
than with vinegar.
*Mit honik ken men khapn mer flign
vi mit esik.* AC

ניט אין זכות-אָבות, ניט אין ירושה –
אין זיך זוך קדושה.

Not in ancestry nor in inheritance
– look into yourself for holiness.
*Nit in skhus-oves, nit in yerushe – in
zikh zukh kedushe.* AC

רעד בעסער וועגן זיך גוטס איידער
וועגן יענעם שלעכטס.

It's better to praise oneself than to
disparage others.
*Red beser vegn zikh guts eyder vegn
yenem shlekhts.* IB

רעד ניט אין די אויגן קיין חניפֿה און
טו ניט אונטער די אויגן קיין רציחה.

Don't flatter people to their faces
or revile them behind their backs.
*Red nit in di oygn keyn khanife un
tu nit unter di oygn keyn retsikhe.* NS

שענק מיר ניט קיין האָניק און גיב
מיר ניט קיין בים.

Don't give me the honey and spare
me the sting.
*Shenk mir nit keyn honik un gib mir
nit keyn bis.* AC

טרײַב ניט דאָס פֿערד מיט געשרײַ
נאָר מיט האָבער און הײ.

Drive the horse with oats, not with
curses and oaths.
*Trayb nit dos ferd mit geshrey nor
mit hober un hey.* NS

וווּ עס זײַנען ניט קיין מענטשן זײַ דו
אַ מענטש.

Where there are no honorable
people, be honorable yourself.
*Vu es zaynen nit keyn mentshn zay
du a mentsh.* AC

זײַ ניט שלעכט אפֿילו ווען דו
ביסט גערעכט.

Don't look for a fight even when
you're right.
*Zay nit shlekht afile ven du bist
gerekht.* NS

EXAGGERATION

א קו איז געפֿלויגן איבערן דאך און
געלייגט אן איי.

A cow flew over the roof and laid
an egg.
*A ku iz gefloygn ibern dakh un
geleygt an ey.* P

ער טראָגט זיך אַרום דערמיט ווי דער
רבונו־של־עולם מיט דער תּורה.

He carries it around like the
Master-of-the-Universe carries the
Torah.
*Er trogt zikh arum dermit vi der
reboyne-shel-oylem mit der toyre.* IB

פֿון אַ וואָרט ווערט אַ קוואָרט.

One word becomes a herd.
Fun a vort vert a kvort. NS

מיט דער צונג קען מען אַלץ מאַכן.

With the tongue anything is
possible.
Mit der tsung ken men alts makhn. P

EXCESS

אַן איבעריק וואָרט האָט קיין אָרט.

A superfluous word has no place.
[A superfluous word should not be heard.]
An iberik vort hot keyn ort. NS

ער וויל דאָס טעלערל פֿון הימל.

He wants the saucer out of heaven.
Er vil dos telerl fun himl. IB

אז עס איז צו פיל פעלט עפעם.

Where there's too much –
something's missing.
Az es iz tsu fil – felt epes. AC

ביי טאטע-מאמע איז קיין קינד
ניט איבעריק.

To parents no child is superfluous.
*Bay tate-mame iz keyn kind nit
ibernik.* P

„לא תבושי ולא תכלמי" – בענטש מיך
ניט און שעלט מיך ניט.

"Don't shame me and don't curse
me" – don't bless me and don't
curse me either.
*"Lo sevushi v'lo tekolmi" – bentsh
mikh nit un shelt mikh nit.* IB

שוואך פארביי און עסט פאר דריי!

Weak is he but eats for three!
Shvakh farbay un est far dray! IF

צו פיל עסן און טרינקען טוט מען אין
דלות זינקען.

Excessive eating and drinking
leads to poverty.
*Tsu fil esn un trinken tut men in
dales zinken.* NS

צו שיין איז אמאל א חסרון.

Too beautiful is sometimes a flaw.
Tsu sheyn iz amol a khisorn. P

צווישן דער קימפעטאָרין און דער
וואַרטערין ווערט דאָס קינד
דערשטיקט.

Between the expectant mother and
the midwife the child suffocates.
*Tsvishn der kimpetorin un der
varterin vert dos kind dershtikt.* IB

וואָס צו איז איבעריק (אומגעזונט).

Excess is superfluous (unhealthy).
Vos tsu iz iberik (umgezunt). P

EXCUSES

אבי א פערד – א ביַיטש געפינט
מען שוין.

If there's a horse – you can
always find a whip.
*Abi a ferd – a baytsh gefint men
shoyn.* NS

די וואָס פעלן זַיַינען שטענדיק
שולדיק.

The absent are always to blame.
Di vos feln zaynen shtendik shuldik. AC

אַז מען וויל אַ הונט אַ זעץ נעבן
געפֿינט מען שוין אַ שטעקן.

When you want to beat the dog,
the stick comes to hand.
*Az men vil a hunt a zets gebn gefint
men shoyn a shtekn.* NS

ער דרייט זיך ווי רש״י אין „בהעלותך״.

He squirms like a Rashi trying to
explain a difficult Biblical passage.
*Er dreyt zikh vi rashi in
b'haloysekho.* IB

„אין לי׳ איז די בעסטע טענה.

'I haven't got' is the best excuse.
'Eyn li' iz di beste tayne. IB

געפֿין דעם דין, דער היתר קומט
שפּעטער.

Find the rule, the exception comes
later.
*Gefin dem din, der heter kumt
shpeter.* IB

צען תירוצים האָבן וויניקער ווערט
ווי איינער.

Ten excuses are less persuasive
than one.
*Tsen terutsim hobn veyniker vert vi
eyner.* NS

EXPECTATIONS

אַז מען דאַרף האָבן פֿײַער זוכט מען
עס אין אַש.

If you need fire look in the ashes.
*Az men darf hobn fayer zukht men
es in ash.* NS

אַז מען ריכט זיך אויף אַ גרויסן עולם
קומט קיין הונט ניט.

When you expect a big crowd, not
even a dog shows up.
*Az men rikht zikh oyf a groysn
oylem kumt keyn hunt nit.* IB

ביסטו אין באָד דאַרפֿסטו שוויצן.

When you go to the steam-bath
expect to sweat.
Bistu in bod darfstu shvitsn. NS

אײן שײַטל האָלץ מאַכט ניט
וואַרעם דעם אויוון.

A single log won't heat the
fireplace.
*Eyn shaytl holts makht nit varem dem
oyvn.* NS

פֿאַרוואָם קומט ניט משיח? ווײַל אַ
בלינדער שוסטער נייט אים שיך.

Why doesn't the Messiah come?
Because a blind shoemaker sews
his shoes.
*Farvos kumt nit meshi'ekh? vayl a
blinder shuster neyt im shikh.* NS

פֿון ,נו לחם נו?' ווערט נאָך ניט קיין
ברויטעניו.

From 'where's the bread?' you
don't get fed.
*Fun 'nu lekhem nu?' vert nokh nit
keyn broytenyu.* NS

אין שיסל קען ניט זײַן מער ווי
אין טאָפּ.

Don't expect more on the plate
than what's in the pot.
In shisl ken nit zayn mer vi in top. P

מען וואַרט אויף אַ
מלאך און עס קומט אַ גלח.

One expects an angel, at the very
least, but all one gets is the priest.
*Men vart oyf a malekh un es kumt a
galekh.* IB

ווער עס וואַגט ניט קריגט ניט זײַן
חלק.

If you don't aspire you won't acquire.
Ver es vagt nit krigt nit zayn kheylek. AC

EXPERTS

ער איז אַ מבֿין ווי אַ קאַץ אויף הייוון.

He's an expert like a cat knows
about yeast.
Er iz a meyvn vi a kats oyf heyvn. AC

איינער איז אַ מבֿין אויף אַ פּשעטל,
דער צווייטער איז אַ מבֿין אויף חזיר
האָר אָבער אַלע זײַנען מבֿינים
אויף אַ חזן.

One is an expert in scholarly
discourse, another is an expert on
pig's bristles, but all are experts
on the merits of cantors.
*Eyner iz a meyvn oyf a pshetl, der
tsveyter iz a meyvn oyf khazer hor
ober ale zaynen meyvinim oyf a
khazn.* NS

זינגען קען איך ניט אָבער אַ מבֿין
בין איך.

I can't sing but I'm an expert anyway.
*Zingen ken ikh nit ober a meyvn bin
ikh.* P

FALSEHOOD

א גוטער ליגן איז אמָאל אויך ווערט געלט.

A good lie can sometimes be worth money.
A guter lign iz amol oykh vert gelt. AC

א ליגן טאָר מען ניט זאָגן, דעם אמת איז מען ניט מחויב צו זאָגן.

A lie you must not tell, the truth you're not obliged to tell.
A lign tor men nit zogn, dem emes iz men nit mekhu'yev tsu zogn. AC

א ליגנער גלייבט קיינעם ניט.

A liar doesn't believe anybody.
A ligner gleybt keynem nit. NS

א ליגנער הערט זיך זיַינע ליגנס אזוי לאַנג איַין ביז ער גלייבט זיך אַליין.

A liar tells his lie so often until he believes it himself.
A ligner hert zikh zayne ligns azoy lang ayn biz er gleybt zikh aleyn. NS

דער בעסטער ליגן איז דער אמת.

The best lie is the truth.
Der bester lign iz der emes. NS

אמת מיט ליגן צעריבן איז גאָרניט געבליבן.

Truth with lies mixed together means no truth whatever.
Emes mit lign tseribn iz gornit geblibn. NS

ליגן טאָר מען ניט זאָגן, דעם אמת
דאַרף מען ניט זאָגן.

One must not lie but it isn't necessary to tell the whole truth either.
*Lign tor men nit zogn, dem emes
darf men nit zogn.* AC

מיט ליגן קומט מען וויַיט אָבער
ניט צוריק.

You can go far with lies but you
can't return.
*Mit lign kumt men vayt ober nit
tsurik.* NS

FEAR

אַ לייב האָט ניט מורא פֿאַר קיין
פֿליג.

A lion doesn't fear a fly.
A leyb hot nit moyre far keyn flig. NS

„אתה בחרתנו מכל העמים" – און
פֿאַרן שייגעץ האָסטו מורא?

"Thou didst choose us from
among all peoples" – and You're
afraid of the Gentile boys?
*"Ata bekhartanu mikol ha'amim" –
un farn sheygets hostu moyre?* NS

דער אינהו-הדין איז ערגער ווי
דער דין אַליין.

Fear is worse than the ordeal itself.
Der inuhadin iz erger vi der din aleyn. NS

פֿאַר אַ געשלאָגענעם הונט טאָר
מען קיין שטעקן ניט וויַיזן.

Don't show a beaten dog the stick.
*Far a geshlogenem hunt tor men
keyn shtekn nit vayzn.* NS

FLATTERY

אַ חונף טאָר אין כּעם ניט ווערן.

A flatterer shouldn't lose his temper.
A khoynef tor in kas nit vern. NS

אַ קוש דעם קינד איז אַזוי גוט ווי דער מאַמען.

Kissing the child is as good as kissing the mother.
A kush dem kind iz azoy gut vi der mamen. IB

צו חנפֿנען איז צו גנבֿענען.

To flatter is to steal.
Tsu khanfenen iz tsu ganvenen. NS

רעד ניט אין די אויגן קיין חניפֿה און טו ניט אונטער די אויגן קיין רציחה.

Don't flatter people to their faces or revile them behind their backs.
Red nit in di oygn keyn khanife un tu nit unter di oygn keyn retsikhe. NS

FOOD AND DRINK

אַ גוטן ביסן וילט זיך יעדערן גענישן.

A tasty bite is everyone's delight.
A gutn bisn vilt zikh yedern genisn. NS

אַ קעמל טרינקט מען אָן מיט וואַסער איידער ער שלעפּט די משׁא.

A camel is allowed to wet his throat before he is expected to tote.
A keml trinkt men on mit vaser eyder er shlept di mase. NS

אַ סך תפֿילות – ווייניק לאָקשן.

Lots of prayers – few noodles!
A sakh tfiles – veynik lokshn! AC

אַ יוון ווערט קלוג נאָך וואַרעמס.

A soldier smartens up after eating warm food.
A yovn vert klug nokh varems. NS

אַלץ קען דער מענטש פֿאַרגעסן נאָר ניט עסן.

A person's memory is fleeting about everything except eating.
Alts ken der mentsh fargesn nor nit esn. AC

אַז דער מאָגן איז ליידיק איז דער
מוח אויך ליידיק.

When the stomach is empty so is the brain.
Az der mogn iz leydik iz der moyekh oykh leydik. NS

אַז עס איז ניטאָ קיין פֿלייש גריזשעט
מען ביינער.

If you don't have meat, you gnaw on bones.
Az es iz nito keyn fleysh grizhet men beyner. NS

אַז מען באַקט ברויט איז די גאַנצע
שטוב זאַט.

When you bake bread, the whole house is sated.
Az men bakt broyt iz di gantse shtub zat. NS

אַז מען לייגט אַרײַן אין די ציינער
געפֿינט מען אין די ביינער.

If the teeth do the chewing, the bones will do the renewing.
Az men leygt arayn in di tseyner gefint men in di beyner. NS

בשׂר ודגים איז אַן עונג שבת – אין
דער וואָכן איז עס אויך ניט שלעכט.

Meat and fish are Sabbath delights – it's also not bad on other nights.
Boser vedogim iz an oneg shabes – in der vokhn iz es oykh nit shlekht. IB

דער ערשטער קוילעטש קומט אַרויס
ניט גער—אָטן.

The first challah doesn't bake well. [a comment on problems with old-time ovens]
Der ershter koyletsh kumt aroys nit gerotn. NS

די שטאַרקסטע משקה איז וואַסער.

The strongest drink is water.
Di shtarkste mashke iz vaser. AC

עס איז גוט צו פֿאַסטן מיט אַ פּולקע
פֿון אַ גאַנדז און מיט אַ האַלב בוטעלקע

Feasting is easy with a goose leg and half-bottle of wine.
Es iz gut tsu fastn mit a pulke fun a gandz un mit a halb'butelke. NS

עס ניט קיין ביינער וועלן דיר ניט ווײ
טאָן די ציינער.

Of bones don't partake and your teeth won't ache.
Es nit keyn beyner veln dir nit vey ton di tseyner. NS

אײַדער האַרצווייטיק איז בעסער
בויכווייטיק.

Better stomach-ache than heart-ache.
*Eyder hartsveytik iz beser
boykhveytik.* NS

אײַדער צו שטאַרבן פֿון הונגער איז
שוין בעסער צו עסן געבראָטנס.

**Rather than starve it's better to
eat a roast.**
*Eyder tsu shtarbn fun hunger iz
shoyn beser tsu esn gebrotens.* AC

עסן גייט ניט פֿאַר קיין טאַנץ.

Eating doesn't come before dancing.
Esn geyt nit far keyn tants. P

פֿון אַ טיש אַליין ווערט מען ניט זאַט,
עס מוז זײַן וואָס אויפֿן טיש אויך.

**The table alone won't satisfy
hunger, only what's placed upon it.**
*Fun a tish aleyn vert men nit zat, es
muz zayn vos oyfn tish oykh.* NS

פֿון אַלע מילכיקע מאכלים
איז דאָס בעסטע אַ שטיקל פֿלייש.

**Of all the dairy delicacies the best
is a piece of meat.**
*Fun ale milkhike maykholim iz dos
beste a shtikl fleysh.* AC

פֿון מעל אַליין מאַכט מען קיין
ברויט ניט.

Bread doesn't come from flour alone.
*Fun mel aleyn makht men keyn broyt
nit.* AC

קאַלבפֿלייש איז האַלבפֿלייש.

Calf meat is half meat.
Kalbfleysh iz halbfleysh. NS

„אַז אין קמח אין תורה" – אַז ס'איז
ניטאָ אין טאָפּ איז ניטאָ אין קאָפּ.

"Where there is no flour there can
be no Torah" – not fed, empty head.
*"Im eyn kemakh eyn toyre" – az
s'iz nito in top iz nito in kop.* NS

מען דערקענט נאָך די באַקן ווי די
ציינער קנאַקן.

The cheeks show what the teeth chew.
*Men derkent nokh di bakn vi di
tseyner k'nakn.* NS

אויף יענעמס שׂימחה האָט מען אַ
גוטן אפּעטיט.

One brings a good appetite to
someone else's feast.
*Oyf yenems simkhe hot men a gutn
apetit.* AC

ס'איז נאָך אַ נס וואָס דער מאָגן איז
ניט פֿון גלאָז.

It's a miracle the stomach isn't
made of glass.
[Or everyone could witness the abuses to
which it is subjected.]
*S'iz nokh a nes vos der mogn iz nit
fun gloz.* IB

צו ברויט געפֿינט מען שוין אַ מעסער.

If you have bread you can always
find a knife.
Tsu broyt gefint men shoyn a meser. AC

ווען דאָס מויל זאָל ניט דאַרפֿן עסן וואָ
דער קאָפּ אין גאָלד גענאַנגען.

If the mouth didn't have to eat,
the head could be clothed in gold.
*Ven dos moyl zol nit darfn esn volt
der kop in gold gegangen.* NS

ווער עס עסט אין צײַט איז אַ לײַט.

Who eats when he should knows
what's good.
Ver es est in tsayt iz a layt. IB

FOOLS AND FOLLY

אַ גאַנצער נאַר איז אַ האַלבער נביא.

A whole fool is half a prophet.
[Only half of what he says can be believed.]
A gantser nar iz a halber novi. IB

אַ האַלבער נאַר איז אַ גאַנצער חכם.

Half a fool is a complete sage.
A halber nar iz a gantser khokhem. NS

אַ נאַר בלײַבט אַ נאַר.

A fool remains a fool.
A nar blaybt a nar. P

אַ נאַר דאַרף קיין מוסר ניט.

A fool won't benefit from a scolding.
A nar darf keyn muser nit. NS

אַ נאַר גייט אין באָד אַרײַן און פֿאַרגעסט זיך דאָס פּנים אָפּצוּוואַשן.

A fool goes to the baths and forgets to wash his face.
A nar geyt in bod arayn un fargest zikh dos ponim optsuvashn. P

אַ נאַר האָט אַ שיינע וועלט (האָט חירות).

A fool has a beautiful world (can take liberties).
A nar hot a sheyne velt (hot kheyrus). P

אַ נאַר איז ערגער ווי אַ ממזר.

A fool is worse than a bastard.
A nar iz erger vi a mamzer. NS

אַ נאַר קען מען ניט אויסנאַרן.

A fool can't be outwitted.
A nar ken men nit oysnarn. P

אַ נאַר וואַקסט אָן רעגן (הייוון).

A fool grows without rain (yeast).
A nar vakst on regn (heyvn). P

אַ נאַר זעצט מען ניט איבער אייער.

You don't seat a fool over eggs.
[He'll hatch more fools.]
A nar zetst men nit iber eyer. NS

אַז אַ קלוגער רעדט צו אַ נאַר רעדן צוויי נאַראָנים.

When a wise man talks to a fool, two fools are conversing.
Az a kluger ret tsu a nar redn tsvey naronim. P

אַז אַ נאַרישקייט גערָאָט אפֿילו אַמאָל איז עס פֿאָרט אַ נאַרישקייט.

Even when foolishness succeeds, it's still foolishness.
Az a narishkeyt gerot afile amol iz es fort a narishkeyt. AC

אַז אַ נאַר האָט ליב זיסע זאַכן –
דאָס האָבן די קלוגע אויסגעטראַכט.

That a fool craves sweets is an
invention of the clever.
[To keep one from nibbling]
*Az a nar hot lib zise zakhn – dos
hobn di kluge oysgetrakht.* IB

אַז מען האַלט זיך פֿאַר אַן אייזל זאָל
מען זיך ניט באַליידיקן אַז מענטשן
רײַטן אויף אים.

If you act like an ass don't get
insulted if people ride you.
*Az men halt zikh far an eyzl zol men
zikh nit baleydikn az mentshn raytn
oyf im.* AC

אַז מען שיקט אַ נאַר פֿאַרמאַכן די
לאָדן פֿאַרמאַכט ער זיי איבער
דער גאַנצער שטאָט.

If you send a fool to close the shutters,
he'll close them all over town.
*Az men shikt a nar farmakhn di lodn
farmakht er zey iber der gantser
shtot.* NS

אַז מען שטויסט דעם נאַר אין אַ
שטױסל זאָגט ער אַז מען מיינט גאָר
ניט אים נאָר דעם פֿעפֿער.

Grind a fool in a mortar and he says
you don't mean him but the pepper.
*Az men shtoyst dem nar in a shtoysl
zogt er az men meynt gor nit im nor
dem fefer.* NS

בעסער אַ גאַנצער נאַר איידער אַ
האַלבער חכם.

Better a complete fool than half a sage.
*Beser a gantser nar eyder a halber
khokhem.* NS

בײַ אַ שימחה און בײַ אַ לוויה זאָל מען
אַ נאַר ניט געבן דאָס וואָרט ווײַל
ער קען נאָך אַרויספּלאַפּלען דעם
אמתן אמת.

At a feast and at a funeral one
shouldn't allow a fool to make a
speech because he might babble
out the real truth.
*Bay a simkhe un bay a levaye zol
men a nar nit gebn dos vort vayl er
ken nokh aroysplaplen dem emisn
emes.* AC

ביסטו שלעכט זײַ כאָטש נישט נאַריש,
ביסטו נאַריש זײַ כאָטש נישט
שלעכט.

If you're wicked, at least don't be
foolish; if you're foolish, at least
don't be wicked.
*Bistu shlekht zay khotsh nisht narish,
bistu narish zay khotsh nisht shlekht.* NS

דער נאַר ליגט אין דר׳ערד און
באַקט בײגל.

The fool's gone to hell and is still
baking bagel.
Der nar ligt in dr'erd un bakt beygl. P

דער נאַר מעסט וואַסער אין אַ זײַער.

The fool measures water in a sieve.
Der nar mest vaser in a zayer. AC

דער נאַר זוכט אַ פּגימה אויף דער זעג.

The fool searches for a flaw in the saw
Der nar zukht a p'gime oyf der zeg. NS

דער נאַר זוכט דעם פֿאַראַיאָריקן שנײ.

The fool searches for last year's snow.
Der nar zukht dem farayorikn shney. P

די כעלעמער זײַנען גאָר קיין נאַראָנים
ניט נאָר אַלע נאַרישקייטן
טרעפֿן זיך בײַ זיי.

People of Chelm are no fools, it's only
that foolish things happen to them.
*Di khelemer zaynen gor keyn
naronim nit nor ale narishkeytn trefn
zikh bay zey.* NS

ער איז ניט קיין גרויסער חכם און
ניט קיין קליינער נאַר.

He's no great sage and no small fool.
*Er iz nit keyn groyser khokhem un
nit keyn kleyner nar.* P

ער איז טאַקע אַ גרויסער למדן אָבער
ניט קיין איבעריקער חכם.

It's true he's a great scholar but
he's not overly intelligent.
*Er iz take a groyser lamdn ober nit
keyn iberiker khokhem.* NS

ער קלערט צי די קוליקאָװער בייגל
זײַנען גרעסער װי די לעמבערגער.

He wonders if the Kulikov bagels
are bigger than the ones from Lemberg.
*Er klert tsi di kulikover beygl zaynen
greser vi di lemberger.* IB

ער לערנט אן אַלטן טאַטן קינדער
מאַכן!

He teaches an experienced father
how to make children!
Er lernt an altn tatn kinder makhn! WZ

ער לויפֿט אַרום און זוכט זײַן ריפֿ!

He runs around looking for his rib!
Er loyft arum un zukht zayn rip! IB

איין נאַר מאַכט אַ סך נאַראָנים.

One fool breeds many fools.
Eyn nar makht a sakh naronim. NS

פֿון איין חמור האָט מען אַ סך.

From one donkey you get many.
Fun eyn khamer hot men a sakh. AC

גאָט זאָל װעלן צוהערן די נאַראָנים
װאָלט די װעלט געהאַט אַן אַנדער
פּנים.

If God would listen to the fools, the
world would look entirely different.
*Got zol veln tsuhern di naronim volt
di velt gehat an ander ponim.* IB

הױך און דאַר און שמעקט מיט נאַר!

Tall and skinny and what a ninny!
Hoykh un dar un shmekt mit nar! NS

מען טאָר ניט װײַזן אַ נאַר אַ
האַלבע אַרבעט.

Don't show a fool a job half-done.
Men tor nit vayzn a nar a halbe arbet. P

אױף אַ נאַר טאָר מען קיין פֿאַריבל
ניט האָבן.

Don't take offense at a fool.
Oyf a nar tor men keyn faribl nit hobn. NS

װען דער נאַר װאָלט ניט געװען מײַנע
װאָלט איך אױך געלאַכט.

If the fool weren't mine, I'd also
laugh.
*Ven der nar volt nit geven mayner
volt ikh oykh gelakht.* P

יעדער נאַר איז קלוג פֿאַר זיך אַליין.

Every fool is smart for himself.
Yeder nar iz klug far zikh aleyn. P

ווו וואקסן נאראָנים? ווו מען
זייט זיי ניט.

Where do fools grow? Where they
aren't planted.
*Vu vaksn varonim? vu men zeyt zey
nit.* NS

זינט גאָט האנדלט מיט נאָראָנים
איז אזאַ נאַר ניט געווען.

Since God has been dealing in fools,
there hasn't been such a fool.
*Zint got handlt mit naronim iz aza
nar nit geven.* AC

CHARACTER OF FOOLS

אַלע חזנים זיַינען נאָראָנים אָבער
ניט יעדער נאַר קען זינגען.

All cantors are fools but not every
fool can sing.
*Ale khazonim zaynen naronim ober
nit yeder nar ken zingen.* P

אַן אייזל דערקענט מען בײַ די לאַנגע
אוירן, אַ נאַר בײַ דער לאַנגער צונג.

A donkey is recognized by its long
ears, a fool by his long tongue.
*An eyzl derkent men bay di lange
oyern, a nar bay der langer tsung.* NS

אַז משיח וועט קומען וועלן אַלע
קראַנקע אויסגעהיילט ווערן נאָר
אַ נאַר וועט בלײַבן אַ נאַר.

When the Messiah comes, all the
sick will be healed but the fool will
remain a fool.
*As meshi'ekh vet kumen veln ale
kranke oysgeheylt vern nor a nar vet
blaybn a nar.* NS

פּורים איז אַלץ פֿריַי אָבער נאָך פּורים
ווייסט מען דאָך ווער ס'איז אַ נאַר.

On Purim anything goes, but after-
wards, you know who remains a fool
*Purim iz alts fray ober nokh purim
veyst men dokh ver s'iz a nar.* AC

COMPARISON

אַ קלוגער באַהאַלט דעם שכל, אַ
נאַר באַוויַיזט זיַין נאַרישקייט.

A wise person conceals his
intelligence, a fool displays his
foolishness.
*A kluger bahalt dem seykhl, a nar
bavayzt zayn narishkeyt.* P

אַ נאַר ווערט ניט עלטער און
קאַלטע וואַסער ווערט ניט קעלטער.

A fool grows no older and cold
water gets no colder.
*A nar vert nit elter un kalte vaser
vert nit kelter.* AC

אַ קלוגער ווייסט וואָס ער זאָגט, אַ
נאַר זאָגט וואָס ער ווייסט.

A wise man knows what he says, a
fool says what he knows.
*A kluger veyst vos er zogt, a nar
zogt vos er veyst.* AC

אַז אַ נאַר האַלט די קו בײַ די הערנער
קען זי אַ קלוגער מעלקן.

When a fool holds the cow by the
horns, a clever person can milk it.
*Az a nar halt di ku bay di herner
ken zi a kluger melkn.* NS

בעסער אַ וויציקער נאַר איידער
אַ נאַרישן וויץ.

Better a wise-cracking fool than a
foolish joke.
*Beser a vitsiker nar eyder a narishn
vits.* NS

דעם קלוגן העלפֿט אַ וואָרט, דעם
נאַר העלפֿט אַפֿילו קיין שטעקן
אויך ניט.

One word aids a wise man, not
even a beating aids a fool.
*Dem klugn helft a vort, dem nar
helft afile keyn shtekn oykh nit.* AC

ווי דעם קלוגן איז ביטער איז דער
נאָר אַלץ פֿרייַ.

What saddens the wise man gladdens the fool.
Vi dem klugn iz biter iz der nar alts fray. NS

זיי זייַנען אונדזערע חכמים ווייַל מיר
זייַנען זייערע נאַראָנים.

They are our wise men because we are their fools.
Zey zaynen undzere khakhomim vayl mir zaynen zeyere naronim. NS

FRAUD

ער האָט אים אָפּגעטאָן אויף
טערקיש.

He dealt with him in the Turkish man
[Double-crossed him.]
Er hot im opgeton oyf terkish. P

ער האָט מיר אַוועקגעקוילעט די
קאַפּאָטע.

He took the shirt off my back.
Er hot mir avekgekoylet di kapote. NS

ער קען צוזאַמענפֿירן אַ וואַנט מיט
אַ וואַנט.

He can bring walls together.
[A smooth talker]
Er ken tsuzamenfirn a vant mit a vant. AC

עס איז אַזוי כּשר ווי אַ חזיר פֿיסל.

It's as kosher as a pig's foot.
Es iz azoy kosher vi a khazer fisl. P

FRIENDS

אַ פֿרייַנד בלייַבט אַ פֿרייַנד
ביז צו דער קעשענע.

A friend is a friend up to his wallet.
A fraynd blaybt a fraynd biz tsu der keshene. NS

אַ גוטער פֿרייַנד איז אָפֿט בעסער
ווי אַ ברודער.

A good friend is sometimes better than a brother.
A guter fraynd iz oft beser vi a bruder. NS

חבֿרשאַפֿט איז שטאַרקער ווי
ברודערשאַפֿט.

Friendship is stronger than kinship.
Khavershaft iz shtarker vi brudershaft. P

בעסער אַ גוטער שׂונא איידער אַ
שלעכטער פֿרײַנד.

Better a good enemy than a bad friend.
Beser a guter soyne eyder a shlekhter fraynd.
NS

איין אַלטער פֿרײַנד איז בעסער
ווי נײַע צוויי.

**One old friend is better than two
new ones.**
Eyn alter fraynd iz beser vi naye tsvey. P

גרינג איז צו קריגן אַ שׂונא, שווער
צו קריגן אַ פֿרײַנד.

**It's easy to acquire an enemy,
hard to acquire a friend.**
*Gring iz tsu krign a soyne shver tsu
krign a fraynd.* NS

היטן זאָל מען זיך פֿאַר די פֿרײַנד
ניט די פֿײַנט.

Beware your friends, not your enemies.
*Hitn zol men zikh far di fraynd nit di
faynt.* NS

אויף אַ שיינעם איז גוט צו קוקן, מיט
אַ קלוגן איז גוט צו לעבן.

**It's good to look at the beautiful
and live with the wise.**
*Oyf a sheynem iz gut tsu kukn, mit a
klugn iz gut tsu lebn.* NS

זײַ ניט צו גוט מיט יענעם – לאָז
אַן אָרט ברוגז צו ווערן.

**Don't get too friendly – leave
room to be on the outs.**
*Zay nit tsu gut mit yenem – loz an
ort broygez tsu vern.* AC

FUTILITY

אַ יחיד קעגן קהל פֿאַרלירט אַלע מאָל.

One against all is certain to fall.
A yokhed kegn ko'ol farlirt ale mol. NS

אַז גאָט מאַכט מיאוס קען דער
מענטש ניט מאַכן שענער.

**If God makes ugly, nobody can
make beautiful.**
*Az got makht mi'es ken der mentsh
nit makhn shener.* NS

ער אַנטלויפֿט פֿון די בערן און פֿאַלט
צווישן די וועלף.

**He flees the bears only to fall
among wolves.**
*Er antloyft fun di bern un falt
tsvishn di velf.* NS

ער וויל איך זאָל אים אויסהיילן
די מילה!

He wants me to restore his
circumcision!
Er vil ikh zol im oys'heyln di mile! IF

עס איז ניטאָ מיט וועמען צום טיש
צו גיין.

There's no one to go to the table
with. [There's nobody worth talking to.]
*Es iz nito mit venem tsum tish tsu
geyn.* P

פאָר אַ טויבן גלח קלינגט מען ניט
צוויי מאָל.

No use ringing bells twice for a
deaf priest.
*Far a toybn galekh klingt men nit
tsvey mol.* NS

פון פאַרטריקנטע ביימער קומען
קיין פרות ניט אַרויס.

You can't get fruit from withered tree
*Fun fartriknte beymer kumen keyn
peyres nit aroys.* AC

גיי קלאַפ זיך קאָפ אין וואַנט!

Go bang your head against the wall!
Gey klap zikh kop in vant! P

מאַך שבת דערפון!

Make Sabath from it!
Makh shabes derfun! IB

מען קען דעם ים מיט אַ לעפל ניט
אויסשעפן.

The ocean can't be emptied with a
spoon.
*Men ken dem yam mit a lefl nit
oys'shepn.* NS

מיטן קאָפ קעגן דער וואַנט – מוז
מען אָבער האָבן אַ וואַנט.

Knock your head against the wall
– first, you must have a wall.
*Mitn kop kegn der vant – muz men
ober hobn a vant.* NS

רעד מיט אַ שוואַנץ חכמות!

Try talking sense to an idiot!
Red mit a shvants khokhmes! WZ

ווער עס יאָגט זיך נאָך אַ ווינט כאַפט
אַ רוח.

If you chase the wind, you nab a devi
*Ver es yogt zikh nokh a vint khapt a
ru'ekh.* NS

וועסט זיך וועלן אויספײַנען פאַר לײַט
וועסטו שטאַרבן פאַר דער צײַט.

If pleasing everyone is your way,
you'll die before your appointed day.
*Vest zikh veln oysfaynen far layt
vestu shtarbn far der tsayt.* NS

GENTILES

אַ גוי בלײַבט אַ גוי.

A Goy remains a goy.
A goy blaybt a Goy. P

אַ משומד איז ניט קיין גוי און ניט
קיין ייד.

An apostate is no Goy and no Jew.
*A meshumed iz nit keyn goy un nit
keyn yid.* NS

"אתה בחרתנו מכל העמים" – און
פֿאַרן שייגעץ האָסטו מורא?

**"Thou didst choose us from
among the nations" – and You're
afraid of the Gentile boys?**
*"Ata bekhartanu mikol ha'amim" –
un farn sheygets hostu moyre?* NS

אַזוי ווי עס קריסטלט זיך, אַזוי
יידלט זיך.

What Gentiles do, Jews ape.
Azoy vi es kristlt zikh, azoy yidelt zikh. P

בעסער דאָס יידישע קעפּל אײדער
דעם גוישן קאָפּ.

**Better the little Jewish brain than
the big Goyish head.**
*Beser dos yidishe kepl eyder dem
goyishn kop.* AC

דער גוי איז צום גלות ניט געוווינט.

Goyim aren't used to Jewish troubles.
Der goy iz tsum goles nit gevoynt. P

איינער רעדט רוסיש ווי אַ ייד, אַן
אַנדערער רעדט יידיש ווי אַ גוי.

**One person speaks Russian like a Jew,
another speaks Yiddish like a Goy.**
*Eyner ret rusish vi a yid, an anderer
ret yidish vi a goy.* NS

אויף אַ שלעכטן גוי טאָר מען קיין
נקמה ניט בעטן.

Don't pray for revenge even on a
wicked Goy.

*Oyf a shlekhtn goy tor men keyn
nekome nit betn.* NS

צום קלענסטן פּגר לייגט דער גלח
ניט צו.

The priest earns his fee even from
the least consequential death.

*Tsum klenstn peyger leygt der galekh
nit tsu.* NS

וווינען זאָל מען צווישן ייִדן, האַנדלען
זאָל מען צווישן גוים.

Live among Jews, do business
among Goyim.

*Voynen zol men tsvishn yidn,
handlen zol men tsvishn goyim.* NS

GIVING AND TAKING

אַ נאַר גיט און אַ קלוגער נעמט.

A fool gives and a clever person takes.

A nar git un a kluger nemt. NS

אַז מען גיט – נעם, אַז מען נעמט –
שריי גוואַלד!

If they give – take; if they take –
shout 'help!'

*Az men git – nem; az men nemt –
shray gevalt!* P

אַז מען וואָלט איינעם געלאָזט נעמען
פֿון דער וועלט וואָס זײַן האַרץ גלוסט
וואָלט ער פֿאַר דעם צווייטן גאָרניט
איבערגעלאָזט.

If everyone were allowed to take
from this world all he desired, there'd
be nothing left for anyone else.

*Az men volt eynem gelozt nemen fun
der velt vos zayn harts glust volt er
far dem tsveytn gornit ibergelozt.* AC

פֿון נעמען ווערט מען ניט אָרעם.

From taking you don't get poor.

Fun nemen vert men nit orem. P

לעולם תקח – אַ מען גיט מיר ריק
איך, אַנישט קיק איך.

Always take – if you give me, I'll
go away, if not, I'll stay.

*L'oylem tikekh, a men git mir rik
ikh, anisht kik ikh.* AC

נעמען זאָל מען שטענדיק!

Always take!

Nemen zol men shtendik! P

וואָס מען כאַפט ניט אַרײַן דאָס האָט מען ניט.

What you don't grab, you won't have.

Vos men khapt nit arayn dos hot men nit. P

GOD

אַ געפֿאַלענעם העלפֿט גאָט.

God helps the defeated.

A gefalenem helft got. NS

„אתה בחרתנו מכל העמים" – וואָס האָסטו זיך אָנגעזעצט אויף אונדז?

"Thou hast chosen us from among the nations" – what, O Lord, did you have against us?

"Ata bekhartanu mikol ha'amim" – vos hostu zikh ongezetst oyf undz? NS

אַז גאָט וויל, מאַכט קאָמעץ בית באָ.

If God wills it, it's ABC.

Az got vil makht komets beyz bo. P

אַז גאָט וואָלט געלעבט אויף דער ערד וואָלט מען אים אַלע פֿענסטער אויסגעשלאָגן.

If God lived on earth, all His windows would be broken.

Az got volt gelebt oyf der erd volt men im ale fenster oysgeshlogn. NS

דער גאָט וואָס האָט געשפּאָלטן דעם ים וועט שפּאַלטן דעם קאָפּ אויך.

The God who split the sea will split one's head also.

Der got vos hot geshpoltn dem yam vet shpaltn dem kop oykh. AC

דרײַ מענטשן האָט גאָט פֿײַנט: אַן עושר אַ גנבֿ, אַן אָרעמאַן אַ בעל-גאווה און אַן אַלטן נואף.

God dislikes three kinds of people: a rich thief, an arrogant pauper, and an old lecher.

Dray mentshn hot got faynt: an oysher a ganef, an oreman a balgayve un an altn noyef. NS

פֿאַר דער תליה האָבן מענטשן מער מורא ווי פֿאַר גאָט אַליין.

People fear the gallows more than they fear God Himself.

Far der tli'e hobn mentshn mer moyre vi far got aleyn. NS

גאָט גיט ניט דעם טויט אין די הענט
ווייל אַניט וואָלט זיך איטלעכער
גענומען דאָס לעבן.

God doesn't give death into one's
hands – otherwise, everyone would
take his own life.
*Got git nit dem toyt in di hent vayl
anit volt zikh itlekher genumen dos
lebn.* AC

גאָט הייסט אויך קיין נאַר ניט זײַן.

God never told anyone to be stupid.
Got heyst oykh keyn nar nit zayn. P

גאָט האָט ליב דעם אָרעמאַן און
העלפֿט דעם נגיד.

God loves the poor but He helps
the rich.
*Got hot lib dem oreman un helft
dem noged.* NS

גאָט האָט זיך באַשאַפֿן
אַ וועלט מיט קלײנע וועלטעלעך.

God created a world full of many
little worlds.
*Got hot zikh bashafn a velt mit
kleyne veltelekh.* NS

גאָט איז איינער, וואָס ער טוט זעט
קיינער.

God is one and always was, none
can witness what he does.
Got iz eyner, vos er tut zet keyner. NS

גאָט נעמט מיט איין האַנט און
גיט מיט דער אַנדערער.

God gives with one hand and takes
with the other.
*Got nemt mit eyn hant un git mit der
anderer.* NS

גאָט שיקט די רפֿואה פֿאַר דער מכה.

God sends the remedy before the dise
Got shikt di refu'e far der make. P

גאָט שטראָפֿט,
דער מענטש איז זיך נוקם.

God punishes, man takes revenge.
*Got shtroft, der mentsh iz zikh
noykem.* NS

גאָט וואַרט לאַנג און צאָלט מיט
פּראָצענט.

God waits long and pays with interest
Got vart lang un tsolt mit protsent. NS

גאָט ווייסט שוין אויך ניט וואָס
ער טוט.

God Himself doesn't even know
what He does.
Got veyst shoyn oykh nit vos er tut. AC

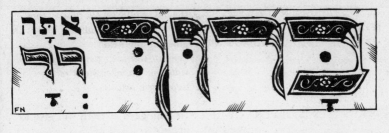

איטלעכער פֿאַר זיך, גאָט פֿאַר אונדז אַלעמען.

Everyone for himself, God for all of us.
Itlekher far zikh, got far undz alemen. NS

אָן גאָטס װילן רירט זיך ניט אַ פֿליג פֿון דער װאַנט.

If God doesn't approve, a fly won't make a move.
On gots viln rirt zikh nit a flig fun der vant. NS

אויף גאָט טאָר מען קיין קשיות ניט פֿרעגן, װײַל ער קען זאָגן: דו װילסט װיסן דעם תּירוץ? קום צו מיר.

Don't question God; He's likely to reply: if you're so anxious for answers, come here to me.
Oyf got tor men keyn kashes nit fregn, vayl er ken zogn: du vilst visn dem terets? kum tsu mir. NS

רבונו-של-עולם, אַ װעלט האָסטו באַשאַפֿן – אַזאַ יאָר אויף מיר, פֿירן פֿירסטו אַ װעלט – אַזאַ יאָר אויף מײַנע שונאים!

Master-of-the-Universe, a world You've created - woe to me; a world you rule - woe to my enemies!
Reboyne-shel-oylem, a velt hostu bashafn - aza yor oyf mir, firn firstu a velt - aza yor oyf mayne sonim! AC

װען פֿרײט זיך גאָט? אַז אַן אָרעמאַן געפֿינט אַ מציאה און גיט עס אָפּ.

When does God rejoice? When a pauper finds a treasure and returns it.
Ven freyt zikh got? az an oreman gefint a metsi'e un git es op. IB

גאָט זיצט אויבן און פֿאָרט אונטן.

God sits on high and pairs off couples below.
Got zitst oybn un port untn. IB

ווען גאָט וואָלט אונדז פון הימל
געוואָרפן וואָלטן מיר ארומגעגאַנגען
מיט צעלעכערטע קעפ.

If God would throw down from
heaven, we'd all walk around with
holes in our heads.
*Ven got volt undz fun himl gevorfn
voltn mir arumgegangen mit
tselekherte kep.* NS

ווער עם האָט געגעבן ציין דער וועט
געבן ברויט.

He who gave us teeth will give us
bread.
*Ver es hot gegebn tseyn der vet gebn
broyt.* NS

וואָם גאָט גיט דאַרף מען אָננעמען
פאַר ליב, ווייל אַ ברירה האָט מען?

What God does, we must willingly
accept; do we have a choice?
*Vos got git darf men on'nemen far
lib, vayl a breyre hot men?* AC

וואָם גאָט טוט איז מסתמא גוט.

What God doth dispose, is good, I
suppose.
Vos got tut iz mistome gut. NS

„יושב בשמים ישחק" – אים איז
גוט צו לאַכן.

"He that sitteth in heaven,
laugheth" – it's easy for Him!
*"Yoyshev bashomayim yiskhak" -
im iz gut tsu lakhn.* NS

GOOD AND BAD

אַ טוב לכל איז אַ רע לכל.

Good for all, bad for all.
A toyv lakol iz a ra lakol. IB

אַז מען זינגט איידער מען שטייט
אויף וועט מען ווינען איידער
מען לייגט זיך שלאָפן.

Sing before seven, cry before eleven.
*Az men zingt eyder men shteyt oyf
vet men veynen eyder men leygt zikh
shlofn.* NS

בעסער דאָם שלעכטע פון גוטן
איידער דאָם גוטע פון שלעכטן.

Better bad from good than good
from bad.
*Beser dos shlekhte fun gutn eyder
dos gute fun shlekhtn.* NS

דאָם גוטע קען מען ניט אויסברענגען
און דאָם שלעכטע ניט איינקאַרגן.

The good you can't squander and
the bad you can't economize.
*Dos gute ken men nit oysbrengen un
dos shlekhte nit aynkargn.* AC

פרייַדן און לייַדן טוען אָפֿט צוזאַמען
זיך קלייַדן.

Joy and distress are often clothed
in the same dress.
*Fraydn un laydn tu'en oft tsuzamen
zikh klaydn.* NS

גוטע צאָלן, שלעכטע מאָנען.

The good pay, the bad demand.
Gute tsoln, shlekhte monen. NS

שלעכט לערנט מען זיך באַלד אויס.

'Bad' is quickly learnt.
Shlekht lernt men zikh bald oys. P

ווען עם גייט דיר גוט נעם זיך ניט
איבער, ווען עם גייט דיר שלעכט
זייַ זיך ניט מצער.

When things go well, don't get
carried away; when they go badly,
don't grieve.
*Ven es geyt dir gut nem zikh nit
iber, ven es geyt dir shlekht zay zikh
nit metsa'er.* AC

GOSSIP

אַ בייזע צונג איז ערגער ווי אַ
שלעכטע האַנט.

A wicked tongue is worse than an
evil hand.
*A beyze tsung iz erger vi a shlekhte
hant.* NS

אַז איך טו וואָם איך וויל, מעג דאָך
יענער זאָגן וואָם ער וויל.

If I do as I choose, then another
may say what he pleases.
*Az ikh tu vos ikh vil, meg dokh
yener zogn vos er vil.* AC

דער רמז שלאָגט שטאַרקער ווי
דער אמת.

What is inferred is worse than
what is heard.
*Der remez shlogt shtarker vi der
emes.* NS

הינטער די אויגן קען מען רעדן אַפֿילו
אויפֿן קייסער.

Behind his back you can even
malign the tsar.
*Hinter di oygn ken men redn afile
oyfn keyser.* AC

פֿאַר מײַן טיר וועט אמאָל אויך
זײַן אַ בלאָטע.

There may be mud before my
door someday too.
*Far mayn tir vet amol oykh zayn a
blote.* NS

פֿון איטלעכן הויז טראָגט מען
עפּעס אַרויס.

From every household something
can be told.
Fun itlekhn hoyz trogt men epes aroys.

פֿון רכילות און פֿון סודות אַנטלויף
ווי פֿון שדים.

From gossip and from secrets flee
as if from demons.
*Fun rekhiles un fun soydes antloyf vi
fun sheydim.* NS

אין די אויגן הייסט גערעדט,
אונטער די אויגן הייסט באַרעדט.

What's said to your face is
conversation; behind your back,
it's vilification.
*In di oygn heyst geret, unter di oygn
heyst baret.* NS

מען קען דער וועלט דאָם מויל ניט
פֿאַרמאַכן.

You can't stop the world from talking.
*Men ken der velt dos moyl nit
farmakhn.* P

שיק דײַנע אויערן אין די טויערן.

Send your ear out to hear.
Shik dayne oyern in di toyern. NS

שטײ ניט הינטער דער וואַנט וועסטו
ניט הערן דײַן אייגענע שאַנד.

**Don't put your ear to the wall and
you won't hear about your faults at all.**
*Shtey nit hinter der vant vestu nit
hern dayn eygene shand.* IB

ווענט האָבן אויערן, גאַסן האָבן אויגן.

Walls have ears, streets have eyes.
Vent hobn oyern, gasn hobn oygn. IB

GREED

אַ קליין קינד איז אַ חזיר און אַ גרויס
קינד איז אַ וואָלף.

**A young child is a pig and a
grown one is a wolf.**
*A kleyn kind iz a khazer un a groys
kind iz a volf.* NS

אַז מען וואָלט איינעם געלאָזט נעמען
פֿון דער וועלט וואָם זײַן האַרץ גלוסט
וואָלט ער פֿאַר דעם צווייטן
גאָרניט איבערגעלאָזט.

**If everyone were allowed to take
from the world all his heart
desired, there would be nothing
left for anyone else.**
*Az men volt eynem gelozt nemen fun
der velt vos zayn harts glust volt er
far dem tsveytn gornit ibergelozt.* NS

סאַמע גוטס נאָר אַליין קען אין
דער וועלט ניט באַשטיין.

**Everything good for oneself alone
is impossible to own.**
*Same guts nor aleyn ken in der velt
nit bashteyn.* NS

GREETINGS

א װינטש קען מען אין קעשענע
ניט לײגן.

You can't pocket a good wish.
A vintsh ken men in keshene nit leygn.

פֿון װינטשן װערט מען ניט זאַט.

Well-wishing won't satisfy hunger.
Fun vintshn vert men nit zat. P

מיר זאָלן זיך באַגעגענען נאָר אױף
שׂימחות.

May we meet only on festive
occasions!
*Mir zoln zikh bagegenen nor oyf
simkhes!* P

װינטשן און שײַסן איז אַלץ אײן
פֿאַרבײַסן.

Well-wishing and shitting are both
the same dessert.
*Vintshn un shaysn iz alts eyn
farbaysn.* AC

װאָס הערט זיך? די באָבע יערט זיך!

What's new? Grandma's due! [pregnan
Vos hert zikh? di bobe yert zikh! AC

זײַ מיר געזונט און שטאַרק און האָב
געלט װי אַ באַרג!

Be strong and healthy and have
enough money to be wealthy!
*Zay mir gezunt un shtark un hob
gelt vi a barg!* AC

GUESTS

אַ גאַסט אױף אַ װײַל זעט אױף אַ
מײַל.

A guest for a while sees a mile.
A gast oyf a vayl zet oyf a mayl. P

אַן אָפֿטער גאַסט פֿאַלט צו לאַסט.

A frequent guest becomes a pest.
An ofter gast falt tsu last. NS

אַז מען פֿרייט זיך מיט אַ
גוטער װעטשערע טראָגנט
דער טײַװל אָן אַ גאַסט.

Just as you start enjoying a tasty
meal, the devil sends a guest.
*Az men freyt zikh mit a guter
vetshere trogt der tayvl on a gast.* AC

דורך אורחים גיט מען אויס קינדער.

Through visitors we marry off our children.

Durkh orkhim git men oys kinder. IB

גיי נישט צו דײַן שכן ווען ער עסט,
ווען ער שלאָפֿט און ווען ער
האַנדלט.

Don't disturb your neighbor when he's eating, sleeping, or doing business.

Gey nisht tsu dayn shokhn ven er est, ven er shloft un ven er handlt. AC

לאָז נאָר זײַן דער טיש צוגעגרייט,
געסט וועלן זיך שוין געפֿינען.

Once the table is prepared, guests will soon appear.

Loz nor zayn der tish tsugegreyt, gest veln zikh shoyn gefinen. AC

מיט אַ גוטן גאַסט פֿרייט מען זיך ווען
ער קומט אַרײַן, מיט אַ שלעכטן
ווען ער גייט אַוועק.

A welcome guest gladdens when he arrives, an unwelcome one when he leaves.

Mit a gutn gast freyt men zikh ven er kumt arayn, mit a shlekhtn ven er geyt avek. NS

נעבן גוטע געסט פּאַשיוועט מען
זיך אַליין.

Alongside welcome guests one also fares well.

Nebn gute gest pashivet men zikh aleyn. IB

וווּ צוויי עסן עסט אַ דריטער.

Where two eat, a third eats.

[An uninvited guest soon appears.]

Vu tsvey esn est a driter. IB

זײַ נאָך ניט געזונט, איך פֿאָר נאָך
ניט אַוועק.

Don't say: 'be well,' I'm not leaving yet.

Zay nokh nit gezunt, ikh for nokh nit avek. AC

HAPPINESS

אַז מען האָט קינדער, געזונט און געלט
האָט מען אַ שיינע וועלט.

If one has children, health, and
money, life will be sunny.
*Az men hot kinder, gezunt un gelt
hot men a sheyne velt.* NS

איינעם דאַכט זיך אַז בײַ יענעם
לאַכט זיך.

Many calculate that others
celebrate.
*Eynem dakht zikh az bay yenem
lakht zikh.* AC

כאָטש איין מינוט, נאָר לעבן גוט.

Even if only for a while, as long
as it's in good style.
Khotsh eyn minut, nor lebn gut. NS

ווען דאָס האַרץ איז פֿריילעך
זײַנען די פֿיס גרייט צו טאַנצן.

When the heart is glad, the feet
are ready to dance.
*Ven dos harts iz freylekh zaynen di
fis greyt tsu tantsn.* AC

HASTE

אַ יוצא בחפּזון פֿאַרלירט דאָס
געלט און די הויזן.

"Speed and spurt," you lose
money and shirt.
*A yoytse b'khipoyzn farlirt dos gelt
un di hoyzn.* NS

אז מען אײלט זיך האָט מען אַ מיידל.

If you rush, you'll have a daughter.
Az men aylt zikh hot men a meydl. IB

עס איז לײַכט צו מאַכן און שװער צו טראַכטן.

Quick to do, hard to think through.
Es iz laykht tsu makhn un shver tsu trakhtn. NS

פֿון כאַפּ-לאַפּ צעבראַכט מען דעם קאָפּ.

Slap-dash and your head will crash.
Fun khap-lap tsebrakht men dem kop. AC

געשװינד איז נאָר גוט פֿליגן צו כאַפּן.

Speed is only good for catching flies.
Geshvind iz nor gut flign tsu khapn. P

צװישן אַ חכם און אַ נאַר איז דער אונטערשייד איטלעכע מינוט.

Between a sage and a fool the difference is several minutes.
Tsvishn a khokhem un a nar iz der untersheyd itlekhe minut. AC

HEALTH

אז מען איז נאָר געזונט איז מען שױן רײַך.

If you're healthy, you're wealthy.
Az men iz nor gezunt iz men shoyn raykh. NS

אבי געזונט – דאָס לעבן קען מען זיך
אַליין נעמען.

As long as you're healthy – you
can always kill yourself later.
*Abi gezunt – dos lebn ken men zikh
aleyn nemen.* P

געזונט קומט פֿאַר פרנסה.

Health comes before livelihood.
Gezunt kumt far parnose. NS

קענצער, שמעענצער – אבי געזונט!

Cancer, shmancer – as long as
you're healthy!
Kentser, shmentser – abi gezunt! P

HEART

אַ ביטער האַרץ רעדט אַ סך.

An embittered heart talks a lot.
A biter harts ret a sakh. AC

אַ האַרץ איז אַ שלאָס, אָבער אַ שלאָס
עפֿנט מען מיט אַ נאָכגעמאַכטן
שליסל.

A heart is a lock, but a lock can
be opened with a duplicate key.
*A harts iz a shlos, ober a shlos efnt
men mit a nokhgemakhtn shlisl.* NS

אַ יתום עסט אַ סך און אַ ביטער
האַרץ רעדט אַ סך.

An orphan eats a lot and an
embittered heart talks a lot.
*A yosem est a sakh un a biter harts
ret a sakh.* NS

אַז מען רעדט זיך אַראָפֿ פֿון האַרצן
ווערט גרינגער.

When one pours out one's heart,
one feels easier.
*Az men ret zikh arop fun hartsn vert
gringer.* AC

דאָס האַרץ איז אַ האַלבער נביא.

The heart is half a prophet.
Dos harts iz a halber novi. AC

דאָס קליינע האַרץ נעמט אַרום די
גרויסע וועלט.

The heart, however small,
embraces all.
*Dos kleyne harts nemt arum di
groyse velt.* NS

אײן האַרץ פֿילט דאָס אַנדערע.

One heart sympathizes with another.

Eyn harts filt dos andere. IB

HEAVEN AND HELL

אַ שעה אין גן-עדן איז אויך גוט.

Even an hour in paradise is worth while.

A sho in ganeydn iz oykh gut. AC

בעסער אין גן-עדן אין שמאַטעס אײדער אין נהינום אויסגעפּוצט.

Better to go to heaven in rags than to hell in finery.

Beser in ganeydn in shmates eyder in gehenem oysgeputst. AC

דער נהינום איז ניט אַזוי שלעכט ווי דאָס קומען צו אים.

Hell is not so bad as the getting there.

Der gehenem iz nit azoy shlekht vi dos kumen tsu im. IB

HEREDITY

אַז די מוטער איז אַ קו איז די טאָכטער אַ קאַלב.

If the mother is a cow, the daughter is a calf.

Az di muter iz a ku iz di tokhter a kalb. NS

דאָס עפּעלע פֿאַלט ניט ווײַט פֿון בײמעלע.

The apple doesn't fall far from the tree.

Dos epele falt nit vayt fun beymele. P

טאַטע-מאַמע ווי די רוחות, קינדער ווי די שדים.

Parents like devils, children like demons.

Tate-mame vi di rukhes, kinder vi di sheydim. NS

ווי די גענדז אַזוי די גריוון.

Like the geese, so the cracklings.

Vi di gendz azoy di grivn. P

HERESY

אַן אויפֿגעקלערטער אין אַ קליין
שטעטל עסט שנויץ מיט ברויט.

An enlightened person in a small town eats pork with bread.
An oyfgeklerter in a kleyn shtetl est shnoyts mit broyt. NS

אַז אַ חסיד ווערט אויפֿגעקלערט
שעלט ער גאָט אין טאַטן אַרײַן.

When a Hassid becomes enlightened he curses God.
Az a khosed vert oyfgeklert shelt er got in tatn arayn. IB

אַז גאָט וויל שטראָפֿן אַן אפיקורס
גיט ער אים אַ פֿרום ווײַב.

When God wants to punish an unbeliever, He gives him a pious wife.
Az got vil shtrofn an apikoyres git er im a frum vayb. IF

בּאַדאַי אַ שלעכטער באָרשט אַבי
די שיסל איז טרפֿה.

Even a vile soup as long as the bowl is treyf.
[Comment on an unbeliever's need to flaunt his heresy by eating non-kosher]
Baday a shlekhter borsht abi di shisl iz treyfe. IB

HOLIDAYS

אַ סך המנס און נאָר איין פּורים.

So many Hamans and only one Purim.
A sakh homens un nor eyn purim. P

אַז עס זאָל ניט קומען דער ליבער
פּסח וואָלט מען פֿון דער בלאָטע
ניט אַרויס.

If not for the beloved Passover, we'd never get out of the mud.
Az es zol nit kumen der liber peysekh volt men fun der blote nit aroys. IB

פּורים איז דאָ לאָקשן אין באָד אויך.

On Purim you get noodles in the bath-house too.
Purim iz do lokshn in bod oykh. IF

שׂימחת-תּורה זײַנען אַלע שיכּורים
ניכטער.

On Simkhat-Torah all drunkards become sober.
[when it is appropriate to take a drink.]
Simkhes-toyre zaynen ale shikurim nikhter. AC

ווענן אַזאַ ביסל בוימל מאַכט מען
אַזאַ גרוֹיסן יום-טובֿ?

Over so little oil you make such a big festival? [Refers to Channukhah.]
Vegn aza bisl boyml makht men aza groysn yontev? IB

HOME

אײדער מיט אַ שלעכטן מאַן אויף אַ
יריד און מיט קינדער אויף אַ חתונה
איז שוין בעסער צו זיצן אין
דער היים.

Rather than accompany a difficult husband to a fair or small children to a wedding, it's better to stay at home.
Eyder mit a shlekhtn man oyf a yarid un mit kinder oyf a khasene iz shoyn beser tsu zitsn in der heym. AC

האַלט דיר דעם כּבֿוד און זיץ אין
דער היים.

Hang on to your dignity and stay at home. [Rather than be humiliated]
Halt dir dem koved un zits in der heym. AC

אומעטום איז גוט און אין דער היים
איז בעסער.

It is good everywhere but home is better.
Umetum iz gut un in der heym iz beser. AC

וווֹיל איז דעם וואָס זיצט אין דער הײב

Good for them who stay at home.
Voyl iz dem vos zitst in der heym. NS

HONESTY

אַ שלאָס איז נאָר גוט פֿאַר אַן
אָרענטלעכן מענטשן.

A lock keeps out only the honest.
A shlos iz nor gut far an orentlekhn mentshn. NS

דער חזיר האָט געשוווירן אַז ער
עסט נישט קיין דרעק.

The pig swore that he doesn't eat shit.
Der khazer hot geshvoyrn az er est nisht keyn drek. IF

אויב זײַן וואָרט וואָלט געדינט אַלס
בריק וואָלט מען מורא געהאַט
אַריבערצוגיין.

If his word were a bridge, we'd be afraid to cross.
Oyb zayn vort volt gedint als brik volt men moyre gehat aribertsugeyn. NS

שווער זיך צען מאָל איבער וועל איך
דיר גלייבן אָן אַ שבֿועה.

Swear ten times and I'll believe you without an oath.
Shver zikh tsen mol iber vel ikh dir gleybn on a shvu'e. NS

HONOR

אַ כּפּרה געלט – אַבי כּבֿוד איז גרויס!

To hell with money – as long as honor is great.
A kapore gelt – abi koved iz groys! NS

אַ מאָלצײַט אין צוויִען שפּאַלטן,
אַבי זיך ערלעך האַלטן.

A meal you may share as long as you honorably fare.
A moltsayt in tsveyen shpaltn, abi zikh erlekh haltn. IB

אַ שם טובֿ איז בעסער ווי אַן אבֿן טובֿ.

A good name is better than a precious stone.
A shem tov iz beser vi an even tov. IB

בעסער צו זײַן גוט איידער פֿרום.

Better honorable than pious.
Beser tsu zayn gut eyder frum. AC

די מלאָכה דאַרף מען קענען און יושר
דאַרף מען האָבן.

A trade one should learn, honor one should have.
Di melokhe darf men kenen un yoysher darf men hobn. IB

גאָט איז גאָר קיין מענטש ניט!

God Himself isn't a decent human being!
Got iz gor keyn mentsh nit! AC

אין דרײַ ערטער גיט מען קיין כּבֿוד
ניט אָפּ: אין תּפֿיסה, אין
בית-הכּסא און אין מרחץ.

One is without honor in three
places: in prison, in the outhouse,
and in the bath-house.
*In dray erter git men keyn koved nit
op: in tfise, in beysakise un in
merkhets.* AC

ער איז געווען אַ גוטער מענטש –
לויט זײַן מצבֿה.

He was an honorable person –
according to his gravestone.
*Er iz geven a guter mentsh – loyt
zayn matseyve.* AC

כּבֿוד און געלט רעגירן די וועלט.

Honor and money rule the world.
Koved un gelt regirn di velt. NS

נאָכן טויט ווערט מען חשובֿ.

After death one becomes honorable.
Nokhn toyt vert men khoshev. AC

שפּײַז קאָכט דער טאָפּ און כּבֿוד
קריגט דער טעלער.

Food is cooked in the pot and the
plate gets the credit.
*Shpayz kokht der top un koved krigt
der teler.* NS

ווויל איז דעם וואָס פֿירט אויס
בכּבֿוד זײַן וועלט.

Happy is he who conducts himself
honorably.
*Voyl iz dem vos firt oys b'koved
zayn velt.* IB

ווו איך זיץ איז אויבן אָן.

Wherever I sit is the head of the table.
Vu ikh zits iz oybn on. P

HOPE

אפֿילו ווען דער חלף לינט אויפֿן
האַלדז טאָר מען דעם בטחון
ניט פֿאַרלירן.

Even with the knife at your throat
don't lose hope.
*Afile ven der khalef ligt oyfn haldz
tor men dem bitokhn nit farlirn.* IB

דער בטחון איז אַ האַלבער נצחון.

Confidence is half the victory.
Der bitokhn iz a halber nitsokhn. NS

אַז מען האָט בטחון האָט מען אויף
שבת צו קאָכן.

If you have faith, you'll have food
for the Sabbath.
*Az men hot bitokhn hot men oyf
shabes tsu kokhn.* IB

אַז מען לעבט האָט מען אַ האָפֿנונג
– צו שטאַרבן.

Where there's life, there's hope –
to die.
*Az men lebt hot men a hofnung – tsu
shtarbn.* AC

דער טאָג איז נאָך גרויס!

The day is yet young!
Der tog iz nokh groys! P

די זון שײַנט ליכטיקער נאָך אַ רעגן.

The sun shines brighter after a
shower.
Di zun shaynt likhtiker nokh a regn. NS

פֿון לויטער האָפֿנונג ווערט מען
משוגע.

With hope alone you can go crazy.
*Fun loyter hofnung vert men
meshuge.* NS

האָפֿן און האַרן מאַכן מענטשן צו
נאַרן.

Wait and hope make a person a
dope.
Hofn un harn makhn mentshn tsu narn.

אָדער דער פֿריץ וועט פּגרן אָדער
דער הונט וועט פּגרן.

Either the landowner will die or
his dog will.
*Oder der porets vet peygern oder
der hunt vet peygern.* AC

ווען משיח וועט קומען וועלן אַלע
קאָרטן זײַן גלעזערנע.

When the Messiah arrives, all the
playing cards will be made of glass.
[Then everyone will see through them and be
a winner.]
*Ven meshi'ekh vet kumen veln ale
kortn zayn glezerne.* AC

זאָג ניט קיינמאָל אַז דו גייסט
דעם לעצטן וועג.

Never say that you travel the last
road.
*Zog nit keynmol az du geyst dem
letstn veg.* P

HUNGER

א ליידיקע קישקע האָט פֿײַנט אַ
לאַנגע דרשה.

An empty belly detests a lengthy sermon.
A leydike kishke hot faynt a lange droshe. AC

אַז דער מאָגן איז לער איז דער
שלאָף שווער.

If the stomach is bare, sleep is full of care.
Az der mogn iz ler iz der shlof shver. IB

אַז מען איז הונגעריק עסט מען ברויט.

If you're hungry, eat bread.
Az men iz hungerik est men broyt. AC

בײַ דעם עסן קען מען קוים דעם
הונגער פֿאַרגעסן.

With such a meal, you can barely forget your hunger.
Bay dem esn ken men koym dem hunger fargesn. AC

דער הונגער קען צו אַלץ ברענגען.

Hunger can lead to anything.
Der hunger ken tsu alts brengen. AC

פֿאַראַן מער אַפּעטיט ווי עסן.

There's more appetite than food.
Faran mer apetit vi esn. AC

פֿון הונגער שטאַרבט מען נאָר
אין אַ הונגער יאָר.

One dies of hunger only in a famine.
Fun hunger shtarbt men nor in a hunger yor. NS

פֿון ווינטשן ווערט מען ניט זאַט.

Well-wishing won't satisfy hunger.
Fun vintshn vert men nit zat. P

אין אַ הונגער יאָר זאָל מען עסן מער.

In a famine eat more!
In a hunger yor zol men esn mer. NS

מאָל דיר אויס אַ טאָפּ מיט סמעטענע.

Imagine you have a pot of cream.
Mol dir oys a top mit smetene. IB

פּורים נאָך דער סעודה איז קיין ייִד
ניט הונגעריק.

After the feast of Purim, no Jew is hungry.
Purim nokh der sude iz keyn yid nit hungerik. IB

ווען עס פֿליט אַרײַן דער הונגער דורך
דער טיר פֿליט אַרוים די ליבע
דורכן פֿענצטער.

When hunger flies in the door,
love flies out the window.
*Ven es flit arayn der hunger durkh
der tir flit aroys di libe durkhn fenster.* N

וואָס האָט מען פֿון דער שיינער שיסל
אַז זי איז ליידיק?

What use is a beautiful bowl if it's
empty?
*Vos hot men fun der sheyner shisl az
zi iz leydik?* IF

HYPOCRISY

בעסער רעדן מיט אַ ייִדענע און
טראַכטן פֿון גאָט איידער רעדן
מיט גאָט און טראַכטן פֿון אַ ייִדענע.

Better talk to a woman and think
of God than talk to God and think
of a woman.
*Beser redn mit a yidene un trakhtn
fun got eyder redn mit got un
trakhtn fun a yidene.* AC

דער גוי איז טרייף אָבער זײַן
גראָשן איז כּשר.

The Goy is treyf but his money is
kosher.
*Der goy is treyf ober zayn groshn iz
kosher.* IB

דער מגיד שטראָפֿט קהל און
אַליין טוט ער פֿאַרקערט.

The preacher scolds the community
and does the reverse of what he says.
*Der magid shtroft ko'ol un aleyn tut
er farkert.* AC

די מסירה האָט מען ליב – דעם
מוסר האָט מען פֿײַנט.

One enjoys the report but despises
the informant.
*Di mesire hot men lib – dem moyser
hot men faynt.* AC

ער איז אַזאַ זגאַל מענטש: ס'ערשטע
גרייט ער צו די רפֿואה דערנאָך
דערלאַנגט ער די מכּה.

He is the sort of person who first
prepares the remedy, then inflicts
the wound.
*Er iz aza zgal mentsh: s'ershte greyt
er tsu di refu'e dernokh derlangt er
di make.* AC

ער מיינט ניט די הגדה נאָר די
קניידלעך.

He isn't interested in the
Haggadah, only in the dumplings.
Er meynt nit di hagode nor di k'neydlekh. P

ער שלאָגט זיך על-חטא און באַלעקט
זיך דערבייַ.

He beats himself for his sins and
enjoys the exercise.
*Er shlogt zikh al khet un balekt zikh
derbay.* NS

הינטערן קייסערס מאָנטל מעג מען
אַ פֿייַג ווייַזן.

Under the tsar's cloak you may
make a sign of contempt.
*Hintern keysers mantl meg men a
fayg vayzn.* IB

מאַך מיר ניט קיין לאָך אין קאָפּ און
לייג מיר ניט צו קיין פֿלאַסטער.

Don't give me a hole in the head
and don't apply the bandage.
*Makh mir nit keyn lokh in kop un
leyg mir nit tsu keyn flaster.* AC

שענק מיר ניט קיין האָניק און גיב
מיר ניט קיין בים.

Don't give me any honey and
spare me the sting.
*Shenk mir nit keyn honik un gib mir
nit keyn bis.* NS

וואָס ער זאָגט דאָס מיינט ער ניט און
וואָס ער מיינט דאָס זאָגט ער ניט.

What he says, he doesn't mean,
and what he means, he doesn't say.
*Vos er zogt dos meynt er nit un vos
er meynt dos zogt er nit.* AC

וואָס מען שעמט זיך צו זאָגן אויף
ייִדיש זאָגט מען אויף לשון-קודש.

What one is ashamed to say in
Yiddish, one says in the Holy
Tongue [Hebrew].
*Vos men shemt zikh tso zogn oyf
yidish zogt men oyf loshn-koydesh.* AC

יושר וויל מען אַז יענער זאָל האָבן.

A sense of justice we want others to have.
Yoysher vil men az yener zol hobn. AC

זייַ מיר ניט קיין פֿעטער און נייַ
מיר ניט קיין שיך.

Don't be my uncle and don't sew
shoes for me.
*Zay mir nit keyn feter un ney mir nit
keyn shikh.* IB

I

IGNORANCE

אַ בלינד פֿערד טרעפֿט גלייך אין
גרוב אַריַן.

A blind horse makes straight for
the ditch.
*A blind ferd treft glaykh in grub
arayn.* AC

אַ הונט וואָס בילט קען ניט בייסן
אָבער זיי אַליין ווייסן ניט פֿון דעם.

Barking dogs don't bite but they
themselves don't know it.
*A hunt vos bilt ken nit baysn ober
zey aleyn veysn nit fun dem.* NS

אַ וואָרעם לינט אין כריין און מיינט
אַז ס'איז קיין זיסערם ניטאָ.

A worm in the horseradish thinks
there's no sweeter place to be.
*A vorem ligt in khreyn un meynt az
s'iz keyn zisers nito.* AC

אַן עם-האָרץ קען קיין
אַפּיקורס ניט זיַן.

An ignoramus isn't smart enough
to be an unbeliever.
*An amorets ken keyn apikoyres nit
zayn.* IB

אַן אָרעמאַן קען ווערן אַן עושר אָבער
אַן עם-האָרץ קען קיין למדן
ניט ווערן.

A pauper can become wealthy but
an ignoramus cannot become a
scholar.
*An oreman ken vern an oysher ober
an amorets ken keyn lamdn nit vern.* AC

אַז גאָט וויל שטראָפֿן אן עם-האָרץ
לייגט ער אים אַרײַן אַ לשון-קודש
וואָרט אין מויל אַרײַן.

If God wants to punish an
ignoramus, He inspires him to
mouth a bit of learning.
*Az got vil shtrofn an amorets leygt
er im arayn a loshn-koydesh vort in
moyl arayn.* IB

אַז גאָט וויל שטראָפֿן אַ לשון-קודש
וואָרט לייגט ער עס אַרײַן בײַ אַן
עם-האָרץ אין מויל.

When God wants to punish the
Holy Tongue [Hebrew], He puts it
into the mouth of an ignoramus.
*Az got vil shtrofn a loshn-koydesh
vort leygt er es arayn bay an
amorets in moyl.* AC

דער גלאָק קלינגט ווײַל ער איז פוסט.

The bell rings because it's empty.
Der glok klingt vayl er iz pust. NS

דער אָקס ווייסט ניט פֿון זײַן גבורה.

The ox doesn't know its own strength.
Der oks veyst nit fun zayn gvure. NS

די גאַליציאַנער זײַנען זייער אַמביציעז:
נאָך איידער זיי קענען
עבֿרי כאַפּן זיי זיך צו דער גמרא.

Galician Jews are very ambitious:
before they even know Hebrew
they're into Talmud.
*Di galitsi'aner zaynen zeyer
ambitsi'ez: nokh eyder zey kenen
ivre khapn zey zikh tsu der gemore.* SM

ער הייסט משה ניסן – ער וויל פֿון
גאָרניט וויסן.

His name is Moshe nut – he knows
not what.
*Er heyst moyshe nisn – er vil fun
gornit visn.* IF

ער איז אַ קענער – ער קען עסן!

He's very knowledgeable – he
knows how to eat!
Er iz a kener – er ken esn. P

ער קען אַלץ – נאָר קיין שבת קען
ער ניט מאַכן!

He knows everything – except how
to prepare for the Sabbath!
*Er ken alts – nor keyn shabes ken er
nit makhn!* P

ער זאָגט עבֿרי װי אַ װאַסער נאָר דאָס
װאַסער לויפֿט און ער שטײט.

Hebrew flows from him like a
river except that a river runs and
he remains.
*Er zogt ivre vi a vaser nor dos vaser
loyft un er shteyt.* IB

פֿון לײדיקע פֿעסער איז דער
ליאַרעם גרעסער.

From an empty drum you get
pandemonium.
Fun leydike feser iz der li'arem greser. N

קײנער איז ניט אַזױ טױב װי דער
װאָס װיל ניט הערן.

None so deaf as those that will not hea
*Keyner iz nit azoy toyb vi der vos vil
nit hern.* P

אָן פּאָדקאָװעס קען ער קײן עבֿרי ניט.

Without horseshoes [pronunciation
marks] he can't read Hebrew.
On podkoves ken er keyn ivre nit. IB

שבת לערנט ער - מכּות קען ער!

To Sabbath studies he goes – but
nothing he knows!
Shabes lernt er – makes ken er! IB

װען אַ חמור רעדט װי אַ מענטש
װוּנדערט זיך די גאַנצע װעלט,
װען אַ מענטש רעדט װי אַ חמור
װוּנדערט זיך קײנער.

When an ass talks like a human
being everyone is surprised, when
a human being talks like an ass no
one is surprised.
*Ven a khamer ret vi a mentsh
vundert zikh di gantse velt, ven a
mentsh ret vi a khamer vundert zikh
keyner.* AC

װער עס האָט ניט קײן מוח דאַרף
האָבן כּוח.

If you have no brain, you need brawn
*Ver es hot nit keyn moyekh darf
hobn koyekh.* P

װאָס דאַרפֿסטו רעדן גױיש? מען זאָל
זען אַז דו ביסט אַ ייִד? רעד
בעסער ייִדיש װעט מען זען
אַז דו ביסט אַ גױ.

Why talk a foreign language? So
others will see that you're a Jew?
Better talk Yiddish so they'll see
that you are a Goy.
*Vos darfstu redn goyish men zol zen
az du bist a yid? red beser yidish vet
men zen az du bist a goy.* NS

קאָך אַ פּױער זיס און זױער
בלײבט ער אַלץ פּױער.

You may cook a peasant with sugar and dill, he remains a peasant still.

Kokh a poyer zis un zoyer blaybt er alts poyer. NS

וואָס טױג גאָלדענע הענט אַז דער
קאָפּ איז אַ לײמענער?

What use golden hands if the head is made of clay?

Vos toyg goldene hent az der kop iz a laymener? AC

זי הײסט לאה און האָט נישט
קײן דעה!

Her name may be Leah but she has no idea!

Zi heyst leye un hot nisht keyn deye! IF

זיבן און זיבן איז עלף – און דער
קאָפּ איז אײַזן.

Seven and seven make eleven – and the head is full of lead.

Zibn un zibn iz elf – un der kop iz ayzn. NS

ILLNESS

אַ געשוויר איז אַ גוטע זאַך בײַ יענעם
אונטערן אָרעם.

A boil is fine under someone else's arm.

A geshvir iz a gute zakh bay yenem untern orem. P

א מכה אונטער יענעמס אָרעם איז
ניט שווער צו טראָגן.

Another person's illness is not
hard to bear.
*A make unter yenems orem iz nit
shver tsu trogn.* IB

אן איַינרעדעניש איז ערגער ווי א
קרענק.

An imagined ailment is worse than
a disease.
An aynredenish iz erger vi a krenk. P

אז א מענטש איז געזונט האָט ער
א סך דאגות, אז ער איז קראַנק
האָט ער נאָר איין דאגה.

A healthy person has lots of
worries, a sick person has only one.
*Az a mentsh iz gezunt hot er a sakh
dayges, az er iz krank hot er nor
eyn dayge.* IB

אז עס קומט אָן א צאָנווייטיק
פאַרגעסט מען דעם קאָפּווייטיק.

With a toothache you forget a
headache.
*Az es kumt on a tsonveytik fargest
men dem kopveytik.* AC

בעסער א געזונטער אָרעמאַן איידער
א קראַנקער עושר.

Better a healthy pauper than a
sick millionaire.
*Beser a gezunter oreman eyder a
kranker oysher.* NS

די אייגענע צוויי פיס זיַינען
בעסער ווי דריַי.

One's own two feet are better than
three. [with a cane]
*Di eygene tsvey fis zaynen beser vi
dray.* AC

גאָט זאָל אָפּהיטן פון די קליינע
פלעשעלעך.

God preserve us from the little
medicine bottles.
*Got zol op'hitn fun di kleyne
fleshelekh.* NS

ווען צו א קרענק איז דאָ א רפואה
איז עס נאָר א האַלבע
קרענק.

If there's a cure, it's only half a
disease.
*Ven tsu a krenk iz do a refu'e iz es
nor a halbe krenk.* P

וווּ מען לייגט דעם קראַנקן טוט
אים אַלץ ווײ.

No matter where you place the
sick person, he's still in pain.
*Vu men leygt dem krankn tut im alts
vey.* AC

IMITATION

אַז מען וויל נאָכטאָן לײַטן וואַרפֿט
מען זיך פֿון אַלע זײַטן.

If you copy another's stride, you'll
end up spending on every side.
*Az men vil nokhton laytn varft men
zikh fun ale zaytn.* NS

אַזוי ווי עס קריסטלט זיך אַזוי
ייִדלט זיך.

What Gentiles do, Jews ape.
*Azoy vi es kristelt zokh azoy yidelt
zikh.* P

קויפֿסט שיך פֿאַר זיך טאָ מעסט
זיי ניט אויף פֿרעמדע פֿיס.

If you want to buy yourself a boot,
don't fit it to someone else's foot.
*Koyfst shikh far zikh, to mest zey nit
oyf fremde fis.* NS

קוק נאָך וואָס אַנדערע מאַכן, קלער
נאָר וועגן אייגענע זאַכן.

What others do you should find,
but make up your own mind.
*Kuk nokh vos andere makhn, kler nor
vegn eygene zakhn.* NS

טו וואָס איך זאָג אָבער ניט וואָס
איך טו.

Do as I say, not as I do.
Tu vos ikh zog ober nit vos ikh tu. AC

INCOMPETENCY

אַ פֿעטער רבֿ און אַ מאָגערער גלח
טויגן ביידע ניט.

A fat rabbi and a skinny priest
are both useless.
*A feter rov un a mogerer galekh
toygn beyde nit.* IB

אַ גרויסער וואָלקן – אַ קליינער רעגן!

A big cloud – a small shower!
A groyser volkn – a kleyner regn! P

אַ שלימזל פֿאַלט אויפֿן רוקן און
צעקלאַפֿט זיך די נאָז.

A shlimazl falls on his back and
bruises his nose.
*A shlimazl falt oyfn rukn un tseklapt
zikh di noz.* NS

אַ שלימזל גלייבט נאָר אין מזל.

A shlimazl believes only in luck.
A shlimazl gleybt nor in mazl. NS

אַ שלימזל וואַנדערט אויס אַלע
לענדער און קומט אַהיים אָן
הויזן און אָן העמדער.

A shlimazl wanders the earth's
expanse and comes back home
without shirt or pants.
*A shlimazl vandert oys ale lender un
kumt aheym on hoyzn un on hemder.* IB

אַז די הענט טויגן ניט זײַנען די פֿיס
ניט שולדיק.

If the hands are useless, the feet
aren't to blame.
*Az di hent toygn nit zaynen di fis nit
shuldik.* P

דער מאָגן גרילט זיך, די מילך בריעט
זיך, די קאַשע פּריעט זיך, און דאָ
בין איך, אײַן מענטש אַליין און
אין מאַרק מוז איך גיין.

The belly grumbles, the milk
bubbles, the groats float, and here
am I, one person all alone and to
the market I must go!
*Der mogn grilt zikh, di milkh bri'et
zikh, di kashe pri'et zikh, un do bin
ikh, eyn mentsh aleyn, un in mark
muz ikh geyn!* SM

ער האָט אויפֿגעהויבן אַ פֿעדער און
געלאָזט פֿאַלן די גאַנצע איבערבעט.

He picked up a feather and let
drop the entire coverlet.
*Er hot oyfgehoybn a feder un gelozt
faln di gantse iberbet.* IB

ער קען אַפֿילו אַ קאַץ אָן עק ניט
צובינדן!

He can't even tie the tail of a cat!
Er ken afile a kats an ek nit tsubindn! A

ער שלעפּט זיך אַרום ווי אַבֿרהם
מיט דער מילה!

He drags himself around like a
newly circumcised Abraham!
*Er shlept zikh arum vi avrum mit
der mile!* AC

ער איז אן אױפֿטױער אַ סכּנה – ער
האָט געשאָסן די לבֿנה!

He's a dangerous guy – he shoots
the moon in the sky!
*Er iz an oyftu'er a sakone – er hot
geshosn di levone!* AC

ער קוקט ווי אַ האָן אין בני אָדם!

He stares like a rooster at people!
Er kukt vi a hon in b'ney odem! P

געפֿאָרן צו דער חתונה און פֿאַרגעסן
דעם חתן אין דער היים!

Went to the wedding and forgot
the bridegroom at home!
*Geforn tsu der khasene un fargesn
dem khosn in der heym!* P

קױם געפּױלט דאָס פֿערדעלע
זאָל ניט עסן נעמט עס און
פּגרט גאָר אַוועק!

Finally convinced the horse to stop
eating and it up and dies!
*Koym gepoylt dos ferdele zol nit esn
nemt es un peygert gor avek!* NS

לױטן פּנים דאַרף ער זײַן אַ חזן, לױטן
קול מוז ער זײַן אַ גרױסער חכם!

According to his face he must be a
cantor, according to his voice he
must be a towering intellect!
*Loytn ponim darf er zayn a khazn,
loytn kol muz er zayn a groyser
khokhem!* AC

צווישן אַלע שוסטערס איז דער
בעסטער שנײַדער יאָסל דער
סטאָליער.

Among the shoemakers, the best
tailor is Yosel the carpenter!
*Tsvishn ale shusters iz der bester
shnayder yosl der stolyer!* NS

צװײ מתים גייען טאַנצן! **Two corpses go dancing!**
Tsvey meysim geyen tantsn! P

װען אַ שלימזל זאָל האַנדלען מיט **If shlimazl sold umbrellas, it**
שירעמס װאָלט אויפֿגעהערט צו **would stop raining; if he sold**
רעגענען, װאָלט ער געהאַנדלט **candles, the sun would never set;**
מיט ליכט װאָלט די זון ניט **and if he dealt in shrouds, people**
אונטערגעגאַנגען און װען ער זאָל **would stop dying.**
האַנדלען מיט תכריכים װאָלטן *Ven a shlimazl zol handlen mit*
מענטשן אויפֿגעהערט צו שטאַרבן. *shirems volt oyfgehert tsu regenen,*
volt er gehandlt mit likht volt di zun
nit untergegangen un ven er zol
handlen mit takhrikhim voltn
mentshn oyfgehert tsu shtarbn. AC

װען אַ שלימזל קוילעט אַ האָן גייט **When a shlimazl slaughters a**
ער, דרייט ער אַ זייגער, שטייט ער. **rooster, it hops; when he winds a**
clock, it stops.
Ven a shlimazl koylet a hon geyt er,
dreyt er a zeyger, shteyt er. NS

װוּ ער װעט זײַן רב שמדט זיך די **Wherever he will be the rabbi, the**
קהילה. **entire community will become**
apostates.
Vu er vet zayn rov, shmat zikh di
kehile. NS

INDIVIDUALITY

אַלע זײַנען טאַקע פֿון זעלבן טייג **Everyone is kneaded out of the**
געקנאָטן אָבער ניט אין זעלבן אויװן **same dough but not baked in the**
געבאַקן. **same oven.**
Ale zaynen take fun zelbn teyg
gek'notn ober nit in zelbn oyvn
gebakn. AC

איטלעכער גייט מיט זײַן װעג. **Everyone goes his own way.**
Itlekher geyt mit zayn veg. NS

איטלעכער ייד האָט זײַן שולחן-ערוך. **Every Jew has his own code of laws.**
Itlekher yid hot zayn shulkhn-orekh. IB

נים אַלע פערד זײַנען גלײַך.

Not all horses are alike.
Nit ale ferd zaynen glaykh. AC

יעדערער מאַכט שבת פֿאַר זיך אַליין.

Every person prepares the Sabbath
in his own way.
Yederer makht shabes far zikh aleyn. P

INEVITABILITY

אַ בלינד פערד טרעפֿט גלײַך אין
גרוב אַרײַן.

A blind horse makes straight for
the ditch.
*A blind ferd treft glaykh in grub
arayn.* P

אַזוי שנעל ווי מען זעצט זיך צו דער
וועטשערע שיקט דער טײַוול
צו אַ גאַסט.

No sooner do you sit down to a
meal then the devil sends a guest.
*Azoy shnel vi men zetst zikh tsu der
vetshere shikt der tayvl tsu a gast.* AC

די זון וועט אונטערגיין אָן דײַן הילף.

The sun will set without your
assistance.
Di zun vet untergeyn on dayn hilf. P

קיינער באַהאַלט נים, ניט דער רשע
זײַן רשעות און ניט דער נאַר
זײַן נאַרישקייט.

Nothing is hidden: not the wicked
from his wickedness nor the fool
from his folly.
*Keyner bahalt nit, nit der roshe zayn
rishes un nit der nar zayn
narishkeyt.* NS

אונטערגענומען הייסט זיך פֿאַרקויפֿט.

Pledge yourself and you're obligated.
Untergenumen heyst zikh farkoyft. NS

וווּ מען וואַרפֿט אַ שטיין איז ער דאָ.

Wherever you throw a stone you
find him.
Vu men varft a shteyn iz er do. AC

וווּ צוויי דאָרט איז אַ דריטער.

Where two, there's soon a third.
Vu tsvey dort iz a driter. IB

INSULT

אַ בהמה קען מען ניט באַליידיקן.

A cow can't be insulted.
A beheyme ken men nit baleydikn. P

ער שטאַמט פֿון אַ גרױסן יחוס! ער
איז דעם אַלטן גנבֿס אַן אוראייניקל.

He comes of a noble line! He is the illustrious old thief's great-grandson.
Er shtamt fun a groysn yikhes! er iz dem altn ganefs an ureynikl. AC

גיי פֿײַפֿן (קאַקן) אױפֿן ים!

Go whistle (shit) on the ocean!
Gey fayfn (kakn) oyfn yam! P

קוש מיך װוּ די ייִדן האָבן גערוט.

Kiss me where the Jews rested.
[i.e. kiss my ass.]
Kush mikh vu di yidn hobn gerut! AC

מען זאָל אים ניט װינטשן אַפֿילו
אױף די שׂונאים.

Don't wish him even on his enemies!
Men zol im nit vintshn afile oyf di sonim

זאָל דער טאַטע דײַנער, עליו השלום,
אױפֿשטײן פֿון קבֿר און דיך אָנקוקן,
װאָלט ער זיך גלײַך צוריקגעלייגט!

If your father, may he rest in peace, rose from the grave and took one look at you, he would promptly return!
Zol der tate dayner, olev hashalom, oyfshteyn fun keyver un dikh onkukn, volt er zikh glaykh tsurikgeleygt! AC

INTERPRETATION

אַ בריװ איז װי מען לייענט אים, אַ
ניגון איז װי מען זינגט אים.

A letter depends on how you read it, a melody on how you sing it.
A briv iz vi men leyent im, a nigun iz vi men zingt im. NS

די שיקסע בײַם רבֿ קען אױך
פּסקענען אַ שאלה.

The rabbi's servant girl can also interpret the law.
Di shikse baym rov ken oykh paskenen a shayle. P

J

JEWS

אַ מלמד – אַ ייד וואָס האַנדלט
מיט גויים.

A Hebrew teacher – a Jew who deals in goyim.
A melamed – a yid vos handlt mit goyim. AC

אַ ייד קען אַלע מלאָכות: פסח איז ער
אַ בעקער, שבועות אַ גערטנער,
תישעה-באָב אַ זעלנער, סוכות
אַ ביימײַסטער, חנוכּה אַ בלײַגיסער
און ראָש-השנה אַ שופֿר-בלאָזער.

A Jew knows all trades: Passover, he's a baker; Shevuoth, a gardener; Tisheh B'av, a soldier; Succoth, a builder; Channukah, he pours lead; and Rosh Hashanah he becomes a shofar-blower.
A yid ken ale melokhes: peysekh iz er a beker, shevu'es a gertner, tishebov a zelner, sukes a boymayster, khanuke a blaygiser un rosheshone a shoyfer-blozer. IB

אַ ייד און אַ וואָלף גייען ניט אַרום
ליידיק.

A Jew and a wolf are never idle.
A yid un a volf geyen nit arum leydik. NS

אַ ייִדן דאַרף מען קיין מאָל ניט חושד
זײַן – ער איז זיכער אַ גנב.

One need never suspect a Jew – he surely is a thief.
A yidn darf men keyn mol nit khoyshed zayn – er iz zikher a ganef. NS

אַ ייִדישע קישקע איז ניט אָפּצושאַצן.

A Jewish gizzard can't be measured.
A yidishe kishke iz nit optsushatsn. P

אַלץ איז בײַ ייִדן צו וויניק נאָר
שׂכל האָט איטלעכער גענוג.

Jews never have enough of
anything except brains.
*Alts iz bay yidn tsu veynik nor
seykhl hot itlekher genug.* AC

אַז דער ייִד איז גערעכט כאַפט ער
ערשט די רעכטע קלעפ.

When a Jew is in the right he gets
flogged with extra might.
*Az der yid iz gerekht khapt er ersht
di rekhte klep.* NS

בעסער אַ ייִד אָן אַ באָרד אײדער
אַ באָרד אָן אַ ייִד.

Better a Jew without a beard than
a beard without a Jew.
*Beser a yid on a bord eyder a bord
on a yid.* AC

בעסער אַ ייִדיש האַרץ מיט אַ גוייִשן
קאָפ אײדער אַ גוייִש האַרץ מיט
אַ ייִדישן קאָפ.

Better a Jewish heart with a
Gentile head than a Gentile heart
with a Jewish head.
*Beser a yidish harts mit a goyishn
kop eyder a goyish harts mit a
yidishn kop.* NS

ברעך אָפן אַ זעמל שפרינגט אַרויס
אַ ייִד.

Break open a roll, out jumps a Jew.
[One finds Jews everywhere.]
Brekh ofn a zeml shpringt aroys a yid.

דעם ייִדן פעלט תמיד אַ טאָג צו
דער וואָך.

A Jew is always short a day in the
week.
*Dem yidn felt tomed a tog tsu der
vokh.* P

דעם ייִדנס ברירה איז אַ
שײנע גזירה.

A Jew's determination is limited
by regulation.
Dem yidns breyre iz a sheyne gezeyre.

דער ים איז אָן אַ גרונט און ייִדישע
צרות אָן אַ ברעג.

The sea has no bottom and Jewish
troubles have no shores.
*Der yam iz on a grunt un yidishe
tsores on a breg.* NS

דער ייד האָט נאָר געלט צו פֿאַרלירן
און צײַט קראַנק צו זײַן.

A Jew has money only to lose and
time only to be sick.
*Der yid hot nor gelt tsu farlirn un
tsayt krank zu zayn.* NS

דער ייד שלאָגט זיך מיט דער דעה
און שיסט מיט דער ראיה.

A Jew fights with his conscience
but shoots with the evidence.
*Der yid shlogt zikh mit der daye un
shist mit der raye.* AC

דו שלאָגסט מײַנע ייִדן? וועל איך
שלאָגן דײַנע ייִדן.

You flog my Jews? Then I will
flog your Jews.
*Du shlogst mayne yidn? vel ikh
shlogn dayne yidn.* NS

עס איז גוט פֿאַר ייִדן?

Is it good for Jews?
Es iz gut far yidn? P

עס איז לײַכטער אַרויסצונעמען דעם
ייִדן פֿון דעם גלות איידער
דעם גלות פֿון דעם ייִדן.

It's easier to take the Jew out of
exile than the exile out of the Jew.
*Es is laykhter aroystsunemen dem
yidn fun dem goles eyder dem goles
fun dem yidn.* AC

גאָט זאָל אָפּהיטן פֿון גוייִשן כּוח
און ייִדישן מוח.

God protect us from Gentile hands
and Jewish wits.
*Got zol op'hitn fun goyishn koyakh
un yidishn moyakh.* NS

איטלעכער ייד האָט זיין פעקל.

Every Jew has his own pack of troubles.
Itlekher yid hot zayn pekl. P

מיט אַ ייִדן איז נאָר גוט קוגל צו עסן, דאַוענען פון איין סידור און ליגן אויף איין בית-הקבֿרות.

Togetherness among Jews is only good for eating pudding, praying from one prayerbook, and lying in one cemetery.
Mit a yidn iz nor gut kugl tsu esn, davenen fun eyn sider un lign oyf eyn beysakvores. AC

משה רבינו האָט מיט די ייִדן אויך ניט געקענט אויסקומען.

Not even Moses Our Teacher could get along with Jews.
Moyshe rabeynu hot mit di yidn oykh nit gekent oyskumen. AC

אָן נסים קען אַ ייד ניט לעבן.

A Jew can't live without miracles.
On nisim ken a yid nit lebn. P

צו וואָס דאַרף אַ ייד האָבן פֿיס? אַז אין חדר מוז מען אים טרייבן, צו דער חופה פֿירט מען אים, צו קבֿורה ברענגט מען אים, אין שול אַריַין גייט ער ניט און צו שיקסעס קריכט ער, איז צו וואָס דאַרף ער האָבן פֿיס?

Why does a Jew need legs? To school he must be forced, to marriage he must be led, to burial he is brought, to synagogue he won't go, and after Gentile girls he crawls. So why does he need legs?
Tsu vos darf a yid hobn fis? az in kheyder muz men im traybn, tsu der khupe firt men im, tsu kvure brengt men im, in shul arayn geyt er nit un tsu shikses krikht er, iz tsu vos darf er hobn fis? MS

צו זיַין אַ ייד דאַרף מען האָבן דעם כּוח פֿון אַ גוי.

To be a Jew one needs the strength of a Goy.
Tsu zayn a yid darf men hobn dem koyekh fun a goy. AC

ייִדישע עשירות איז ווי שניי אין מאַרץ.

Jewish wealth is like snow in March.
Yidishe ashires iz vi shney in marts. NS

וואָס עם וועט זײַן מיט כּל ישׂראל
וועט זײַן מיט רב ישׂראל.

Whatever befalls the People of Israel will befall Mr Israel.
Vos es vet zayn mit kol yisro'el vet zayn mit reb yisro'el. IB

וואָס גרעסער דער סוחר אַלץ
קלענער דער ייד.

The bigger the merchant the smaller the Jew.
Vos greser der soykher alts klener der yid. P

וווינען זאָל מען צווישן יידן, האַנדלען
זאָל מען צווישן גויים.

Live among Jews, do business among Goyim.
Voynen zol men tsvishn yidn, handlen zol men tsvishn goyim. NS

ייִדישע עשירות, מישטיינס געזאָגט
– פֿון תּעניתים ווערט מען רײַך.

Jewish wealth, alas – from fasting you get rich.
Yidishe ashires, mishteyns gezogt – fun taneysim vert men raykh. NS

ייִדן זײַנען געוווען צו פֿאַרנומען קינדער
האָבן צו זאָרגן זיך וועגן סעקס.

Jews were too busy having children to worry about sex.
Yidn zaynen geven tsu farnumen kinder hobn tsu zorgn zikh vegn seks. AC

ייִדישער חן איז אומעטום שיין.

Jewish charm is everywhere beautiful.
Yidisher kheyn iz umetum sheyn. P

JUSTICE

אַ ריכטער מוז זײַן ניכטער.

A judge must be sober.
A rikhter muz zayn nikhter. AC

אַז דער דיין וויל ניט פּסקנען מעג
דער שולחן-ערוך צעזעצט ווערן.

If the judge won't make a decision, then the Code of Laws can go to hell.
Az der dayen vil nit paskenen meg der shulkhn-orekh tsezetst vern. IF

אז מען טוט זיך לאָדן קומט מען צו שאָדן.

If you go to litigation, you get tribulation.
Az men tut zikh lodn kumt men tsu shodn. NS

דעם בעסטן ביסן קריגט דער ערגסטער הונט.

The best morsel often goes to the worst dog.
Dem bestn bisn krigt der ergster hunt. NS

דער עושר האָט ניט קיין יושר.

The rich have no sense of justice.
Der oysher hot nit keyn yoysher. P

עס איז אַ קוליקאָווער מישפּט!

It's a Kulikov trial!
[Kulikov – a small town near Lemberg. The tale is told that the town contained two tailors and one shoemaker. The shoemaker committed murder, was tried and sentenced to hang, but since there was only one shoemaker and two tailors, one of the tailors was hanged instead.]
Es iz a kulikover mishpet! IB

איינער קריגט פֿאַר אַ קניפ אַ גלעט, אַ צווייטער קריגט פֿאַר אַ גלעט אַ פּאַטש.

One person gets caressed for a pinch, another gets slapped for a caress.
Eyner krigt far a k'nip a glet, a tsveyter krigt far a glet a patsh. AC

מיט אַ נאַר, אַ פּחדן און אַ פּגר זאָל מען ניט מישפּטן.

Don't judge a fool, a coward, or a corpse.
Mit a nar, a pakhdn un a peyger zol men nit mishpetn. AC

וואָס קען ווערן פֿון די שאָף אַז דער וואָלף איז דער ריכטער?

What will become of the sheep if the wolf is the judge?
Vos ken vern fun di shof az der volf iz der rikhter? NS

יושר וויל מען אַז יענער זאָל האָבן.

A sense of justice we want others to have.
Yoysher vil men az yener zol hobn. P

KINSHIP

א ברודער א שונא איז א שונא
אויפֿן לעבן.

A brother turned enemy is an enemy for life.
A bruder a soyne iz a soyne oyfn lebn. NS

אלע ייִדן זײַנען אײן משפּחה.

All Jews belong to one family.
Ale yidn zaynen eyn mishpokhe. NS

אז מען נעמט ניט קיין ירושה זאָגט
מען ניט קיין קדיש.

If you don't receive the inheritance, don't recite the mourner's prayer.
Az men nemt nit keyn yerushe zogt men nit keyn kadesh. AC

בלוט איז דיקער פֿון וואַסער.

Blood is thicker than water.
Blut iz diker fun vaser. IB

די קרובֿים דערקענט מען אז זיי
ווערן רײַך.

You know who your relatives are when they become rich.
Di kroyvim derkent men az zey vern raykh. AC

אייגנס איז ניט פֿרעמד.

One's own is not alien.
Eygns iz nit fremd. P

פֿון בלוט ווערט קיין וואַסער ניט.

Blood doesn't turn into water.
Fun blut vert keyn vaser nit. P

מיַין באָבע און זיַין זיידע ליגן אין
דר'ערד ביידע.

My grandmother and his
grandfather are both in the
ground.

[satirical comment on a questionable kinship]
Mayn bobe un zayn zeyde lign in
dr'erd beyde. AC

מיַין זיידנס האָן האָט אין זיַין באָבעס
הויף אַריַינגעקרייט.

My grandfather's rooster crowed
into his grandmother's yard.

[satirical comment on a questionable kinship]
Mayn zeydns hon hot in zayn bobes
hoyf arayngekreyt. AC

מען מוסרט די טאָכטער און מען
מיינט די שנור.

You scold your daughter but you
mean your daughter-in-law.

Men musert di tokhter un men meynt
di shnur. NS

ריַיכע קרובֿים זיַינען נאָענטע קרובֿים.

Rich kin are close kin.

Raykhe kroyvim zaynen no'ente
kroyvim. AC

ווי גאָט טוט אַבי אין איינעם.

Whatever God wills as long as
we're together.

Vi got tut abi in eynem. NS

זיַי מיר ניט קיין קרובֿ און איך
וועל ניט זיַין דיַין ערובֿ.

Don't be my relative and I won't
be your sponsor.

Zay mir nit keyn korev un ikh vel nit
zayn dayn eruv. IB

KNOWLEDGE

אַ בוים ביינגט זיך נאָר ווען ער
איז יונג.

A tree bends only when it is young.

A boym beygt zikh nor ven er iz
yung. AC

אַ ייִד אַ למדן קען קיין חסיד ניט זיַין.

A learned Jew can't be a blind
believer.

A yid a lamdn ken keyn khosed nit
zayn. IB

ביי שװאַרצע פינטעלעך װאָס מער
גויים איז שװערער און ביי האָלץ
האַקן – פֿאַרקערט.

When it comes to the printed
word, the more Goyim the more
difficulty; with chopping wood it's
the reverse.
*Bay shvartse pintelekh vos mer
goyim iz shverer un bay holts hakn –
farkert.* IB

דער תּלמיד-חכם װײסט װאָס עם
פֿעלט אים נאָך צו װיסן.

The scholar knows what he lacks
knowledge of.
*Der talmed-khokhem veyst vos es felt
im nokh tsu visn.* AC

גאָרנישט איז נישט שװער – מען
דאַרף נאָר קענען.

Nothing is too difficult – you only
need to know how.
*Gornisht iz nisht shver – men darf
nor kenen.* AC

נעם די אױגן אין די הענט אַרײַן און
זע װאָס ס'טוט זיך.

Take your eyes into your hands
and look what's doing!
*Nem di oygn in di hent arayn un ze
vos s'tut zikh.* AC

װאָס חײמקע לערנט ניט קען ניט
חײם.

What little Chaim doesn't learn,
big Chaim won't know.
*Vos khayemke lernt nit ken nit
khayem.* IB

LAND OF ISRAEL

פֿאַרוואָם האָט אַרץ ישראל אַזוי פֿיל
שטיינער? ווייל יעדער ייד
וואָס קומט וואַרפֿט אַרונטער אַ
שטיין פֿון האַרץ.

Why is the Land of Israel so
stony? Because every Jew who
arrives casts off a stone from his
heart.
Farvos hot erets yisro'el azoy fil
shteyner? vayl yeder yid vos kumt
varft arunter a shteyn fun harts. AC

אין אַרץ ישראל האָבן מיר שוין
אייגענע פֿערד גנבֿים, אַלץ וואָס
פֿעלט נאָר איז פֿערד.

In the Land of Israel we now have
our very own horse thieves, all
that's missing are the horses.
In erets yisro'el hobn mir shoyn
eygene ferd ganovim, alts vos felt
nor iz ferd. SM

אין אַרץ ישראל איז דאָ איין פּיאַסטער
מיט אַ לאָך און דער גאַנצער
ישובֿ האַנדלט מיט אים.

The Land of Israel possesses only
one coin and the whole community
trades on it.
In erets yisro'el iz do eyn pi'aster
mit a lokh un der gantser yishuv
handlt mit im. AC

LAUGHTER AND TEARS

אַלצדינג לאָזט זיך אוים מיט אַ
געוויין.

Everything ends in weeping.
Altsding lozt zikh oys mit a geveyn.

א בדחן מאכט אלעמען פֿרײילעך און
אלײן ליגט ער אין דר׳ערד.

The wedding entertainer makes
everyone happy but he himself is
miserable.
*A batkhn makht alemen freylekh un
aleyn ligt er in dr'erd.* IB

ווען אַ יתום לײַדט זעט קיינער ניט, ווע
ער פֿרייט זיך זעט די גאַנצע וועלט.

When an orphan suffers nobody
notices, when he rejoices the whole
world sees.
*Ven a yosem layt zet keyner nit, ven
er freyt zikh zet di gantse velt.* NS

ווי זייף פֿאַרן גוף איז אַ טרער פֿאַר
דער נשמה.

Like soap for the body so are
tears for the soul.
*Vi zeyf farn guf iz a trer far der
neshome.* NS

LAZINESS

אַ פֿוילן איז גוט צו שיקן נאָכן
מלאך־המוות.

It's good to send a lazy person
after the angel of death.
*A foyln iz gut tsu shikn nokhn
malekhamoves.* IB

אַ פֿוילער שליח געפֿינט אַלע
תירוצים.

A sluggard finds every excuse.
A foyler sheli'ekh gefint ale terutsim. P

אַ קאַץ וואָס מיאַוקעט קען קיין
מײַז ניט כאַפֿן.

A meowing cat catches no mice.
*A kats vos mi'avket ken keyn mayz
nit khapn.* IB

אַז די פֿוילע מיידלעך גייען טאַנצן
גייען די כלי־זמרים פּישן.

When the lazy girls start dancing,
the musicians go out to pee.
*Az di foyle meydlekh geyen tantsn
geyen di klezmorim pishn.* NS

אַז מען האָט ניט וואָס צו טאָן איז
קאַקן אויך אַן אַרבעט.

If you don't have enough to do,
shitting is also work.
*Az men hot nit vos tsu ton iz kakn
oykh an arbet.* IB

בײַ אַ פוילן וואָקסט דער וועג
אונטער די פֿיס.

Under the sluggard's feet grass grows.
Bay a foyln vakst der veg unter di fis.

די קאַץ האָט ליב פֿיש. אָבער זי וויל
ניט די פֿים אײַננעצן.

The cat likes fish but won't wet her paws.
Di kats hot lib fish ober zi vil nit di fis ayn'netsn. NS

דער וואָם זוכט לײַכטע אַרבעט
גייט זייער מיד אין בעט.

Whoever looks for easy work goes to bed very tired.
Der vos zukht laykhte arbet geyt zeyer mid in bet. NS

ער דרייט זיך ווי אַ פֿאָרץ אין ראָסל.

He moves like a fart in brine.
Er dreyt zikh vi a forts in rosl. AC

LEARNING

אַ בוים בייגט זיך נאָר ווען ער
איז יונג.

A tree bends only when it is young.
A boym beygt zikh nor ven er iz yung.

אַ גוטער זיצער איז בעסער ווי אַ
גוטער קאָפּ.

A good seat is better than a good head.
A guter zitser iz beser vi a guter kop. P

אַ שיקסע בײַם רֻב קען אויך
פּסקענען אַ שאלה.

The rabbi's servant girl can also interpret the law.
A shikse baym rov ken oykh paskenen a shayle. P

אַז מען וויל לערנען כּסדר מח מען
יונגערהייט גיין אין חדר.

If you want to learn, you must start young.
Az men vil lernen keseyder muz men yungerheyt geyn in kheyder. AC

ביז זיבעציק יאָר לערנט מען שֹכל,
דערנאָך שטאַרבט מען גאָר אַוועק.

Until seventy, one learns wisdom, and then one goes and drops dead.
Biz zibetsik yor lernt men seykhl, dernokh shtarbt men gor avek. NS

די פען שיסט ערנער ווי אַ פֿײַל.

The pen stings worse than an arrow.
Di pen shist erger vi a fayl. NS

פֿיל אין קעפּעלע, פּוסט אין
טעפּעלע.

Full head, empty [cook] pot.
Fil in kepele, pust in tepele. NS

אױף אַ פֿרעמדער באָרד איז נוט
זיך צו לערנען שערן.

**It's good to learn barbering on
someone else's beard.**
*Oyf a fremder bord iz gut zikh tsu
lernen shern.* P

שלעכטס לערנט מען זיך באַלד אױס.

Bad is quickly learnt.
Shlekhts lernt men zikh bald oys. P

תּורה קומט ניט בירושה.

Learning can't be inherited.
Toyre kumt nit b'yerushe. IB

LIFE

אַ מענטש זאָל לעבן נאָר פֿון
נײַגעריקייט װעגן.

**A person should live if only for
curiosity's sake.**
*A mentsh zol lebn nor fun
naygerikeyt vegn.* AC

אַז מען דערמאָנט זיך אָן דעם טױט
איז מען ניט זיכער מיטן לעבן.

**If you start thinking about death,
you're no longer certain about life.**
*Az men dermont zikh on dem toyt iz
men nit zikher mitn lebn.* AC

אַז מען לעבט דערלעבט מען.

**If you live long enough, you live to
see everything.**
Az men lebt derlebt men. P

דאָס לעבן איז אַ גרױסער קאָפּװייטיק
אױף אַ טומלדיקער גאַס.

**Life is a big headache on a noisy
street.**
*Dos lebn iz a groyser kopveytik oyf
a tumldiker gas.* AC

דאָס לעבן איז ניט מער ווי אַ חלום
אָבער וועק מיך ניט אױף.

**Life is no more than a dream –
but don't wake me up.**
*Dos lebn iz nit mer vi a kholem ober
vek mikh nit oyf.* NS

דאָס לעבן איז אַ טאַנץ – מען דאַרף
עס נאָר קענען אָפּטאַנצן.

Life is a dance – you just have to
know the steps.
*Dos lebn iz a tants - men darf es
nor kenen optantsn.* AC

דאָס לעבן איז ווי אַ שמונה עשׂרה –
מ'שטייט, מ'שטייט ביז
וואַנען מען גייט אויס.

Life is like the daily prayers – one
stands and stands until one drops.
*Dos lebn iz vi a shimenesre –
m'shteyt, m'shteyt biz vanen men
geyt oys.* SK

עס איז בעסער צו לעבן אין נחת
איידער צו שטאַרבן אין צער.

It's better to live in joy than to die
in sorrow.
*Es iz beser tsu lebn in nakhes eyder
tsu shtarbn in tsar.* NS

פֿון נחת לעבט מען ניט, פֿון צרות
שטאַרבט מען ניט.

From joy you can't live, from
troubles you can't die.
*Fun nakhes lebt men nit, fun tsores
shtarbt men nit.* IB

געשלאָפֿן איז ניט געלעבט.

Slept isn't lived.
Geshlofn iz nit gelebt. P

היום – חיים, מאָרגן האָב איך עס אין
דר'ערד!

Today – life, tomorrow – the hell
with it!
*Hayom – khayim, morgn hob ikh es
in dr'erd!* IF

מען דאַרף לעבן און לאָזן לעבן.

One ought to live and let live.
Men darf lebn un lozn lebn. P

מען וואָלט געקענט לעבן נאָר מען
לאָזט ניט.

One could live but one isn't
allowed to.
Men volt gekent lebn nor men lozt nit. P

שיטער איז דײַן ברײַ און לעבן
איז כּדאי.

The brew may be slight but life is
still all right.
Shiter iz dayn bray un lebn iz keday. NS

זינט עס איז אויפגעקומען דאָס
שטאַרבן איז מען ניט זיכער
מיטן לעבן.

Since dying became fashionable,
living isn't safe.
*Zint es iz oyfgekumen dos shtarbn iz
men nit zikher mitn lebn.* P

LIQUOR

אַ גאַנץ יאָר שיכּור און פורים ניכטער.

The whole year full of rye and on
Purim dry.
[when it is appropriate to take a drink.]
A gants yor shiker un purim nikhter. P

אַ שיכּור טרינקט אויס דעם בראָנפן
פרײַטיק בײַטאָג און מאַכט שבת
קידוש איבער אַ חלה.

The drunkard drinks all the
brandy Friday afternoon and ends
up making the Sabbath wine
blessing over the challah.
*A shiker trinkt oys dem bronfyn
fraytik baytog un makht shabes
kidesh iber a khale.* IB

אַן איבעריק גלעזל ווײַן מאַכט
שמאַרץ און פּײַן.

A drink too many brings sorrow
aplenty.
*An iberik glezl vayn makht shmarts
un payn.* NS

אַזוי לאַנג ווי דער מענטש לעבט
דאַרף ער מאַכן אַ שהכּל.

As long as one lives, one should
make a blessing over a drink.
*Azoy long vi der mentsh lebt darf er
makhn a shakl.* NS

בעסער טויט שיכּור אײדער טויט
הונגעריק.

Better dead drunk than dead hungry.
*Beser toyt shiker eyder toyt
hungerik.* AC

בראָנפֿן איז אַ פֿױלער שליח: מען
שיקט אים אין בױך און ער קריכט
גלײַך צום קאָפּ.

Brandy is an unreliable
emmissary: send it to the stomach,
it creeps right to the head.
*Bronfn iz a foyler sheli'ekh: men
shikt im in boykh un er krikht glaykh
tsum kop.* AC

בראָנפֿן רעדט און האָבער פֿאָרט.

Brandy talks but oats ride.
Bronfn ret un hober fort. NS

דעם גאַנצן ירדן האָט ער שױן
אױסגעטרונקען!

He's already swallowed up the
entire Jordan River!
*Dem gantsn yardn hot er shoyn
oysgetrunken!* NS

די מלאָכה האָט ליב אַ כּוסע,
זאָל זײַן אַ גרױסע.

A drink gets the work done,
especially a big one.
*Di melokhe hot lib a koyse, zol zayn
a groyse.* AC

דרײַ זאַכן שאַטן קײן מאָל ניט:
שלאָף, בראָנפֿן און אַ באָד.

Three things never hurt: sleep,
brandy, and a bath.
*Dray zakhn shatn keyn mol nit:
shlof, bronfn un a bod.* NS

ער װערט שיכּור פֿון אַ בולבע.

Even a potato makes him drunk.
Er vert shiker fun a bulbe. IB

פֿון אַ לחיים װערט ליהודים.

A drink of brandy makes
everything dandy.
Fun a lekhayim vert layehudim. NS

גאָט איז גאָט און בראָנפֿן איז בראָנפֿן.

God is God but brandy is brandy.
Got iz got un bronfn iz bronfn. AC

קודם כּל איז גוט אַ שהכּל.

First and foremost, let's have a toast!
Koydem kol iz gut a shakl. NS

מיט אַ ביסל נאַריש וואַסער ווערט
פֿון אַ מענטש אַ חזיר.

From a foolish swig one becomes a
pig.
*Mit a bisl narish vaser vert fun a
mentsh a khazer.* AC

אויף צו מאַכן אַ כּוסע איז אַ
מזל-טוב אויך גענוג.

'Mazel-tov' is a good enough
excuse for a drink.
*Oyf tsu makhn a koyse iz a mazl-tov
oykh genug.* AC

שׂימחת-תּורה זײַנען אַלע שיכּורים
ניכטער.

On Simkhat-Torah all drunks
become sober.
[when it is appropriate to take a drink]
*Simkhes-toyre zaynen ale shikurim
nikhter.* P

וואָס בײַ אַ ניכטערן אויפֿן לונג איז
בײַ אַ שיכּורן אויפֿן צונג.

What the sober mind conceals the
drunken tongue reveals.
*Vos bay a nikhtern oyfn lung iz bay
a shikern oyfn tsung.* IB

וואָס דער שיכּור האָט אין קעפּל האָט
דער ניכטערער ניט אין פֿלעשל.

What the drunkard has in his
head, the abstainer doesn't have in
his flask.
*Vos der shiker hot in kepl hot der
nikhterer nit in fleshl.* NS

יין שׂרף איז קיין קרוב.

Gin is no kin.
Yayen soref iz keyn korev. NS

LIVELIHOOD

א גוטער מכשיר איז אַ האַלבער
בעל־מלאָכה.

A good tool is half the artisan.
*A guter makhsher iz a halber bal-
melokhe.* NS

אַ מלאָכה איז אַ מלוכה – אַז מען
דאַרף ברויט פֿאַרזעצט מען
די סליחה.

**A trade is a kingdom – if you
need bread pawn a prayer.**
*A melokhe iz a melikhe – az men
darf broyt farzetst men di slikhe.* IB

אַ מלאָכה איז אַ מלוכה אָבער מען
האָט ניט קיין מינוט מנוחה.

**A trade is fine but interferes with
your time.**
*A melokhe iz a melukhe ober men
hot nit keyn minut menukhe.* IB

אַלע שוסטערס גייען באָרוועס.

All shoemakers go barefoot.
Ale shusters geyen borves. P

אַז אַ ייִד קען ניט ווערן אַ שוסטער
טרוימט ער כאָטש פֿון ווערן אַ
פּראָפֿעסאָר.

**When a Jew can't become even a
shoemaker, he at least dreams of
becoming a professor.**
*Az a yid ken nit vern a shuster troymt
er khotsh fun vern a profesor.* NS

אַז דו וועסט ניט האָרעווען וועסטו
ניט עסן.

If you don't toil, you won't eat.
Az du vest nit horeven vestu nit esn. AC

אַז מען באַקומט שוין דאָס ברויט
קומט דער טויט.

**By the time you earn your bread,
you're dead.**
*Az men bakumt shoyn dos broyt
kumt der toyt.* NS

אַז מען איז אַ מײַסטער איז פֿול דער
טײַסטער.

**If you're skilled, your wallet will
be filled.**
*Az men iz a mayster iz ful der
tayster.* NS

דער מילנער פֿרייט זיך ווען דאָס
רעדל דרייט זיך.

**The miller celebrates when the
wheel rotates.**
*Der milner freyt zikh ven dos redl
dreyt zikh.* NS

דער שוסטער בײַם קאַפּול און דער
טאָפּ איז פֿול.

**If the shoemaker sticks to his last,
he won't have to fast.**
*Der shuster baym kapul un der top
iz ful.* NS

דער בעל-עגלה פֿאָרט אַזוי לאַנג מיטן
פּנים צו די פֿערד ביז ער ווערט
אַליין אַ פֿערד.

**The wagoneer rides facing the
horses for so long that he himself
becomes a horse.**
*Der balegole fort azoy lang mitn
ponem tsu di ferd biz er vert aleyn a
ferd.* MS

ער האָט דאָס לעבן פֿון גאָט און
דאָס עסן פֿון מענטשן.

**He owes his life to God and his
livelihood to people.**
*Er hot dos lebn fun got un dos esn
fun mentshn.* NS

גרינג קומט קיין זאַך ניט אָן.

Nothing comes easy.
Gring kumt keyn zakh nit on. P

איך וועל דאָס ניט פֿאַרדינען אין שיל
וואָס איך וועל פֿאַרלירן אין מיל.

**I won't earn at prayer what I'll
lose at the fair.**
*Ikh vel dos nit fardinen in shil vos
ikh vel farlirn in mil.* AC

אויף פֿרעמדע בערד איז גוט צו
לערנען שערן.

**It's good to learn barbering on
other people's beards.**
*Oyf fremde berd iz gut tsu lernen
shern.* P

פּרנסה איז אַ רפֿואה צו יעדער
קרענק.

Livelihood is a cure for every
ailment.

Parnose iz a refu'e tsu yeder krenk. P

וואָס איינער פֿאַרדינט דאָס האָט ער.

What one earns, one has.

Vos eyner fardint dos hot er. P

LOGIC

אַ משל איז נאָך ניט קיין ראיה.

An example isn't proof.

A moshl iz nokh nit kayn raye. IB

ביינער אָן פֿלייש איז דאָ, פֿלייש אָן
ביינער איז ניטאָ.

Bones without meat are possible,
meat without bones is impossible.

*Beyner on fleysh iz do, fleysh on
beyner iz nito.* NS

עס איז אָן אַ טעם און אָן אַ ראַם.

It's without taste or reason.

[It's without rhyme or reason.]

Es iz on a tam un on a ram. P

ווען די באָבע וואָלט געהאַט אַ באָרד
(ביצים) וואָלט זי געווען אַ זיידע.

If grandma had a beard (balls)
she'd be grandpa.

*Ven di bobe volt gehat a bord
(beytsim) volt zi geven a zayde.* AC

ווען די באָבע וואָלט געהאַט רעדער
וואָלט זי געווען אַ וואָגן.

If grandma had wheels, she'd be a
wagon.

*Ven di bobe volt gehat reder volt zi
geven a vogn.* P

יעדער משל האָט זײַן נימשל.

Every subject has its object.

Yeder moshl hot zayn nimshl. IB

LONELINESS

אַפֿילו אין גן-עדן איז ניט גוט צו זײַן
אַליין.

Even in paradise it's not good to
be alone.

*Afile in ganeydn iz nit gut tsu zayn
aleyn.* P

אַז מען האָט ניט קיין קלינגער
איז מען אַליין ווי אַ פֿינגער.

If you've no money to jingle,
you'll remain single.
*Az men hot nit keyn klinger iz men
aleyn vi a finger.* NS

אײדער אַ שטײן איז שױן בעסער
אַליין.

Rather than like a stone – it's
better to be alone.
Eyder a shteyn iz shoyn beser aleyn. NS

אײנער איז קיינער.

One is none.
Eyner iz keyner. P

נאָר אַ שטײן זאָל זײַן אַליין.

Only a stone should be alone.
Nor a shteyn zol zayn aleyn. AC

LOVE

אַ ליבע איז געגליכן צו אַ סוכּה – אין
זיבן טעג פֿאַלט זי אײַן.

Love is comparable to a succah –
in seven days it topples over.
*A libe iz geglikhn tsu a suke – in
zibn teg falt zi ayn.* NS

אַלטע ליבע זשאַװערט ניט.

Old love doesn't rust.
Alte libe zhavert nit. AC

די ליבע איז זיס נאָר זי איז בעסער
מיט ברויט.

Love is sweet but better with
bread.
*Di libe iz zis nor zi iz beser mit
broyt.* NS

עס איז לײַכטער צו היטן אַ זאַק פֿליי
אײדער אַ פֿאַרליבטע מיידל.

It's easier to guard a sack of fleas
than a girl in love.
*Es iz laykhter tsu hitn a zak fley
eyder a farlibte meydl.* AC

אײן האָר פֿון אַ מיידלס קאָפּ שלעפּט
שטאַרקער פֿון צען אָקסן.

One hair from a girl's head pulls
stronger than ten oxen.
*Eyn hor fun a meydls kop shlept
shtarker fun tsen oksn.* NS

פֿון ליבע באַקומט ער קאָפּווייטיק
און זי בויכווייטיק.

From love he gets a headache and she a bellyache.
Fun libe bakumt er kopveytik un zi boykhveytik. NS

האָב מיך ווייניק ליב נאָר האָב מיך
לאַנג ליב.

Love me a little but love me long.
Hob mikh veynik lib nor hob mikh lang lib. AC

ליבע איז ווי פּוטער, ס'איז גוט
מיט ברויט.

Love is like butter, it's good with bread.
Libe iz vi puter, s'iz gut mit broyt. NS

ליבע און הונגער וווינען ניט אין
איינעם.

Love and hunger make poor companions.
Libe un hunger voynen nit in eynem. AC

משוגעת אָן ליבע קען זיין אָבער ליבע
אָן משוגעת איז אוממעגלעך.

Lunacy without love is possible but love without lunacy is impossible.
Meshugas on libe ken zayn ober libe on meshugas iz ummeglekh. AC

ווען עס פֿליט אַריַין דער הונגער
דורך דער טיר פֿליט אַרוים די
ליבע דורכן פֿענצטער.

When hunger flies in the door, love flies out the window.
Ven es flit arayn der hunger durkh der tir fli aroys di libe durkhn fenster. NS

LUCK

אַ שטיקל מזל איז ווערט מער ווי אַ
טאָן גאָלד.

A bit of luck is worth more than a
ton of gold.
*A shtikl mazl iz vert mer vi a ton
gold.* NS

אַז דאָס מזל גייט קעלבט זיך דער
אָקס.

With luck even your ox will calve.
Az dos mazl geyt kelbt zikh der ox. IB

אַז דאָס מזל איז קליין העלפֿט ניט
קיין געוויין.

If your luck is small it won't help
to bawl.
*Az dos mazl is kleyn helft nit keyn
geveyn.* NS

בעסער אַ לויט מזל איידער אַ פֿונט
גאָלד.

Better an ounce of luck than a
pound of gold.
Beser a loyt mazl eyder a funt gold. NS

דער איז קלוג וואָס דאָס מזל גייט
אים נאָך.

He is clever whom luck follows.
Der iz klug vos dos mazl geyt im nokh. NS

דאָס גליק איז ווי אַ שנירל פּערל –
פֿאַלט אַראָפּ איינס צעשיטן
זיך אַלע.

Luck is like a string of pearls – if
one breaks, all scatter.
*Dos glik iz vi a shnirl perl – falt
arop eyns tseshitn zikh ale.* NS

ער שלאָפֿט און זײַן מזל ליגט אויף.

He sleeps yet his luck remains
awake.
Er shloft un zayn mazl ligt oyf. P

איינעמס מזל איז דעם אַנדרערנס
שלימזל.

One's good luck is another's
misfortune.
*Eynems mazl iz dem anderns
shlimazl.* P

גליק אָן שכל איז אַ
לעכערדיקער זאַק.

Luck without brains is a
perforated sack.
Glik on seykhl iz a lekherdiker zak. NS

אַז עס איז איינעם צו גוט גייט ער
זיך גליטשן אויף אײַז.

If someone has it too good, he tempts fate by skating on ice.
Az es iz eynem tsu gut geyt er zikh glitshn oyf ayz. NS

„משנה מקום משנה מזל" – אַמאָל
צום גליק אַמאָל צום שלימזל.

"Change your place, change your luck" - sometimes for better, sometimes for worse.
"Meshane makoym meshane mazl" – amol tsum glik amol tsum shlimazl. P

מיט מזל קען מען אַלעם.

Everything is possible with luck.
Mit mazl ken men ales. AC

אָן מזל טויג גאָר ניט.

Without luck nothing will succeed.
On mazl toyg gor nit. P

אָן מזל זאָל מען גאָרניט געבוירן
ווערן אויף דער וועלט.

Without luck one shouldn't even be born.
On mazl zol men gornit geboyrn vern oyf der velt. NS

צום שלימזל דאַרף מען אויך האָבן מזל.

Even for bad luck you need luck.
Tsum shlimazl darf men oykh hobn mazl. AC

ווען דאָם מזל קומט שטעל אים אַ
שטול.

When luck calls, offer it a seat.
Ven dos mazl kumt shtel im a shtul. IB

וואָם מער גוי אלץ מער מזל.

The more of a Goy the better the
luck.
Vos mer goy alts mer mazl. AC

וואָם טויג שיינקייט אָן מזל?

What use beauty without luck?
Vos toyg sheynkeyt on mazl? IB

LUNACY

אַ משוגענער מעג אַלץ טאָן.

A lunatic can get away with anything.
A meshugener meg alts ton. AC

אז דרײַ זאָגן משוגע דאַרף דער
פֿערטער זאָגן: בים באָם.

When three say crazy, the fourth
should say: 'bim bom.'
*Az dray zogn meshuge darf der
ferter zogn: bim bom.* NS

ביסטו משוגע? טאָ לאָז זיך בינדן.

Are you crazy? If so, let yourself
be restrained.
Bistu meshuge? to loz zikh bindn. IB

ער איז פֿריש און געזונט – און משוגע!

He is hale and hearty – and crazy!
Er is frish un gezunt – un meshuge! P

איטלעכער מענטש האָט זײַן שגעון.

Every person has his quirk.
Itlekher mentsh hot zayn shigo'en. NS

משוגע מטורף און פֿאַרדרייט נאָר
יענעם דעם קאָפּ!

Stark, raving mad and drives
everyone else crazy!
*Meshuge meturef un fardreyt nor
yenem dem kop!* IB

יעדער מענטש האָט זײַן אייגענעם
משוגעת.

Every person has his own brand of
lunacy.
*Yeder mentsh hot zayn eygenem
meshugas.* P

MAJORITY

אַ כפרה אַ יחיד פֿאַר אַ רבים!

To hell with the individual in
favor of the majority!
A kapore a yokhed far a rabim! IB

אַז די וועלט לאַכט איז דאָ פֿון
וועמען און פֿון וואָם.

When the world laughs in deri-
sion, it's usually for a very good
reason.
*Az di velt lakht iz do fun vemen un
fun vos.* NS

אַז איינער זאָגט דיר: האָסט אויערן
פֿון אַן אייזל מאַך זיך ניט וויסנדיק,
אַז צוויי זאָגן שוין דאַרף מען
קויפֿן אַ זאָטל.

If one person says you have the
ears of an ass, pay no attention; if
two say so, better buy a saddle.
*Az eyner zogt dir: host oyern fun an
ayzl makh zikh nit visndik az tsvey
zogn shoyn darf men koyfn a zotl.* NS

אַז צוויי זאָגן שיכּור, זאָל דער
דריטער גיין שלאָפֿן.

If two say 'drunk,' the third
should go to sleep.
*Az tsvey zogn shiker, zol der driter
geyn shlofn.* IB

MARRIAGE

א פֿרוי אָן אַ מאַן איז ווי אַ הויז אָן אַ
דאַך און אַ מאַן אָן אַ פֿרוי איז ווי
אַ דאַך אָן אַ הויז.

A woman without a man is like a
house without a roof and a man
without a woman is like a roof
without a house.
*A froy on a man iz vi a hoyz on a
dakh un a man on a froy iz vi a
dakh on a hoyz.* NS

אַ חתונה איז ווי אַ לוויה נאָר מיט
כּלי-זמרים.

A wedding is like a funeral but
with musicians.
*A khasene iz vi a levaye nor mit
klezmorim.* AC

אַ מאַן גייט צו דער חופּה
לעבעדיקערהייט און קומט
צוריק אַ מת.

A man goes to the bridal canopy
alive and returns a corpse.
*A man geyt tsu der khupe
lebedikerheyt un kumt tsurik a mes.* NS

אַ שידוך און אַ טשאָלנט געראָטן
זעלטן.

A match and a cholent seldom succeed.
A shidekh un a tsholnt gerotn zeltn. NS

אַ ייִדישע טאָכטער טאָר מען
ניט נייטן.

A Jewish daughter should not be
forced to marry.
A yidishe tokhter tor men nit neytn. AC

אַפֿילו פֿון קרומע שידוכים קומען
אַרויס גלײַכע קינדער.

Even from bad matches good
children can be born.
*Afile fun krume shidukhim kumen
aroys glaykhe kinder.* NS

אַז אַן אַלטער בחור שטאַרבט האָבן
מיידלעך אַ נקמה.

When an old bachelor dies the
spinsters are avenged.
*Az an alter bokher shtarbt hobn
meydlekh a nekome.* IB

אַז מען שלאָפֿט ניט אונטערן בעט
ווייסט מען גאָר ניט.

If you don't sleep under their bed,
you can't know their affairs.
*Az men shloft nit untern bet veyst
men gor nit.* P

אַז מען האָט חתונה בינדט מען צו אַ
קניפ מיט דער צונג וואָס מ'קען
שפּעטער ניט אויפֿבינדן אַפֿילו מיט
די ציין.

When one marries one ties a knot
with the tongue that cannot later
be undone even with the teeth.
*Az men hot khasene bint men tsu a
k'nip mit der tsung vos m'ken
shpeter nit oyfbindn afile mit di
tseyn.* AC

אַז מען טוט אַ שידוך מוז מען זען מיט
וועמען מען וועט זיך שפּעטער צעגניין.

Before you marry, make sure you
know whom you will later divorce.
*Az men tut a shidekh muz men zen
mit vemen men vet zikh shpeter
tsegeyn.* AC

אַז צוויי ליגן אויף איין קישן זאָל אַ
דריטער נישט מישן צווישן.

When two on a pillow are fixed, a
third should not mix betwixt.
*Az tsvey lign oyf eyn kishn zol a
driter nisht mishn tsvishn.* AC

בעסער אַ מיאוס ווײַב פֿאַר זיך
איידער אַ שיין ווײַב פֿאַר יענעם.

Better a homely wife for yourself
than a pretty wife for others.
*Beser a mi'es vayb far zikh eyder a
sheyn vayb far yenem.* NS

דער שדכן שטראָפֿט מען ניט פֿאַר
זײַנע ליגנס.

The matchmaker isn't punished
for his lies.
*Der shatkhn shtroft men nit far
zayne ligns.* NS

דער טויט און די נויט ברענגען דעם
שידוך צונויף.

Death and need make the marriage agreed.
*Der toyt un di noyt brengen dem
shidekh tsunoyf.* NS

פֿון חתונה האָבן האָט מען פֿיל לײַדן
אָבער פֿון ניט חתונה האָבן האָט
מען ניט קיין פֿריידן.

Marriage brings much pain but
not marrying brings no pleasure.
*Fun khasene hobn hot men fil laydn
ober fun nit khasene hobn hot men
nit keyn fraydn.* AC

פֿאַרװאָם האָט די מיטה נאָר צװײ
שטאַנגען און די חופּה פֿיר? װײַל
דורך דער מיטה באַגראָבט מען נאָר
אײן מענטשן און אונטער דער
חופּה צװײ.

Why does a stretcher have only
two poles and the bridal canopy
four? Because with a stretcher you
bury only one person and under
the bridal canopy you bury two.
*Farvos hot di mite nor tsvey
shtangen un di khupe fir? vayl durkh
der mite bagrobt men nor eyn mentshn
un unter der khupe tsvey.* NS

חתונה געהאַט אין גיך און געבליבן
אָן שטיך.

Married in haste and stuck like paste.
*Khasene gehat in gikh un geblibn on
shtikh.* NS

חתונה האָבן און שטאַרבן איז קײן
מאָל ניט צו שפּעט.

It's never too late for marrying or
for dying.
*Khasene hobn un shtarbn iz keyn
mol nit tsu shpet.* NS

מען טאָר ניט עסן די חלה פֿאַר
דער המוציא.

Don't sample the challah before
you make the blessing.
*Men tor nit esn di khale far der
hamoytse.* AC

מיט שלום-בית איז מען צופֿרידן
מיט אַ כּזית.

With peace in the house a bit will
suffice.
*Mit sholem-bayes iz men tsufridn mit
a kezayes.* NS

שײן איז די ליבע מיט אַ
געשמאַקער װעטשערע.

Love is beautiful accompanied by
a tasty meal.
*Sheyn iz di libe mit a geshmaker vet-
shere.* IB

װען אַן אַלטער מאַן נעמט אַ בתולה
האָבן בײדע ניט קײן גדולה.

When an old man takes a virgin to
wife, neither will have joy in their
life.
*Ven an alter man nemt a p'sule
hobn beyde nit keyn g'dule.* IB

נאָך דער חופה איז שפּעט די חרטה.

After the wedding it's too late for regretting.
Nokh der khupe iz shpet di kharote. NS

ווי נאַריש מענטשן זיַינען, באַגראָבן
זיי איינעם וויינט מען, באַגראָבן
זיי צוויי טאַנצט מען.

How foolish people are – when they bury one person they cry, when they bury two, they dance.
Vi narish mentshn zaynen, bagrobn zey eynem veynt men, bagrobn zey tsvey tantst men. AC

יעדער זיווג איז נאָך נישט קיין פּאָר.

Every couple is not necessarily a pair.
Yeder ziveg iz nokh nisht keyn por. P

BRIDES AND GROOMS

אַ חתן אַ ידען גייט ניט אָן נדן.

A groom of attainment can't be had without a dowry payment.
A khosn a yadn geyt nit on nadn. NS

אַז אַלע זוכן שײנע כּלות איז וו
קומען אַהין די מיאוסע מיידן?

If everyone looks for pretty brides, where do the ugly girls disappear to?
Az ale zukhn sheyne kales iz vu kumen ahin di mi'ese meydn? P

אויף איין אויג נאָר איז די קו בלינד.

The cow is blind in only one eye.
Oyf eyn oyg nor iz di ku blind. NS

אַז די כּלה איז ניט שײן האָט זי
אַנדערע מעלות.

If the bride is not pretty, then she
has other virtues.
*Az di kale iz nit sheyn hot zi andere
mayles.* NS

שפּיל דעם חתן װײנענדיקס, ער האָט
זיך זײַנס אין זינען.

Play the groom a melancholy tune,
he's got good reason to be sad.
*Shpil dem khosn veynendiks, er hot
zikh zayns in zinen.* SK

װען עס איז דאָ דער גראָשן װעט זיך
שױן געפֿינען אַ חתן.

If the money is here, the groom
will appear.
*Ven es iz do der groshn vet zikh
shoyn gefinen a khosn.* NS

װאָס מיאוסער דאָס שטיק אַלץ
גרעסער די גליק.

The uglier the piece [bride], the
luck will increase.
*Vos mi'eser dos shtik alts greser di
glik.* NS

זאָל זײַן אַ בעדער אַבי פֿון דער
פֿרעמד.

Even a bath-house attendant, as
long as he's from out of town.
Zol zayn a beder abi fun der fremd. IB

COURTSHIP

אַז עס קומט דער באַשערטער װערט
עס אין צװײי װערטער

When the right mate comes into
view, two words will do.
*Az es kumt der basherter vert es in
tsvey verter.* NS

אין אַ טשאָלנט און אין אַ שידוך
קוקט מען ניט צו פֿיל אַרײַן.

It doesn't pay to look too closely
into a cholent or into a bridal
match.
*In a tsholnt un in a shidekh kukt
men nit tsu fil arayn.* NS

מיט זאַבאָנגעס כאַפּט מען פֿײגעלעך
און מיט מתנות
– מײדעלעך.

With nets you snare birds, with
gifts – girls.
*Mit zabonges khapt men feygelekh
un mit matones – meydelekh.* NS

אַ בייזע ווייב איז ווי אַ שלעכטער
אויוון – עס גייט קיין היץ ניט נאָר
אַ רויך און קריגן קריגט מען
נאָר אַ קאָפּווייטיק.

**A shrewish wife is like a defective
stove – it gives no heat, smokes a
lot, and all you get is a headache.**
*A beyze vayb iz vi a shlekhter oyvn
– es geyt keyn hits nit nor a roykh
un krign krigt men nor a kopveytik.*
AC

אַ מאַן אַפֿילו אַז ער זינדיקט איז ער
אַלץ אַ מאַן.

**A sinning husband is still a
husband.** [better than none]
*A man afile az er zindikt iz er alts a
man.* AC

אַ מאַן ווי אַ מויז און אַ ווייב ווי אַ
הויז איז נאָך ניט גלייַך.

**A man like a mouse and a wife
like a house, they're still not
equal.**
*A man vi a moyz un a vayb vi a
hoyz iz nokh nit glaykh.* IB

אַ שלעכטע ווייב איז אויך אַמאָל
גערעכט.

**Even a shrewish wife can
sometimes be right.**
*A shlekhte vayb iz oykh amol
gerekht.* AC

אַ ווייב אַ מרשעת איז אַ נגע-צרעת.

A shrewish wife is like a leper.
A vayb a marshas iz a negetsora'as. NS

אַ ווייב מאַכט פֿון דעם מאַן אַ נאַר
און אַ האַר.

**A wife can make of her husband a
fool or a lord.**
*A vayb makht fun dem man a nar un
a har.* IB

אַ „זיווג מן השמים"– דער חתן אויף
איין אויג בלינד און די כּלה
אויף איין אויער טויב.

**"A pair made in heaven" – the
groom blind and the bride deaf.**
*A "ziveg min hashomayim" – der
khosn oyf eyn oyg blind un di kale
oyf eyn oyer toyb.* IB

א וויילע געשפילט מיט א מיידל און
א גאנץ לעבן געליטען פֿון א ווײַב.

Flirted a while with a girl and suffered life long with a wife.
*A vayle geshpilt mit a meydl un a
gants lebn gelitn fun a vayb.* AC

אז בײַ א מאן גייט שוין גוט נעמט
ער און זוכט זיך אוים א ווײַב.

Just when things are going well, a
man goes and takes a wife.
*Az bay a man geyt shoyn gut, nemt
er un zukht zikh oys a vayb.* AC

אז דער מאן איז צו גוט פֿאַר דער
וועלט איז ער שלעכט פֿאַר דער
ווײַב.

If a man is good to the whole
world, he will be unkind to his
own wife.
*Az der man iz tsu gut far der velt iz
er shlekht far der vayb.* NS

אז דאָס ווײַב הייסט ברכה איז זי
אויך אמאָל קיין ברכה ניט.

Just because her name is Brachah
doesn't mean she's always a blessing.
[Brachah: feminine name meaning blessing]
*Az dos vayb heyst brokhe iz zi oykh
amol keyn brokhe nit.* NS

אז דאָס ווײַב איז א זייגערין איז דער
מאַן א זייגער.

If the wife is a wet-nurse the husband sucks. [play on words]
*Az dos vayb iz a zeygerin iz der man
a zeyger.* IB

אז מען האָט א שיין ווײַב איז מען
א שלעכטער חבֿר.

If you have a pretty wife, you'll be
a bad friend.
*Az men hot a sheyn vayb iz men a
shlekhter khaver.* NS

אז מען שלאָגט די ווײַב מיט א
קולטעווע ווערט דערפֿון די גרעט
ניט ווײַס.

Beating your wife with a paddle
won't make the linen white.
*Az men shlogt di vayb mit a kulteve
vert derfun di gret nit vays.* NS

דער מאַן איז דער בעל-הבית – אז די
ווײַב זײַנע לאָזט.

The husband is the boss – if his
wife allows.
*Der man iz der balebos – az di vayb
zayne lozt.* AC

די ליבע גייט אַוועק ווי דער ליבער
שבת קודש – און די ווײַב בלײַבט.

Love disappears like the beloved
Holy Sabbath disappears – but
one's wife remains.
*Di libe geyt avek vi der liber shabes
koydesh – un di vayb blaybt.* NS

דאָס ערשטע ווײַב איז געטרײַ ווי אַ
הונט, דאָס צווייטע ווי אַ קאַץ
און דאָס דריטע ווי אַ מויז וואָס
קלערט נאָר וועגן עסן.

The first wife is as devoted as a
dog, the second as a cat, and the
third as a mouse that thinks only
of food.
*Dos ershte vayb iz getray vi a hunt,
dos tsveyte vi a kats un dos drite vi
a moyz vos klert nor vegn esn.* IB

דאָס צווייטע ווײַב איז ווי אַ מאַרצאָווע
זון – זי מאַכט נישט וואַרעם, זי
מאַכט נישט קאַלט.

The second wife is like the sun in
March – she neither warms nor
cools.
*Dos tsveyte vayb iz vi a martsove
zun – zi makht nisht varem, zi makht
nisht kalt.* IB

‏„את הכל יקח האֿפל" – נאָר אַ שלעכט
ווײַב גיט ער און נעמט ניט צוריק.

"God gives and takes everything"
– except a shrewish wife whom He
gives but won't take back.
*"Es hakol yikakh ha'ofel" – nor a
shlekht vayb git er un nemt nit tsurik.* ?

פֿאַרוואָס טאַנצט דער בער? ווײַל ער
האָט ניט קיין ווײַב, גיב אים אַ
ווײַב וועט ער אויפֿהערן צו
טאַנצן.

Why does the bear dance? Because
he has no wife, give him a wife
and he'll stop dancing.
*Farvos tantst der ber? vayl er hot
nit keyn vayb, gib im a vayb vet er
oyfhern tsu tantsn.* NS

פֿון אַן אַלטער מויד ווערט אַ
געטרײַע ווײַב.

An old maid becomes a faithful wife.
*Fun an alter moyd vert a getraye
vayb.* NS

פֿון אַן אַלטער מיידל ווערט אַ יונג
ווײַבל.

An old maid becomes a young wife.
*Fun an alter meydl vert a yung
vaybl.* AC

געטרוי ניט א פֿערד אין וועג און א
ווײַב אין דער היים.

Don't trust a horse on the road or
a wife at home.
*Getroy nit a ferd in veg un a vayb
in der heym.* AC

מאַמע-לשון: אז די מאַמע רעדט
פֿאַרלירט דער טאַטע דאָם לשון.

Mother-tongue: when mother
speaks, father loses his tongue.
*Mame-loshn: az di mame ret farlirt
der tate dos loshn.* AC

מאַן און ווײַב זײַנען טאַקע איין לײַב
אָבער קעשענעם האָבן זיי צוויי.

Husband and wife are truly one
flesh but their pockets are
separate.
*Man un vayb zaynen take eyn layb
ober keshenes hobn zey tsvey.* AC

מען וואָלט געקענט נאַנץ רויִק לינן
ווען ניט די ווײַב און די פֿליגן.

A man could easily rest his eyes if
not for his wife and the flies.
*Men volt gekent gants ru'ik lign ven
nit di vayb un di flign.* NS

מיט א קינד אויף א חתונה און מיט
א ווײַב אויף א יריד איז שלעכט
צו גיין.

It's no good to go to a wedding
with small children or to a fair
with one's wife.
*Mit a kind oyf a khasene un mit a
vayb oyf a yarid iz shlekht tsu geyn.* AC

שלעכט צום ווײַב גוט צו לײַט.

To his wife he's base, to others he
shows a good face.
Shlekht tsum vayb gut tsu layt. NS

ווען דער מאַן איז א בעל-עגלה האָט ער
ניט מורא פֿאַר דער ווײַבם קללה.

When the husband is a wagoneer,
he's not afraid of his wife's jeer.
[The wagoneer is the epitome of the tough guy.]
*Ven der man iz a balegole hot er nit
moyre far der vaybs klole.* NS

ווער איז דער „והוא" איך אָדער דו?

Who is the "he," you or me?
Ver iz der "vehu" ikh oder du? IB

MASSES

אַ יחיד קעגן קהל פֿאַרלירט אַלע מאָל.

One against all is sure to fall.
A yokhed kegn ko'ol farlirt ale mol. NS

דער עולם איז אַ גולם.

The masses are asses.
Der oylem iz a goylem. P

דער עולם איז ניט קיין גולם.

The masses are no asses.
Der oylem iz nit keyn goylem. P

די גאַנצע וועלט איז נאָך ניט משוגע.

The whole world hasn't yet gone crazy.
Di gantse volt iz nokh nit meshuge. P

וואָס עס וועט זיַין מיט דער כּלה וועט זיַין מיט אונדז אַלע.

What becomes of the bride will become of us all.
Vos es vet zayn mit der kale vet zayn mit undz ale. NS

וואָס עס וועט זיַין מיט כּל ישראל וועט זיַין מיט רב ישראל.

What befalls the People of Israel will befall Mr Israel.
Vos es vet zayn mit kol yisro'el vet zayn mit reb yisro'el. IB

MEASURE

אַ ביסל שאַט נאָר אַ ביסל.

A little matters a little.
A bisl shat nor a bisl. NS

אַ קליין שטיינדל קען אויך מאַכן אַ גרויסע לאָך.

A small stone can also make a big wound.
A kleyn shteyndl ken oykh makhn a groyse lokh. NS

אַז אַ ביסל איז גוט איז אַ סך נאָך בעסער.

If a little is good, then a lot is even better.
Az a bisl iz gut iz a sakh nokh beser.

דאָרט וווּ מען איז איין מאָל איז מען צוויי מאָל.

Where once, there twice.
Dort vu men iz eyn mol iz men tsvey mol. NS

דער ערשטער ביסן איז אָן עגבער,
דער צווייטער מאַכט אַ לאָך, דער
דריטער שרייט: גיב נאָך!

The first bite is a bore, the second
makes a hole, the third shouts:
'give more!'
*Der ershter bisn iz an egber, der
tsveyter makht a lokh, der driter
shrayt: gib nokh!* NS

עס איז אַזוי לאַנג ווי דער ייִדישער
גלות.

It's as long as the Jewish exile.
Es iz azoy lang vi der yidisher goles. P

עס איז גענוג אויף אַ לעק און אַ שמע

It's enough for a lick and a smell.
Es iz genug oyf a lek un a shmek. P

איין מאָל איז געוועזן אַ חכמה.

Once, it's clever.
Eyn mol iz geven a khokhme. P

איין מאָל איז קיין מאָל.

Once is nonce.
Eyn mol iz keyn mol. P

הונדערט און הונדערט און איינס איז
אַלץ איינס.

Between 100 and 101, the difference
is none.
*Hundert un hundert un eyns iz alts
eyns.* AC

כמעט האָט אַמאָל דעם טײַטש
פֿון גאָרניט.

Almost sometimes means nothing.
Kimat hot amol dem taytsh fun gornit. NS

מיט שניי קען מען קיין געמאָלקעם
ניט מאַכן.

You can't make cheesecakes out of
snow.
*Mit shney ken men keyn gemolkes nit
makhn.* IB

אָדער אַ קלאַפּ, אָדער אַ פֿאָרץ!

Either a wallop or a fart!
[Too much or not enough!]
Oder a klap, oder a forts! P

צו גוט איז ניט גוט.

Too good is no good.
Tsu gut iz nit gut. P

וואָס ווייניקער, אַלץ געזינטער.

Least is best.
Vos veyniker, alts gezinter. P

MIRACLES

אַז גאָט װיל, שיסט אַ בעזעם אױך.

If God so wills, even a broom can shoot.
Az got vil, shist a bezem oykh. P

דער װוּנדער זאָל דיר קײן װוּנדער ניט זײַן.

The marvel should be no marvel to you.
Der vunder zol dir keyn vunder nit zayn. AC

ניט יעדן פּורים טרעפֿט זיך אַ נס.

Not on every Purim is a miracle performed.
Nit yedn purim treft zikh a nes. P

אָן נסים קען אַ ייִד ניט לעבן.

A Jew can't live without miracles.
On nisim ken a yid nit lebn. P

אױף קײן נסים טאָר מען זיך ניט פֿאַרלאָזן.

Don't rely on miracles.
Oyf keyn nisim tor men zikh nit farlozn. AC

װען טױזנטער חסידים זאָלן זיך דרײען אַרום אַ קלאָץ װאָלט עס אױך באַװיזן נסים.

If thousands of the devout gathered round a block of wood, it too could perform miracles.
Ven toyznter kh'sidim zoln zikh dreyen arum a klots volt es oykh bavizn nisim. AC

MISERLINESS

אַ קאַרגער ליגט אױפֿן געלט װי אַ הונט אױפֿן בײן.

A miser guards his money like a dog a bone.
A karger ligt oyfn gelt vi a hunt oyfn beyn. IB

אַז אַ קאַרגער װערט מילד װערט אַ זעענדיקער בלינד.

When the miser becomes kind, the seeing become blind.
As a karger vert mild vert a ze'endiker blind. IF

ער דארף האבן דעם קרעכץ פאר זיך.

He needs the sigh for himself.
Er darf hobn dem krekhts far zikh. AC

ער מאכט שבת פאר זיך אליין.

He prepares the Sabbath for himself alone.
Er makht shabes far zikh aleyn. AC

ער וועט דיר זאגן שלום-עליכם מיט
א פולן מויל געבן דיר תקיעת כף
מיט צען פינגער נאר א פעני וועט
ער דיר ניט געבן.

He will greet you with a full mouth [of talk], shake hands with ten fingers, but a penny he won't give you.
Er vet dir zogn sholem-aleykhem mit a fuln moyl, gebn dir tki'es kaf mit tsen finger, nor a peni vet er dir nit gebn. AC

פון א קארגן גביר און א פעטן באק
געניסט מען ערשט נאכן טויט.

A miser and a fatted calf are useful only after death.
Fun a kargn gvir un a fetn bok genist men ersht nokhn toyt. NS

MISFORTUNE

די ווייב אויקעט און דער הונט
קאנויקעט, דאס קינד כליפעט
און דער דלות ריפעט.

The wife wails and the dog yowls, the child whines and poverty howls.
Di vayb oyket un der hunt kanoyket, dos kind khlipet un der dales ripet. NS

איינעמס מזל איז דעם אנדערנס
שלימזל.

One's good luck is another's misfortune.
Eynems mazl iz dem anderns shlimazl. P

צום שלימזל דארף מען אויך האבן מזל.

Even for bad luck you need luck.
Tsum shlimazl darf men oykh hobn mazl. AC

MONEY

אַ בײַטל אָן געלט איז נאָר אַ שטיק
לעדער.

A wallet without money is only a
piece of leather.
A baytl on gɛlt iz nor a shtik leder. IB

אַ פֿאַלשע מטבע פֿאַרלירט מען ניט.

A bad penny never gets lost.
A falshe matbeye farlirt men nit. IB

אַ חילוף איז אַ חלף.

Exchanging money is like going to
the slaughter.
A khilef iz a khalef. NS

אַ נגיד קומט אָפּ און אַן אָרעמאַן
קומט אויף איז נאָך ניט גלײַך.

A rich man's fortune down and a
poor man's fortune up, they're
still not equal.
*A noged kumt op un an oreman
kumt oyf iz nokh nit glaykh.* NS

אַ שווערער בײַטל מאַכט אַ לײַכט
געמיט.

A heavy wallet makes for a light
spirit.
A shverer baytl makht a laykht gemit.

אַלע שלעסער קען מען עפֿענען מיט
אַ גאָלדענעם שליסל.

All locks open with a golden key.
*Ale shleser ken men efenen mit a
goldenem shlisl.* NS

אַרײַן און אַרויס קאָסט געלט.

'In' and 'out' costs money.
Arayn un aroys kost gelt. IB

אַז מען האָט די מטבע האָט
מען די דעה.

With money in hand you can deman
*Az men hot di matbeye hot men di
deye.* IB

אַז מען האָט מעות איז מען אַ
בעל-הבית.

If you have the dough, it's your
show.
Az men hot mo'es iz men a balebos. N

אַז מען שמירט פֿאָרט מען.

When you grease palms, you ride.
Az men shmirt fort men. P

עס סטייעט גענוג די באָבע חתונה
צו מאַכן.

Enough money can marry off even
a grandmother.
*Es stayet genug di bobe khasene tsu
makhn.* NS

אזוי גייט אויף דער וועלט: איינער
האָט דעם בײַטל דער צווייטער האָט
דאָס געלט.

The world has always been so: one
has the wallet, the other has the dough.
*Azoy geyt oyf der velt: eyner hot
dem baytl der tsveyte hot dos gelt.*
NS

עס איז ניט אַזוי גוט מיט געלט
ווי עס איז שלעכט אָן דעם.

It's not so good with money as it's
bad without it.
*Es iz nit azoy gut mit gelt vi es iz
shlekht on dem.* AC

געלט פֿירט די גאַנצע וועלט.

Money rules the world.
Gelt firt di gantse velt. P

געלט גייט צו געלט.

Money goes to money.
Gelt geyt tsu gelt. P

געלט איז די בעסטע זייף וואָס נעמט
אַרויס דעם גרעסטן פֿלעק.

Money is the best soap – it
removes the greatest stain.
*Gelt iz di beste zeyf vos nemt aroys
dem grestn flek.* NS

גאָלד שײַנט אַרויס פֿון דער בלאָטע.

Gold shines out of the mud.
Gold shaynt aroys fun der blote. NS

גאָלד האָט אַ מיאוסן טאַטן און
איז פֿאָרט אַ יחסן.

Gold has a dirty origin but is
nevertheless treated with honor.
*Gold hot a mi'esn tatn un iz fort a
yakhsn.* IB

קהילישע געלט האָט אין זיך אַ
מאַגנעט.

Community funds are a magnet.
Kehilishe gelt hot in zikh a magnet. IB

מיט אַ וװענדקע כאַפּט מען פֿיש און
מיט אַ קערבל כאַפּט מען מענטשן.

With bait you catch fish and with
a coin you catch people.
*Mit a vendke khapt men fish un mit
a kerbl khapt men mentshn.* IB

אָן געלט איז קיין וועלט.

Without money it's not much of a
world.
On gelt iz keyn velt. P

אויף דרײַ זאַכן שטייט די וועלט: אויף
געלט, אויף געלט און אויף געלט.

The world stands on three things:
on money, on money, and on
money.
[play on words on a traditional saying]
*Oyf dray zakhn shteyt di velt: oyf
gelt, oyf gelt un oyf gelt.* AC

תּחת אויפֿן טיש!

Ass on the table!
[Put up or shut up!]
Tokhes oyfn tish! P

צו האָבן געלט איז אײַ-אײַ-אײַ
אָבער אָן געלט איז אוי-אוי-אוי.

Having money is not so bad but
without money it's pretty sad.
*Tsu hobn gelt iz ay-ay-ay ober on
gelt iz oy-oy-oy.* AC

NECESSITY

אַ ייִד אַ למדן גיט זיך ניט אַן עצה – אַז
ער האָט ניט קיין שטיוול גייט ער
באָרוועס.

A Jew with brains can always manage – if he has no boots he goes barefoot.
A yid a lamdn git zikh an eytse – az er hot nit keyn shtivl geyt er borves. NS

אַז מען קען ניט אַריבער מוז מען
אַרונטער.

If you can't go over, you must go under.
Az men ken nit ariber muz men arunter. P

אַז מען מוז קען מען.

When one must, one can.
Az men muz ken men. P

עס פֿעלט ניט קיין געלט אויף מצות
און תכריכים.

For matzoth and shrouds money is found.
Es felt nit keyn gelt oyf matses un takhrikhim. IB

פֿאַר נויט עסט מען ווייַס ברויט.

When in need, on white bread feed.
Far noyt est men vays broyt. NS

פֿאַרן שוואַרץ יאָר געפֿינט מען.

Out of desperation, one finds.
Farn shvarts yor gefint men. AC

נויט ברעכט אייַזן.

Need breaks iron.
Noyt brekht ayzn. AC

ווו מען דאַרף האָבן זאַלץ טויג ניט
קיין צוקער.

When you need salt, sugar won't do.
Vu men darf hobn zalts toyg nit keyn tsuker. NS

OLD AND NEW

אַ נײַער בעזעם קערט גוט.

A new broom sweeps clean.
A nayer bezem kert gut. NS

דער בגד איז אַלט – נאָר די לעכער
זײַנען נײַ.

The coat is old – only the holes are new.
Der beged iz alt – nor di lekher zaynen nay. AC

נײַ איז געטרײַ.

New is true.
Nay iz getray. AC

OWNERSHIP

אַ גוטער בעל-הבית שטעקט
אומעטום אַרײַן די נאָז.

A good proprietor sticks his nose into every corner.
A guter balebos shtekt umetum arayn di noz. IB

נאָר בײַ זײַן אייגענעמס טיש קען
מען זאַט ווערן.

Only at your own table can your appetite be sated.
Nor bay zayn eygenem tish ken men zat vern. NS

אויף פֿרעמדע קברים טאָר מען ניט
קריכן.

Don't crawl to the graves of strangers.
Oyf fremde kvorim tor men nit krikhn. NS

PAIN

פֿאַלשע צײן טוען ניט וויי.

False teeth don't hurt.
Falshe tseyn tu'en nit vey. NS

מען רעדט פֿון פֿיין אַזױ װי פֿון װײַן.

**From drink and pain one speaks
in the same vein.**
Men ret fun payn azoy vi fun vayn. NS

ניט װיסן פֿון קײן יסורים הײסט ניט
זײַן קײן מענטש.

**If you haven't experienced pain,
you are not fully human.**
*Nit visn fun keyn yesurim heyst nit
zayn keyn mentsh.* NS

יעדער װײסט װוּ ס'דריקט אים דער
שוך.

**Everyone knows where the shoe
pinches.**
Yeder veyst vu s'drikt im der shukh. AC

PARENTS

בײַ טאַטע-מאַמע איז קײן קינד ניט
איבעריק.

To parents no child is superfluous.
*Bay tate-mame is keyn kind nit
iberik.* P

דורך אַ שלעכט קינד קומען עלטערן
צו זינד.

**Through a wayward child parents
sin.**
*Durkh a shlekht kind kumen eltern
tsu zind.* NS

פֿאַר געלט באַקומט מען אַלץ - נאָר
ניט טאַטע-מאַמע.

You can get anything for money
except parents.
*Far gelt bakumt men alts – nor nit
tate-mame.* NS

פֿאַר קינדער צערײַסט מען אַ
וועלט.

For the sake of our children we
would tear the world apart.
Far kinder tserayst men a velt. P

טאַטע-מאַמע איז אַ קונץ צו זײַן און
אַלע נעמען עס זיך אונטער.

To be a parent takes know-how,
everyone undertakes it anyhow.
*Tate-mame iz a kunts tsu zayn un
ale nemen es zikh unter.* NS

ווען די קינדער זײַנען יונג דערצײַלן
די עלטערן זייערע חכמות, ווען
די עלטערן ווערן אַלט דערצײַלן די
קינדער זייערע נאַרישקייטן.

When children are young, their
parents tell of their brilliance;
when parents grow old, their
children relate their foolishness.
*Ven di kinder zaynen yung dertseyln
di eltern zeyere khokhmes, ven di
eltern vern alt dertseyln di kinder
zeyere narishkeytn.* NS

FATHERS

אַ רײַכן טאַטן איז כּדאַי צו באַגראָבן,
אַן אָרעמען איז ניט כּדאַי צו האָבן.

A rich father is worth burying, a
poor one isn't worth having.
*A raykhn tatn iz keday tsu bagrobn,
an oremen iz nit keday tsu hobn.* AC

אז דער טאטע שענקט דעם זון לאכן
ביידע, אז דער זון שענקט דעם טאטן
ווײנען ביידע.

When a father supports his son,
both laugh; when a son supports
his father, both cry.
*Az der tate shenkt dem zun lakhn
beyde, az der zun shenkt dem tatn
veynen beyde.* NS

בעסער א פאטש פֿון א טאטן
אײדער א קוש פֿון א פֿרעמדן.

Better a slap from a father than a
kiss from a stranger.
*Beser a patsh fun a tatn eyder a
kush fun a fremdn.* NS

אײדער דער טאטע ווערט געבוירן
שטײט שוין דער זון אויפֿן דאך.

Before the father is even born, the
son is already standing on the roof.
[comment on bastardy]
*Eyder der tate vert geboyrn shteyt
shoyn der zun oyfn dakh.* IF

IN-LAWS

א שנור איז א שטיקל שוויגער.

A daughter-in-law has a bit of the
mother-in-law in her.
A shnur iz a shtikl shviger. AC

די שוויגער האט פֿארגעסן אז זי איז
אויך אמאל געווען א שנור.

The mother-in-law has forgotten
that she was once a daughter-in-
law.
*Di shviger hot fargesn az zi iz oykh
amol geven a shnur.* AC

אדם איז געווען א גליקלעכער
מענטש – ער האט ניט געהאט
קיין שוויגער.

Adam was a lucky man – he
didn't have a mother-in-law.
*Odem iz geven a gliklekher mentsh –
er hot nit gehat keyn shviger.* AC

MOTHERS

א מאמע איז א דעקטוך: זי פֿארדעקט
די חסרונות פֿון די קינדער.

A mother is like a veil: she hides
the faults of her children.
*A mame iz a dektukh: zi fardekt di
khesroynes fun di kinder.* NS

אַז די מוטער שרײַט אױפֿן קינד
'ממזר' מעג מען איר גלײבן.

When a mother shouts at her child
'bastard,' you can believe her.
Az di muter shrayt oyfn kind
'mamzer' meg men ir gleybn. P

בײַ אַ מאַמען איז ניטאָ קיין מיאוס
קינד.

To a mother no child is ugly.
Bay a mamen iz nito keyn mi'es kind.

דאָס װאַרעמסטע בעט איז דער
מאַמעם.

The warmest bed is mother's.
Dos varemste bet iz der mames. NS

אױף דער זון איז גוט צו זיצן און לעבן
דער מאַמע איז גוט צו װױנען.

It's good to bask in the sun and to
live close to one's mother.
Oyf der zun iz gut tsu zitsn un lebn
der mame iz gut tsu voynen. NS

יעדער מוטער דענקט אַז אירע
קינדער זײַנען די געראָטנסטע.

Every mother thinks her children
are the most talented.
Yeder muter denkt az ire kinder
zaynen di gerotnste. P

PARTNERSHIP

אַ דאָקטער און אַ קבֿרות-מאַן זײַנען
שותּפֿים.

Doctors and grave diggers are
partners.
A dokter un a kvures-man zaynen
shutfim. NS

איינער האַקט האָלץ און
דער צװייטער שרײַט: ,אײ'.

One chops the wood and the other
does the grunting.
Eyner hakt holts un der tsveyter
shrayt: 'ey!' NS

שותּפֿות איז גוט – אַ מכּה.

Sharing is a good idea – for an
abscess.
Shutfes iz gut – a make. AC

װאָם מער שותּפֿות אַלץ מער טעַנות.

The more partners the more
arguments.
Vos mer shutfes alts mer taynes. IB

PEDIGREE

אַ פֿרישע בולקע איז בעסער ווי אַן
אַלטע.

A fresh bun is better than a stale one.
A frishe bulke iz beser vi an alte. AC

אַ מענטש מיט גוטע מאַנירן שלאָגט
זיך דורך אַלע טירן.

All doors open to a person of good breeding.
A mentsh mit gute manirn shlogt zikh durkh ale tirn. NS

אָן אָרעמער מיוחס איז געגליכן צו
די שובֿרי-לוחות.

A fallen aristocrat is comparable to the broken tablets.
[Refers to the Biblical account of Moses at Mount Sinai.]
An oremer meyukhes iz geglikhn tsu di shivre – lukhes. IB

בעט אַ פֿאַרך צום מנין ווערט ער
בײַ זיך גרויס.

Ask an inferior to the minyan and he becomes conceited.
Bet a parekh tsum minyen vert er bay zikh groys. IB

די מאַמע איז אַ צדקת און די
טאָכטער איז אויך אַ זונה.

The mother is a saintly one and the daughter is also a tainted one.
[Play on words.]
Di mame iz a tsedeykes un di tokhter iz oykh a zoyne. AC

פֿון אַ פֿאַרכל ווערט מען רב פֿאַרך.

A little scab becomes Mister Scab.
Fun a parekhl vert men reb parekh. AC

שענד ניט מעך, איך שענד ניט דעך,
מיר זײַנען בײדע פֿון אײן צעך.

Don't shame me, I won't shame thee; we both belong to the same party.
Shend nit mekh, ikh shend nit dekh, mir zaynen beyde fun eyn tsekh. NS

צווישן פֿערד איז ייחום וויכטיק.

Among horses pedigree is important.
Tsvishn ferd iz yikhes vikhtik. NS

ייחוס אויפֿן בית-הקבֿרות און אין דער
היים איז צרות.

In the cemetery, a great name; at
home, troubles all the same.
*Yikhes oyfn beysakvores un in der
heym iz tsores.* AC

PEOPLE

אַ מענטש איז נעבעך, ניט מער ווי אַ
מענטש און אַמאָל דאָס אויך ניט.

A person is only a person and
sometimes, not even that.
*A mentsh iz nebekh, nit mer vi a
mentsh un amol dos oykh nit.* AC

בראָנפֿן איז גענוג – נאָר עולם איז
צו פֿיל!

There's enough brandy – there's
just too many people!
Bronfn iz genug – nor oylem iz tsu fil!

דער מענטש וואָס איז ניט גוט פֿאַר
זיך איז ניט גוט פֿאַר אַנדערע.

Who is not good for himself is no
good for others.
*Der mentsh vos iz nit gut far zikh iz
nit gut far andere.* NS

דער וואַלד איז שיין נאָר די ביימער
טויגן ניט.

The forest is beautiful but the
trees are useless.
*Der vald iz sheyn nor di beymer
toygn nit.* AC

איינער וויל לעבן און קען ניט, דער
צווייטער קען לעבן און וויל ניט.

One person wants to live and
can't, another can live and won't.
*Eyner vil lebn un ken nit, der
tsveyter ken lebn un vil nit.* AC

ווען מענטשן זאָלן וויסן וואָס איינער
אויף דעם אַנדערן טראַכט
וואָלטן זיי זיך אומגעבראַכט.

If people knew what others
thought of them, the result would
be murder and mayhem.
*Ven mentshn zoln visn vos eyner oyf
dem andern trakht voltn zey zikh
umgebrakht.* NS

מערסטנס האָבן מענטשן זיך ליב
פֿון דערווײַטנס.

As a rule, people love each other
from a distance.
*Merstns hobn mentshn zikh lib fun
dervaytns.* AC

פאראן פארשידענע מענטשן אויף
דער וועלט: בהמות און אייזלען,
הינט און חזירים – און אויך
ווערעם.

There are all sorts of people in this world: cows and asses, dogs and hogs, also worms.

Faran farshidene mentshn oyf der velt: beheymes un eyzlen, hint un khazeyrim – un oykh verem. NS

ווער עס טויג ניט פאר זיך טויג ניט
פאר יענעם.

He who is no good for himself is no good for others.

Ver es toyg nit far zikh toyg nit far yenem. AC

וואָס דער מענטש קען זיך אליין
טאָן, קענען אים צען שונאים
ניט ווינטשן.

What a person thinks up for himself, ten enemies couldn't wish on him.

Vos der mentsh ken zikh aleyn ton, kenen im tsen sonim nit vintshn. P

וואָס מען האָט וויל מען ניט און וואָס
מען וויל האָט מען ניט.

What one has, one doesn't want, and what one wants, one doesn't have.

Vos men hot vil men nit un vos men vil hot men nit. P

PIETY

אַ ייד איז פרום נאָר ניט אומעטום.

A Jew may act religiously but not continuously.

A yid iz frum nor nit umetum. AC

א שיינע באָרד און פּאות אָבער
וויניק דעות.

A fine beard and sidecurls on
display but little of worth does he
have to say.
*A sheyne bord un peyes ober veynik
deyes.* IB

אַז אַ חסיד ווערט אויפֿגעקלערט
שעלט ער גאָט אין טאַטן אַריַין.

When a Hassid becomes enlightened, he curses God.
*Az a khosed vert oyfgeklert shelt er
got in tatn arayn.* IB

בעסער זיַין גוט איַידער פֿרום.

Better to be good than pious.
Beser zayn gut eyder frum. NS

ער מעג עסן פֿאַרן דאַוװענען – ער
דאַװנט סיַי װי ניט.

It's permissible for him to eat
before praying – he doesn't pray
anyway.
*Er meg esn farn davenen – er davnt
say vi nit.* AC

PITY

אַ גוטער געהערט אויפֿן גוטן אָרט.

A good person belongs in a good
place [cemetery].
A guter gehert oyfn gutn ort. AC

דער גרעסטער רחמנות איז אויף
אַן אָרעמער מויד וואָס ליגט
אין קימפּעט.

The most pitiable is a penniless
maid in childbirth.
*Der grester rakhmones iz oyf an
oremer moyd vos ligt in kimpet.* NS

אויף אַ מענטש איז ניט קיין רחמנות,
אַ רחמנות איז אויף ניט
קיין מענטש.

A human being is not to be pitied,
pitiable is one who is not even a
human being.
*Oyf a mentsh iz nit keyn rakhmones,
a rakhmones iz oyf nit keyn mentsh.* AC

רחמנות האָט ריינע כּוונות.

Pity has pure intentions.
Rakhmones hot reyne kavones. NS

טו אַ הונט גוטס, בילט ער נאָך.

Do a dog a favor and he still barks.
Tu a hunt guts bilt er nokh. AC

ווארף ארוים דעם ארעמאן, איך
קען דאָס רחמנות ניט צוזען – א
מיצווה וועל איך פֿאַרדינען.

**Throw the pauper out, I can't
stand the pity I feel – I might be
tempted to do a good deed.**
*Varf aroys dem oreman, ikh ken dos
rakhmones nit tsuzen – a mitsve vel
ikh fardinen.* AC

יענער האָט אויך א נשמה.

Another also has a soul.
Yener hot oykh a neshome. P

POVERTY

אַ פֿרעמדער אָרעמאַן טוט דעם
היימישן קיין טובֿה ניט.

**An imported pauper does the
home-grown one no favor.**
*A fremder oreman tut dem heymishn
keyn toyve nit.* IB

אַ לוסטיקער דלות גייט איבער אַלעם.

Poor but gay has its way.
A lustiker dales geyt iber ales. NS

אַלע אָרעמעלײַט האָבן גוטע
הערצער.

All paupers are good-hearted.
Ale oremelayt hobn gute hertser. IB

אַן אָרעמאַן האָט ניט וואָס אָנצוווערן.

A pauper has nothing to lose.
An oreman hot nit vos ontsuvern. IB

אַן אָרעמאַן איז אַ ותרן אויף אַ
פֿרעמדן בײַטל.

**A pauper is generous with someone
else's purse.**
*An oreman iz a vatren oyf a fremdn
baytl.* IB

אַן אָרעמאַן שטאַרבט נישט, ער
בײַט זיך נאָר דאָס געלעגער.

**A pauper doesn't die, he just
trades beds.**
*An oreman shtarbt nisht, er bayt
zikh nor dos geleger.* IF

אין ארץ ישראל איז דאָ איין פיאַסטער
מיט אַ לאָך און דער גאַנצער
יישובֿ האַנדלט מיט אים.

**The Land of Israel possesses only
one coin and the whole community
trades on it.**
*In erets yisro'el iz do eyn pi'aster
mit a lokh un der gantser yishuv
handlt mit im.* SM

אַז אַן אָרעמאַן דערזעט אַ גראָשן
שפרינגט ער פֿון דער הויט
אַרויס.

When a pauper sees a penny, he
jumps out of his skin.
*Az an oreman derzet a groshn
shpringt er fun der hoyt aroys.* AC

אָרעם איז ניט קיין שאַנד אָבער
ניט קיין גרויסער כּבֿוד אויך.

Poverty is no disgrace but no great
honor either.
*Orem iz nit keyn shand ober nit keyn
groyser koved oykh.* P

מען זאָל זיך קענען אויסקויפֿן פֿון
טויט וואָלטן די אָרעמעלייַט
שיין פּרנסה געהאַט.

If we could hire others to die for
us, the poor would make a very
nice living.
*Men zol zikh kenen oyskoyfn fun toyt
voltn di oremelayt sheyn parnose
gehat.* NS

אָרעמעלייַט קאָכן מיט וואַסער.

Poor people cook with a lot of water.
Oremelayt kokhn mit vaser. IB

ס'איז שלעכט צו עסן פֿרעמדע
ברויט.

It's hard to eat someone else's bread.
S'iz shlekht tsu esn fremde broyt. NS

צוויי קבצנים קענען קיין איין שבת
ניט מאַכן.

Two paupers can't afford to
prepare one Sabbath.
*Tsvey kaptsonim kenen keyn eyn
shabes nit makhn.* NS

אונדזער שטעטל איז אַזוי אָרעם אַז
טאָמער וויל שוין אַ ייִד אויסטוישן
אַ הונדערטער, לאָזט זיך אויס, אַז
ער האָט גאָר קיין הונדערטער ניט.

Our town is so poor that if someone wants to exchange a
hundred-ruble note, it turns out
that he doesn't even own one.
*Undzer shtetl iz azoy orem az tomer
vil shoyn a yid oystoyshn a
hunderter, lozt zikh oys, az er hot
gor keyn hunderter nit.* SM

וווּ מען גייט און וווּ מען שטייט
דרייט זיך דער קבצן אין מיטן.

No matter which way you turn,
the pauper is always in the middle.
*Vu men geyt un vu men shteyt dreyt
zikh der kaptsn in mitn.* MS

אַז אַן אָרעמאַן עסט אַ הון איז אָדער
ער איז קראַנק אָדער די הון.

When a pauper eats chicken, one
of them is sick.
*Az an oreman est a hun iz oder er iz
krank oder di hun.* AC

אַז מען האָט ניט קיין געלט שלאָפֿט
מען אין דער פֿינצטער.

If you have no money, you sleep
in the dark.
*Az men hot nit keyn gelt shloft men
in der fintster.* AC

אַז מען פֿאַרזעצט דעם טלית איז
שוין אַ סימן דלות.

When you pawn your prayer
shawl - that's real poverty!
*Az men farzetst dem tales iz shoyn a
simen dales.* IB

בײַם אָרעמאַן ווערט די חכמה
דערשלאָגן.

A pauper's wisdom is buried in
troubles.
*Baym oreman vert di khokhme der-
shlogn.* IB

ביסט אַ שנײַדער – נײ, ביסט אַ
פֿערד – נײַי, ביסט אַן אָרעמאַן –
אין דר׳ערד אַרײַן!

If you're a tailor - sew, if you're
a horse - go, if you're a pauper -
to hell with you!
*Bist a shnayder - ney, bist a ferd -
gey, bis an oreman - in dr'erd arayn!* IF

דלות ברעכט שלעסער.

Poverty breaks locks.
Dales brekht shleser. NS

דעם אָרעמאַן פֿעלט שטענדיק אַ
טאָג צו דער וואָך.

The pauper is always short a day
in the week.
*Dem oreman felt shtendik a tog tsu
der vokh.* AC

דער דלות לייגט זיך צום ערשטנס
אויפֿן פֿנים.

Poverty is first revealed on the
face.
*Der dales leygt zikh tsum ershtns
oyfn ponim.* IB

דער דאָקטער האָט אַ רפֿואה צו
אַלעם אָבער ניט צום דלות.

The doctor has a remedy for
everything except poverty.
*Der dokter hot a refu'e tsu ales ober
nit tsum dales.* MS

דער נגיד עסט ווען ער וויל, דער
אָרעמאַן ווען ער קען.

The rich eat when they want, the
poor when they can.
*Der noged est ven er vil, der
oreman ven der ken.* NS

דער אָרעמאַן האָט ניט קיין מורא
פאַרן גנב.

The poor fear no thieves.
*Der oreman hot nit keyn moyre farn
ganef.* NS

דער רייכער עסט דאָם פלייש און
דער אָרעמאַן די ביינער.

The rich eat the meat and the
poor get the bones.
*Der raykher est dos fleysh un der
oreman di beyner.* NS

דער עושר בלאָזט זיך און דער
אָרעמאַן ווערט געשוואָלן.

The rich puff themselves up and
the poor become swollen.
*Der oysher blozt zikh un der oreman
vert geshvoln.* AC

דאָם לעבן איז אַ חלום פאָרן חכם,
אַ שפיל פאָרן נאָר, אַ
קאָמעדיע פאָרן נגיד און אַ טראַגעדיע
פאָר די אָרעמעלייט.

Life is a dream for the wise, a
game for the fool, a comedy for
the rich, and a tragedy for the poor.
*Dos lebn iz a kholem farn khokhem, a
shpil farn nar, a komedye farn noged un a tragedye far di oremelayt.* NS

ער האָט ניט אויף וואַסער אויף
קאַשע.

He hasn't the water to cook his
gruel.
Er hot nit oyf vaser oyf kashe. AC

ער איז אַ קבצן אין זיבן פאָלעם.

He's a pauper in seven shreds.
Er iz a kaptsn in zibn poles. AC

ער ווי אַ לולב, זי ווי אַן אתרוג און
קינדערלעך ווי סכך!

He like a twig, she like a citron,
and children like straws!
[similes taken from the holiday of Succoth]
*Er vi a lulev, zi vi an esreg un
kinderlekh vi s'khakh!* NS

אײן אויג מוז אויך שלאָפֿן.

One eye also needs sleep.
Eyn oyg muz oykh shlofn. IB

אײנער האָט ניט קיין אַפּעטיט צום
עסן, דער צווייטער האָט ניט
קיין עסן צום אַפּעטיט.

One person has no appetite for his food, another has no food for his appetite.
Eyner hot nit keyn apetit tsum esn, der tsveyter hot nit keyn esn tsum apetit. AC

פֿאַראַן מער שוחטים ווי הינער.

There are more slaughterers than hens.
Faran mer shokhtim vi hiner. AC

פֿון נעמען ווערט מען נישט רײַך.

You don't get rich from handouts.
Fun nemen vert men nisht raykh. AC

הוליע קבצן – צרות קאָסט קיין
געלט ניט!

Rejoice, pauper – troubles don't cost money!
Hulye kaptsn – tsores kost keyn gelt nit! NS

PRAYER

אַכילה איז די בעסטע תּפֿילה.

Eating is the best kind of praying.
Akhile iz di beste tfile. IB

דער קצבֿ בעט אויף כּשר, דער בעדער
בעט אויף טריפֿה.

The butcher prays for kosher, the bath-house attendant prays for the forbidden. [unclean]
Der katsef bet oyf kosher, der beder bet oyf treyfe. IB

פֿון דײַן מויל אין גאָטס
אויערן.

From your mouth into God's ear.
Fun dayn moyl in gots oyern. P

גאָט, שיק אונדז די רפֿואה, די
מכּה האָבן מיר שוין אַליין.

God, send us the remedy, the affliction we managed on our own.
Got, shik undz di refu'e, di make hobn mir shoyn aleyn. AC

הלוואי וואָלט עס יאָ געווען ווי עס
וועט ניט זײַן.

Would it were what I know it will not be.
Halevay volt es yo geven vi es vet nit zayn. P

גאָט זאָל אָפּהיטן פֿון גויישע הענט
און יידישע רייד.

God protect us from Gentile hands and Jewish tongues.
Got zol op'hitn fun goyishe hent un yidishe reyd. NS

מען זאָל ניט דאַרפֿן אָנקומען צו
קינדער.

May we never become a burden to our children.
Men zol nit darfn onkumen tsu kinder. AC

רבונו-של-עולם, איך בעט דיר נאָר
„לחם לאכל ובגד ללבש" – אַ טרונק
וועל איך מיר שוין אליין
באַזאָרגן.

Master-of-the-Universe, I ask you only for "bread to eat and clothes to wear" – a drink I'll manage on my own.
Reboyne-shel-oylem, ikh bet dir nor "lekhem lekhol uveged lilbosh" - a trunk vel ikh mir shoyn aleyn bazorgn. AC

ווען עס זאָל העלפֿן גאָט בעטן, וואָלט
מען שוין צוגעדונגען מענטשן.

If prayer did any good, they'd be hiring people to pray.
Ven es zol helfn got betn, volt men shoyn tsugedungen mentshn. AC

נאָט זאָל אָפּהיטן פֿון גוטע פֿרײַנד,
פֿאַר שׂונאים וועט מען זיך שוין
אַליין היטן.

God protect us from our friends,
from our enemies we can protect
ourselves.
*Got zol op'hitn fun gute fraynd, far
sonim vet men zikh shoyn aleyn hitn.* AC

נאָט זאָל אָפּהיטן פֿון איין העמד,
איין אויג און איין קינד.

God protect us from having only
one shirt, one eye, and one child.
*Got zol op'hitn fun eyn hemd, eyn
oyg un eyn kind.* NS

רבונו־של־עולם, קוק אַראָפּ פֿון דײַן
הימל און קוק דיר אָן דײַן וועלט.

Master-of-the-Universe, look down
from Your heaven and take a good
look at Your world.
*Reboyne-shel-oylem, kuk arop fun
dayn himl un kuk dir on dayn velt.*
NS

PREPARATION

אַז מען בעט זיך גוט דאָ ליגט מען
גוט דאָרט.

If you make your bed well here,
you'll lie well there. [in the next world]
*Az men bet zikh gut do ligt men gut
dort.* IB

אַז מען קאָכט ניט אין דער וואָכן
האָט מען שבת ניט צו עסן.

If you don't cook mid-week, you
won't have food on the Sabbath.
*Az men kokht nit in der vokhn hot
men shabes nit tsu esn.* NS

עס איז כּדאַי אַ גאַנצע נאַכט בעטן
און איין שעה שלאָפֿן.

Even if it takes all night to make
the bed, an hour of sleep makes it
worth while.
*Es iz keday a gantse nakht betn un
eyn sho shlofn.* AC

פֿון הימל פֿאַלט גאָרניט אַראָפּ.

Nothing falls from heaven.
Fun himl falt gornit arop. AC

האַלטן שבת איז גרינגער ווי מאַכן
שבת.

Keeping the Sabbath is easier than
preparing it.
*Haltn shabes iz gringer vi makhn
shabes.* AC

מיט נאָר גענעראַלן קען מען קיין
מלחמות ניט געווינען.

With generals alone you don't win
wars.

*Mit nor generaln ken men keyn
milkhomes nit gevinen.* AC

ווי מען בעט זיך אויס אַזוי
שלאָפֿט מען.

How you prepare your bed, that's
how you sleep.

Vi men bet zikh oys azoy shloft men. P

PRIDE

אַז אַ לויז קריכט אַרײַן אין פּאַרך
ווייסט זיך דער פּאַרך ניט וווּ צו
קראַצן.

When a louse invades a scabhead,
the scabhead doesn't know where
first to scratch.

*Az a loyz krikht arayn in parekh
veyst zikh der parekh nit vu tsu
kratsn.* AC

די נאווה קען פֿאַרדאַרבן אָבער פֿון
תאווה וועט מען ניט שטאַרבן.

Corruption can come from pride,
but none from pleasure has yet died.

*Di gayve ken fardarbn ober fun
tayve vet men nit shtarbn.* NS

נאווה און אַ ליידיקער טײַסטער
זײַנען ניט קיין פּאָר.

Pride and an empty wallet are not
fit companions.

*Gayve un a leydiker tayster zaynen
nit keyn por.* NS

מען טאָר זיך ניט לאָזן שפּײַען אין
דער קאַשע.

Don't allow anyone to spit into
your porridge.

*Men tor zikh nit lozn shpayen in der
kashe.* P

נאַרישקייט און שטאָלץ וואַקסן אויף
איין האָלץ.

Foolishness and pride grow side by
side.

*Narishkeyt un shtolts vaksn oyf eyn
holts.* NS

PROMISES

„נעשה ונשמע" – אַ ייִד זאָגט אַלץ
צו.

"We shall do and we shall obey"
– a Jew will promise anything.
"Nase venishma" – a yid zogt alts tsu. NS

אויף דעם וואָס מען שווערט איז
אָפֿט פּונקט פֿאַרקערט.

That to which you attest is often
just the opposite.
Oyf dem vos men shvert iz oft punkt
farkert. NS

שווערן איז ערלעך, האַלטן איז
שווערלעך.

A promise is honorable enough but
keeping it is tough.
Shvern iz erlekh, haltn iz shverlekh. NS

PROPHECY

אַ גאַנצער נאַר איז אַ האַלבער נבֿיא.

A whole fool is half a prophet.
A gantser nar iz a halber novi. IB

דער לוח טרעפֿט אויך אַמאָל.

The calendar sometimes prophesies
correctly.
Der lu'akh treft oykh amol. NS

דאָס האַרץ איז אַ האַלבער נבֿיא.

The heart is half a prophet.
Dos harts iz a halber novi. AC

ווען אַלע וואָלטן געווען נבֿיאים וואָלט
מען ניט באַדאַרפֿט קיין עיניים.

If everyone were a prophet there'd
be no need for eyes.
Ven ale voltn geven nevi'im volt men
nit badarft keyn eynayim. NS

PUNISHMENT

אַ נאַכט אָן שלאָף איז די גרעסטע
שטראָף.

A sleepless night is the worst
blight.
A nakht on shlof iz di greste shtrof. NS

אַז אַ קינד כאַפּט איז עם אַ חכמה,
אַז אַ גרויסער כאַפּט ניט מען
אים איבער די הענט.

When a child grabs, it's cute;
when an adult grabs, he gets a
slap.
*Az a kind khapt iz es a khokhme, az
a groyser khapt git men im iber di
hent.* NS

אַז מען האַלט בײַם שמײַסן, שאַט
ניט נאָך אַ שמיץ.

If you've a mind to give a beating,
one more slap won't hurt.
*Az men halt baym shmaysn, shat nit
nokh a shmits.* AC

אַז מען שלאָגט, לויפֿט מען.

When the blows fall, everyone runs.
Az men shlogt, loyft men. IB

די טאָכטער שטראָפֿט מען, די
שנור מיינט מען.

The daughter is punished but the
daughter-in-law is meant.
*Di tokhter shtroft men, di shnur
meynt men.* NS

איך וועל דיר געבן נײַן מאָל נײַן
וויפֿל עם וועט אין דיר אַרײַן.

I'll give you nine times nine,
enough to make you feel it fine.
*Ikh vel dir gebn nayn mol nayn vifl
es vet in dir arayn.* IB

וואָס איז דער חילוק צי דער נאַר
שלאָגט אָדער דער חכם שלאָגט
– וויי טוט עם דאָך.

What difference if a fool or a
clever person beats you – it hurts
just the same.
*Vos iz der khilek tsi der nar shlogt
oder der khokhem shlogt – vey tut es
dokh.* IB

QUARRELS

אַ געקריג איז ווי אַ קרעץ, וואָס מער
מען קראַצט אַלץ מער
בײַסט עם.

A quarrel is like an itch; the more
you scratch, the more it itches.
*A gekrig iz vi a krets, vos mer men
kratst alts mer bayst es.* NS

אַז דו קריגסט זיך, קריג זיך אַזוי אַז
דו זאָלסט זיך קענען איבערבעטן.

In a quarrel keep the door open
for reconciliation.
*Az du krigst zikh, krig zikh azoy az
du zolst zikh kenen iberbetn.* AC

אַז מען קריגט זיך קושט מען זיך ניט.

Quarrelers don't kiss.
Az men krigt zikh kusht men zikh nit. IB

אַז ייִדן רײַסן זיך איז אַ שימחה
בײַ די המנס.

When Jews quarrel their enemies
rejoice.
*Az yidn raysn zikh iz a simkhe bay
di homens.* AC

דרײַ זאַכן ווינען ניט בשלום:
ווײַבער, הינט און הינער.

Three things can't live together
peaceably: women, dogs, and hens.
*Dray zakhn voynen nit besholem:
vayber, hint un hiner.* NS

פֿון אַ קלײַנער מלחמה ווערט
אַ גרויסע מהומה.

From small rows big strife grows.
*Fun a kleyner milkhome vert a
groyse mehume.* IB

אַז דער מלמד קריגט זיך מיט
דעם ווײַב איז אָך און וויי צו די
תּלמידים.

When the teacher quarrels with
his wife, it's too bad for the pupils.
*Az der melamed krigt zikh mit dem
vayb iz okh un vey tsu di talmidim.* IB

הינט בײַסן זיך איבער אַ ביין און
אבלים איבער אַ ירושה.

Dogs fight over a bone and
mourners over the inheritance.
*Hint baysn zikh iber a beyn un
aveylim iber a yerushe.* NS

איך רעד הוידעם און ער רעדט בוידעם.

I talk cellar and he talks attic.
Ikh red hoydem un er ret boydem. AC

אין תּוך איז יעדער צד גערעכט.

Essentially, each side is right.
In tokh iz yeder tsad gerekht. NS

צוויי שטעט קריגן זיך איבער אַ רב.

Two towns quarrel over the rabbi.
[Neither town wants him.]
Tsvey shtet krign zikh iber a rov. AC

זאָגט ער הודו, זאָגט זי קיש, זאָגט
ער פֿלייש, זאָגט זי פֿיש.

If he says; 'praise be,' 'damn' says
she; if he says: 'meat,' 'fish' she'll
bleat.
*Zogt er hodu zogt zi kish, zogt er
fleysh zogt zi fish.* NS

QUESTIONS

אז מען פרעגט א שאלה ווערט טרייף.

If you ask permission the answer is: forbidden.
Az men fregt a shayle vert treyf. AC

אז מען ווייסט אליין פֿרעגט מען ניט אנדערע.

If you know the answer, don't ask others.
Az men veyst aleyn fregt men nit andere. P

פֿאַר פֿרעגן קומט קיין פּאַטש ניט.

A question doesn't warrent a slap.
Far fregn kumt keyn patsh nit. AC

קלאָץ קשיא: פֿאַרוואָס א קריגל האָט איין אויער און הענגט יאָ און דער מענטש האָט צוויי אויערן און הענגט ניט?

Foolish question: Why is it that a jug has only one ear and can hang and a human being has two ears and cannot hang?
Klots kashe: farvos a krigl hot eyn oyer un hengt yo un der mentsh hot tsvey oyern un hengt nit? AC

קלאָץ קשיא: פֿאַר וואָס אז ס׳איז דאָ א לאָך אין א שוך רינט עם אַרײַן און אז ס׳איז דאָ א לאָך אין א טאָפּ רינט עם אַרויס?

Foolish question: Why, if there's a hole in a shoe, does the water run in and if there's a hole in a pot, the water runs out?
Klots kashe: farvos az s'iz do a lokh in a shukh rint es arayn un az s'iz do a lokh in a top rint es aroys? AC

אויף אַ מעשׂה פֿרעגט מען קיין קשיא ניט.

Don't question a story.
Oyf a mayse fregt men keyn kashe nit. AC

אויף יעדער קשיא איז דאָ א תירוץ.

Every question has an answer.
Oyf yeder kashe iz do a terets. AC

וואָם ווייניקער מען פֿרעגט אַלץ געזונטער איז.

The less you ask, the healthier.
Vos veyniker men fregt alts gezinter iz. P

RABBIS

אַלץ הייסט רבי געלט.

**Everything involves a payment to
the rabbi.**
[Chalk it up to experience.]
Alts heyst rebe gelt. P

אַז מען זיצט לעבן אַ רב מיינט נאָך
ניט אַז מ׳איז אַ רב.

**Sitting next to the rabbi is no
guarantee of becoming one.**
*Az men zitst lebn a rov meynt nokh
nit az m'iz a rov.* AC

בײַ אײַך איז אַ נם וואָס גאָט טוט דעם
רבנס ווילן, בײַ אונדז איז אַ נם
אַז דער רבי טוט גאָטס ווילן.

**To you it's a miracle if God does
what the rabbi wants; to us it's a
miracle if the rabbi does what God
wants.**
*Bay aykh iz a nes vos got tut dem
rebns viln, bay undz iz a nes az der
rebe tut gots viln.* NS

דער מגיד שטראָפֿט קהל און אַליין
טוט ער פֿאַרקערט.

**The preacher scolds the community
and, himself, does what he wants.**
*Der maged shtroft ko'ol un aleyn tut
er farkert.* AC

ער האָט ליב וואָס דער רבי האָט
ניט פֿײַנט.

**He enjoys what the rabbi doesn't
dislike.**
Er hot lib vos der rebe hot nit faynt. AC

אַ חזן נעמט געלט אויף שרײַען און
אַ רבֿ פֿאַר שווײַגן.

A cantor takes money to scream
and a rabbi to keep silent.
*A khazn nemt gelt oyf shrayen un a
rov far shvaygn.* AC

דער רבי האַלט ניט פֿון קיין קאָרטן,
ער האַלט בעסער פֿון קוויטלעך.

The rabbi doesn't approve of playing cards, he prefers praying
cards.
*Der rebe halt nit fun keyn kortn, er
halt beser fun kvitlekh.* AC

מען הערט די מגילה ווי דעם רבֿ, דעם
רבֿ ווי דער מגילה און זיי ביידן ווי
דעם פֿאַראַיאָריקן שניי.

People listen to the megillah like to
the rabbi, to the rabbi like to the
megillah, and to both of them like
to last year's snow.
*Men hert di megile vi dem rob, dem
rov vi der megile un zey beydn vi
dem farayorikn shney.* NS

„מי בחרב ומי ברעבֿ" – ווער עם זאָל
ניכשל ווערן דורכן שווערד און
ווער דורכן רבֿ.

"Who through the sword and who
through hunger" – some will be
knocked off by the sword and
some by the rabbi.
[Play on words: 'rav' has two meanings,
'hunger' and 'rabbi.']
*"Mi b'kherev umi b'rov" – ver es
zol nikhshl vern durkhn shverd un
ver durkhn rov.* AC

ווּ ער וועט זײַן רבֿ שמדט זיך די
קהילה.

Wherever he will be rabbi, the entire community will convert.
*Vu er vet zayn rov shmat zikh di
kehile.* NS

REGIONS

אַ ליטוואַק האָט אַ ברייטן מוח און
אַ שמאָלע קישקע.

A Litvak has a wide brain and a
narrow gut.
*A litvak hot a breytn moyakh un a
shmole kishke.* NS

אַ ליטוואַק איז אַ גנבֿ.

A Litvak is a thief.
A litvak iz a ganef. NS

אַ ליטוואַק טוט תשובֿה איידער ער
זינדיקט.

A Litvak repents even before he sins
A litvak tut tshuve eyder er zindikt. AC

אַ וואַרשעווער איז נאָר קלוג ביז צו
די ראָגאַטקעס.

A person from Warsaw is smart
only as long as he's within the city
limits.
*A varshever iz nor klug biz tsu di
rogatkes.* NS

אַמעריקע איז אַ טײַער לאַנד ווײַל
אַרבעט איז קיין שאַנד.

American is a wonderful place
because work is no disgrace.
*Amerike iz a tayer land vayl arbet iz
keyn shand.* NS

ביסט דאָך ניט קיין ליטוואַק,
פֿאַרוואָס זשע ביסטו אַ חזיר?

You're not a Litvak so why do
you act like a pig?
*Bist dokh nit keyn litvak, farvos zhe
bistu a khazer?* AC

די גאַליציאַנער זײַנען זייער אַמביציעז:
נאָך איידער זיי קענען עבֿרי כאַפֿן
זיי זיך צו דער גמרא.

Galician Jews are very ambitious:
before they even know Hebrew,
they're already into Talmud.
*Di galitsi'aner zaynen zeyer ambit-
si'ez: nokh eyder zay kenen ivre
khapn zey zikh tsu der gemore.* SM

נאָט זאָל אָפּהיטן פֿאַר בערדיטשעווער
נגידים און פֿאַר אומאַנער חסידים,
פֿאַר קאָנסטאַנטינאָוװער משרתים
און פֿאַר מאָהילעווער אפּיקורסים,
פֿאַר קאָמענעצער קאָדאַטײעס
און פֿאַר אָדעסער הולטײעס.

God protect us from the rich of
Berditchev and from the pious of
Uman, from the servants of
Konstantinov and from the
freethinkers of Mohilev, from the
meddlers of Kameniets and from
the debauchers of Odessa.
*Got zol op'hitn far berditshever
negidim un far umaner kh'sidim, far
konstantinover meshorsim un far
mohilever apikorsim, far komenetser
kodatayes un far odeser hultayes.* NS

אין מעזריטש שטאַרבט קיין עושר
ניט.

Nobody rich ever died in Mezritch.
In mezritsh shtarbt keyn oysher nit. NS

אין פּוילן איז אַלץ קרום, נאָר די
טרעפּ זײַנען גלײַך.

In Poland everything is lopsided,
only the stairs are straight.
*In poyln iz alts krum, nor di trep
zaynen glaykh.* NS

לאָצקעווער קהל פֿאַרמאָגט איין
פּאָר הויזן!

The entire community of Lotskov
possesses only one pair of pants!
*Lotskever ko'ol farmogt eyn por
hoyzn!* NS

מיט אַ ליטוואַק שרעקט מען קינדער.

A Litvak is good for scaring little
children.
Mit a litvak shrekt men kinder. NS

וואַרשעווער טויטע רעדן פֿיל
לעבעדיקער ווי ווילנער
לעבעדיקע.

The Warsaw dead are more lively
than the Vilna living.
*Varshever toyte redn fil lebediker vi
vilner lebedike.* AC

וווּ הינט בילן דאָרט איז אַ יישוב.

Where dogs bark, people live.
Vu hint biln dort iz a yishuv. NS

REGRET

גנבֿע ניט און פֿאַסט ניט.

Rob not, repent not.
Ganve nit un fast nit. AC

א פֿרומען ייִדן זאָל מען זוכן צווישן
אַלטע הולטײַעס.

Look for a pious Jew among old
roués.

*A frumen yidn zol men zukhn tsvishn
alte hultayes.* NS

נאָך דער חופּה איז צו שפּעט די
חרטה.

After the wedding it's too late for
regretting.

*Nokh der khupe iz tsu shpet di
kharote.* NS

אויף ,נייין' זאָל מען קיין חרטה ניט
האָבן.

One should never regret saying 'no.'

*Oyf 'neyn' zol men keyn kharote nit
hobn.* NS

שׂכל און חרטה קומען צו שפּעט.

Wisdom and regret come too late.

Seykhl un kharote kumen tsu shpet. P

צוויי מאָל האָט מען ניט חרטה.

You can't repent twice.

Tsvey mol hot men nit kharote. IB

RELATIONSHIP

אַ באַרג מיט אַ באַרג קומען זיך ניט
צונויף אָבער אַ מענטש מיט אַ
מענטש יאָ.

Mountains cannot meet but people
can.

*A barg mit a barg kumen zikh nit
tsunoyf ober a mentsh mit a mentsh yo.*

אַ מוכר-ספֿרים איז ניט קיין למדן אַ
חלפֿן איז ניט קיין עושר און אַ
קבֿרות-מאַן איז קיין צדיק
ניט.

A book-seller is no scholar, a
money-lender is no millionaire,
and a grave-digger is no saint.

*A moykher-sforim iz nit keyn lamdn,
a khalfn iz nit keyn oysher un a
kvores-man iz keyn tsadik nit.* NS

אַז מיך בײַסט דאָ זאָל איך קראַצן
דאָרט?

If it itches here, I should scratch
there?

Az mikh bayst do zol ikh kratsn dort?

עס קלעפּט זיך ניט אַ וואָרט צו אַ
וואָרט.

One word doesn't stick to another.

Es klept zikh nit a vort tsu a vort. P

אײנעם מיטן דריטן איז ניט קײן
מחותן.

One with a third is absurd.
Eyns mitn dritn iz nit keyn mekhutn. IB

װי אַזױ קומט די קאַץ איבערן
װאַסער?

How does the cat cross the ocean?
Vi azoy kumt di kats ibern vaser? AC

װי קומט אַ הונט דײן צו זײן?

How does a dog get to be the judge?
Vi kumt a hunt dayen tsu zayn? IB

װי קומט אַ פּאַטש צו גוט שבת?

How does a slap come to a greeting?
Vi kumt a patsh tsu gut-shabes? AC

װי קומט דער חזיר אױפֿן בית-עולם?

How did the pig get into the cemetery?
Vi kumt der khazer oyfn besoylem? NS

װי קומט הודו צו כּוש?

How does Africa come to India?
Vi kumt hodu tsu kush? IF

װי קומט המן אין דער „מה-נשתנה"
אַרײן?

How does Haman get into the Passover story?
Vi kumt homen in der "ma-nishtane" arayn? NS

װאָס האָט דער כּהן אױפֿן
בית-הקבֿרות צו טאָן?

What's the Kohen doing at the cemetery?
Vos hot der koyen oyfn beysakvores tsu ton? NS

יאָ טאַבאַק – װוּ אַ נאָז?

You have the snuff? Where's the nose?
Yo tabak – vu a noz? IB

REMEDIES

אַמאָל איז די רפֿואה ערגער פֿאַר
דער מכּה.

Sometimes, the cure is worse than the disease.
Amol iz di refu'e erger far der make. AC

פֿון דעם מאַנס רפֿואה ווערט דאָס
ווײַב קראַנק אין נײַן חדשים.

The husband's cure makes the
wife ill nine months later.
*Fun dem mans refu'e vert dos vayb
krank in nayn khodoshim.* NS

גאָט, שיק אונדז די רפֿואה, די
מכה האָבן מיר שוין אַליין.

God, send us the remedy, the affliction we managed on our own.
*Got, shik undz di refu'e, di make
hobn mir shoyn aleyn.* AC

אָדער עס העלפֿט ניט אָדער מען
דאַרף עס ניט.

Either it won't help or you don't
need it.
Oder es helft nit oder men darf es nit.

פרנסה הײלט אַלע מכות.

Livelihood heals all ills.
Parnose heylt ale makes. P

פרנסה איז אַ רפֿואה צו יעדער
קרענק.

Livelihood is a cure for every
disease.
Parnose iz a refu'e tsu yeder krenk. P

ווען צו אַ קרענק איז דאָ אַ רפֿואה
איז עס נאָר אַ האַלבע קרענק.

If there's a cure, it's only half a
disease.
*Ven tsu a krenk iz do a refu'e iz es
nor a halbe krenk.* P

ווען תהילים זאָל זײַן אַ רפֿואה וואָלט
מען שוין צוגעדונגען מענטשן.

If Psalms could cure, they'd have
hired men to recite them.
*Ven tilim zol zayn a refu'e volt men
shoyn tsugedungen mentshn.* NS

REPETITION

אַ חזיר עסט געקײַטע זאַכן.

A pig chews over.
A khazer est gekayte zakhn. NS

אײן מאָל אַ שׂכל, דאָס צווייטע מאָל
חן, דעם דריטן מאָל ניט מען אין
די ציין.

The first time it's smart, the second time it's sweet, the third time
gets you a sock in the teeth.
*Eyn mol a seykhl, dos tsveyte mol
kheyn, dem dritn mol git men in di
tseyn.* NS

די מעשה האָט שוין אַ באָרד.

This story already has a beard.
Di mayse hot shoyn a bord. P

געקײַטע איז נישט געשמאַק.

Chewed-over isn't tasty.
Gekayte iz nisht geshmak. AC

צוויי מאָל זאָגט אַ חזן.

Twice over is for the cantor.
[Refers to practise of singing same passage
more than once before concluding the prayer.]
Tsvey mol zogt a khazn. NS

RESPONSIBILITY

אַז מען לעבט אָן חשבון שטאַרבט
מען אָן תכריכים.

**If you live without account, you
die without a shroud.**
*Az men lebt on kheshbn shtarbt men
on takhrikhim.* NS

עם איז גרינג צו פישן אויף יענעמס
לײַלעך.

**It's easy to pee on someone else's
sheets.**
*Es iz gring tsu pishn oyf yenems
laylekh.* AC

לייג ניט אָפ אויף מאָרגן וואָס דו
קענסט הײַנט באַזאָרגן.

**Don't put off until tomorrow what
you can do today.**
*Leyg nit op oyf morgn vos du kenst
haynt bazorgn.* AC

מען קען ניט קײַען מיט פֿרעמדע צייַן.

**You can't chew with someone
else's teeth.**
Men ken nit kayen mit fremde tseyn. P

אויפֿנאַשן קען מען אַ גאַנצן
מאַיאָנטיק אויך.

**One can nibble away a great for-
tune also.**
*Oyfnashn ken men a gantsn mayontik
oykh.* AC

ווי מען שטעלט זיך דעם שטייגער
אַזוי גייט דער זייגער.

**How you run your life, that's how
your clock will run.**
*Vi men shtelt zikh dem shteyger azoy
geyt der zeyger.* NS

אַז דער קרעמער באַרעכנט ניט די
קראָם באַרעכנט די קראָם דעם
קרעמער.

**If the storekeeper doesn't figure
out his accounts, his accounts will
figure him out.**
*Az der kremer barekhnt nit di krom
barekhnt di krom dem kremer.* AC

זאָל זיך יעדערער אויסרייניקן די
אייגענע נאָז.

**Let each person clean out his own
nose.**
*Zol zikh yederer oysreyniken di
eygene noz.* AC

REVENGE

אַ נקמה - דער טאַטע האָט די
מאַמע גענומען.

**Some revenge! Father married
mother.**
*A nekome! der tate hot di mame
genumen.* AC

אַ נקמה אין די וואַנצן אַז דאָס הײַזל
ברענט!

**A revenge on the roaches when the
hovel burns!**
*A nekome in di vantsn az dos hayzl
brent!* AC

גאָט שטראָפֿט, דער מענטש איז
זיך נוקם.

God punishes, man takes revenge!
*Got shtroft, der mentsh iz zikh
noykem.* NS

נקמה איז אַ גוטער ביסן.

Revenge is a tasty morsel.
Nekome iz a guter bisn. NS

אויף אַ שלעכטן גוי טאָר מען קיין
נקמה ניט בעטן.

**Don't pray for revenge even on a
wicked Goy.**
*Oyf a shlekhtn goy tor men keyn
nekome nit betn.* NS

SECRECY

א גוטע זאך האלט מען פאר זיך.

Something choice one keeps for oneself.
A gute zakh halt men far zikh. AC

א סוד איז קיין ברכה.

A secret is not a blessing.
A sod iz keyn brokhe. NS

ביי א נאר און ביי א קינד איז קיין סוד ניט פאראן.

Children and fools can't keep secrets.
Bay a nar un bay a kind iz keyn sod nit faran. IB

דריי קענען האלטן א סוד אז צוויי זיינען מתים.

Three can keep a secret if two of them are corpses.
Dray kenen haltn a sod az tsvey zaynen meysim. AC

פאראן זאכן וואָס מען טאָר אפילו דעם אייגענעם מאן ניט וויזן.

Some things shouldn't be shown even to your own husband.
Faran zakhn vos men tor afile dem eygenem man nit vayzn. NS

פאר א וויַב איז קיין סוד ניטאָ.

You can't keep a secret from your wife.
Far a vayb iz keyn sod nito. AC

אין נײַן חדשים קומט אַרױס דער סוד.

In nine months the secret will out.
In nayn khadoshim kumt aroys der sod.

פֿאַר צװײ איז שױן ניט קײן סוד.

When two people know, it's no
longer a secret.
Far tsvey iz shoyn nit keyn sod. P

גרינגער איז הערן אַ סוד אײדער
היטן אַ סוד.

It's easier to listen to a secret than
to keep it.
Gringer iz hern a sod eyder hitn a sod.

װאָס איך ניט װײס מאַכט מיר ניט
הײס.

What I know not won't make me hot.
Vos ikh nit veys makht mir nit heys. NS

זאָל נאָר װיסן אײנע װעט שױן װיסן
די שכנה.

As soon as one person hears, it
gets to the neighbor's ears.
*Zol nor visn eyne vet shoyn visn di
shkheyne.* AC

SEX

אַ מת איז פּטור פֿון פּריה ורביה.

A corpse is through with sex.
A mes iz poter fun pri'ye urvi'ye. WZ

אַלע מײדלעך זײַנען בתולות אַזױ
לאַנג דער בױך שװײַגט.

All girls are virgins as long as
their bellies don't tell.
*Ale meydlekh zaynen p'sules azoy
lang der boykh shvaygt.* WZ

אז אַ מיידל פֿאַלט פֿאַלט זי
שטענדיק אױפֿן רוקן.

When a girl falls, she always lands
on her back.
*Az a meydl falt falt zi shtendik oyfn
rukn.* WZ

אז מען לאָזט אַ זכר מיט אַ נקבֿה אַלײן
אין הױז קומט קײן גוטס ניט אַרױס.

If you leave male and female alone
in a room, no good will come of
it, one can safely assume.
*Az men lozt a zokher mit a nekeyve
aleyn in hoyz kumt keyn guts nit
aroys.* NS

די כּלה שעמט זיך אָבער הנאה
האָט זי פֿאָרט.

The bride may be bashful but she
enjoys it anyway.
*Di kale shemt zikh ober hanoye hot
zi fort.* WZ

ער האָט אין די הױזן אַ יריד.

He's got a carnival in his pants.
[Refers to syphilis.]
Er hot in di hoyzn a yarid. WZ

פֿאַר גוטע נעכט האָט מען שלעכטע
טעג.

From good nights you get bad days.
Far gute nekht hot men shlekhte teg. AC

גאָטס װינדער – אַ פֿץ מאַכט קינדער!

God's wonder – a prick makes
children!
Gots vinder – a pots makht kinder! WZ

איבער אַן אָנגעהױבענער חלה מאַכט
מען קײן ברכה ניט.

Over a half-eaten loaf you don't
make a blessing.
*Iber an ongehoybener khale makht
men keyn brokhe nit.* IB

מיאוסע מיידן לאָזן זיך רײדן.

A homely maid can easily be laid.
Mi'ese meydn lozn zikh reydn. NS

שטיף און לאַך און היט אָפּ די זאַך.

Laugh and jest but be wary is
best.
Shtif un lakh un hit op di zakh. NS

אַז דער פּיץ שטייט לינט דער שׂכל אין
דר׳ערד.

When the prick rises, good sense
lies down.
*Az der pots shteyt ligt der seykhl in
dr'erd.* AC

מיט אָן אייגן ווײַב ווען מען וויל, מיט
אַ פֿרעמד ווײַב ווען זי וויל.

With your own wife, whenever you
want, with someone else's wife
when she wants.
*Mit an eygn vayb ven men vil, mit a
fremd vayb ven zi vil.* WZ

צו דער שפּיץ ברוסט האָט
איטלעכער אַ גלוסט.

Every man has a zest for the breast.
*Tsu der shpits brust hot itlekher a
glust.* NS

וויל ער, זי ניט; וויל זי ,ער ניט; ווילן
שוין ביידע, פֿאַלט אַראָפֿ דער
פֿאָרהאַנג.

He wants, she doesn't; she wants,
he doesn't; both finally want and
the curtain comes down.
[comment on the action of a stage play]
*Vil er, zi nit; vil zi, er nit, viln
shoyn beyde, falt arop der forhang.* AC

ווי אַזוי טרעפֿט דער בלינדער צום
ווײַב אין בעט אַרײַן? דער קליינער
פֿירט אים.

How does a blind man locate his
wife in bed? His little one leads
him to her.
*Vi azoy treft der blinder tsum vayb
in bet arayn? der kleyner firt im.* WZ

SIGHT

אַ בלינדער גלייבט אַז מען זאָגט
אים ער האָט אַ שיינע ווייַב.

A blind person will believe when
he's told he has a pretty wife.
*A blinder gleybt az men zogt im er
hot a sheyne vayb.* NS

אַ בלינדער האָט ליב צו הערן אַלע
ווינדער.

A blind person delights in hearing
about wonderful sights.
A blinder hot lib tsu hern ale vinder. NS

די קאַטשקע קוקט נאָר אין אַ זייַט,
אָבער אירע אויגן טראָגן ווייַט.

A duck's eyes are on the side but
it sees far and wide.
*Di katshke kukt nor in a zayt, ober
ire oygn trogn vayt.* NS

דאָס אויג דערצייילט וואָס דאָס
האַרץ מיינט.

The eye reveals what the heart
conceals.
*Dos oyg dertseylt vos dos harts
meynt.* NS

פֿון זען איז קיינער נאָך ניט בלינד
געוואָרן.

Nobody has yet gone blind from
looking.
*Fun zen iz keyner nokh nit blind
gevorn.* P

ווען די אויגן וואָלטן ניט געזען
וואָלטן די הענט ניט גענומען.

If the eyes didn't see, the hands
wouldn't take.
*Ven di oygn voltn nit gezen voltn di
hent nit genumen.* AC

וואָס טויג ליכט און ברילן אַז דער
מענטש ניט זען וויל?

What use can a lamp and glasses
be, if a person doesn't want to see?
*Vos toyg likht un briln az der
mentsh nit zen vil?* AC

SILENCE

קיין ענטפֿער איז אויך אַן ענטפֿער.

No answer is also an answer.
Keyn entfer iz oykh an entfer. P

א בהמה האָט אַ לאַנגע צונג און
קען קיין ברכה ניט זאָגן.

Even though a cow has a long
tongue, it can't recite a blessing.
*A beheyme hot a lange tsung un ken
keyn brokhe nit zogn.* NS

אַ שוויַיגעדיקער נאַר איז אַ
האַלבער חכם.

When a fool holds his tongue, he
A silent fool is half a sage.
*A shvaygediker nar iz a halber
khokhem.* AC

אַז אַ נאַר שוויַיגט ווערט ער אויך
גערעכנט צווישן די קלוגע.

When a fool holds his tongue, he
too can be thought clever.
*Az a nar shvaygt vert er oykh
gerekhnt tsvishn di kluge.* P

אַז מען האָט ניט צו ענטפערן מוז
מען פאַרשוויַיגן.

If one has nothing to say, it's best
to shut up.
*Az men hot nit tsu entfern muz men
farshvaygn.* AC

דער בעל־תפילה איז געגאַנגען אין
מיקווה אריַין?

The prayer leader went to the
ritual bath?
[comment on a lull in the conversation]
*Der bal-tfile iz gegangen in mikve
arayn?* IB

די בעסטע רעדע איז די וואָס מען
האַלט ניט.

The best speech is the one you
don't make.
Di beste rede iz di vos men halt nit. AC

עם שטייט דאָך געשריבן: חכמה ־
שתיקה.

It is written: silence is wisdom.
*Es shteyt dokh geshribn: khokhme –
shtike.* NS

האָסטו ־ האַלט, וויַיסטו ־ שוויַיג!

If you have – hold, if you know –
keep silent!
Hostu – halt, veystu – shvayg! P

רעדן איז גוט, שוויַיגן נאָך בעסער.

Speech is good, silence is even
better.
Redn iz gut, shvaygn nokh beser. P

שווײַגן הייסט אויך גערעדט.

Silence also conveys meaning.
Shvaygn heyst oykh geret. AC

– שווײַגן איז א צוים פֿאַר חכמה
אָבער נאָר שווײַגן איז קיין
חכמה ניט.

Silence is the restraint of wisdom
but mere silence is not necessarily
wisdom.
*Shvaygn iz a tsoym far khokhme –
ober nor shvaygn iz keyn khokhme
nit.* NS

וואָם ווייניקער מען רעדט, אַלץ
געזינטער איז.

The less you speak, the healthier.
Vos veyniker men ret, alts gezinter iz. P

SIN

אַ פֿרעמדער ביסן שמעקט זים.

Stolen pleasures taste sweet.
A fremder bisn shmekt zis. P

אַן עבֿירה קאָסט געלט.

A sin can be costly.
An aveyre kost gelt. AC

אַז מען עסט חזיר זאָל רינען פֿון באָרד.

If you're going to eat pork, let it
overflow your beard.
Az men est khazer zol rinen fun bord. P

באַגיין אַ זינד איז נאָר שווער דאָם
ערשטע מאָל.

Sinning is difficult only the first
time.
*Bageyn a zind iz nor shver dos er-
shte mol.* NS

דער זינדיקער מענטש – ער מוז עסן
און טרינקען, קאַקן און שטינקען.

Sinful human – he must eat and
drink, shit and stink!
*Der zindiker mentsh – er muz esn un
trinken, kakn un shtinken.* WZ

די וועגן פֿון תשובֿה זײַנען ניט
ווייניקער פֿאַרבאָרגן ווי די
וועגן פֿון זינד.

The ways of repentance are as
much hidden as the ways of sin.
*Di vegn fun tshuve zaynen nit
veyniker farborgn vi di vegn fun zind.* NS

ער קלאַפּט זיך „על חטא" און
באַלעקט זיך דערבײַ.

He beats his breast in remorse but
enjoys the exercise.
*Er klapt zikh ''al khet'' un balekt
zikh derbay.* NS

מען איז דיר מוחל די תשובה נאָר
טו ניט די עבֿירה.

Never mind the remorse, don't
commit the sin.
*Men iz dir moykhl di tshuve nor tu
nit di aveyre.* AC

ווען ניט די מורא וואָלט געווען זיס
די עבֿירה.

If not for the fear, the sin would
be sweet.
*Ven nit di meyre volt geven zis di
aveyre.* NS

SPEECH

אַ מענטשן דערקענט מען אין זײַן
רעדן.

A person is recognized by his
speech.
A mentshn derkent men in zayn redn. F

אַ וואָרט איז אַזוי ווי אַ פֿײַל – בײדע
האָבן גרויסע אײַל.

A word and an arrow are the
same – both deliver with speedy
aim.
*A vort iz azoy vi a fayl – beyde
hobn groyse ayl.* NS

אַלע גלידער ווילן רעדן און די צונג
אַלײן שטעלט מען אַרויס.

Every limb wants to speak but the
tongue alone does the talking.
*Ale glider viln redn un di tsung
aleyn shtelt men aroys.* NS

אַז מען רעדט, דערעדט מען זיך.

Talk too much and you give
yourself away.
Az men ret, deret men zikh. IB

אַז מען רעדט אַ סך רעדט מען פֿון זיך.

Talk too much and you reveal
yourself.
Az men ret a sakh ret men fun zikh. AC

דער מענטש לערנט פֿרי רעדן און
שפּעט שוויַיגן.

A human being learns to speak
early and to keep silent late.
*Der mentsh lernt fri redn un shpet
shvaygn.* NS

דער שוסטער רעדט פֿון דער קאָפּעטע
און דער בעקער רעדט
פֿון דער לאָפּעטע.

The shoemaker speaks of his last
and the baker speaks of his
paddle.
*Der shuster ret fun der kopete un
der beker ret fun der lopete.* NS

די גאַנצע וועלט שטייט אויף דעם
שפּיץ צונג.

The whole world rests on the tip
of the tongue.
*Di gantse velt shteyt oyf dem shpits
tsung.* NS

די צונג איז ניט אין גלות.

The tongue is not in exile.
Di tsung iz nit in goles. AC

די צונג איז דער פֿעדער פֿון האַרץ.

The tongue is the pen of the heart.
Di tsung iz der feder fun harts. NS

ער רעדט פֿאַר פֿיַיער און פֿאַר
וואַסער!

He talks like fire and like flood!
[incessantly]
Er ret far fayer un far vaser! P

איינער רעדט רוסיש ווי אַ ייִד, דער
אַנדערער רעדט ייִדיש ווי אַ גוי.

One person speaks Russian like a
Jew, another speaks Yiddish like a
Goy.
*Eyner ret rusish vi a yid, der
anderer ret yidish vi a goy.* NS

פֿון זאָגן פֿאַרנייט מען ניט אין טראָגן.

From talking you don't get
pregnant.
Fun zogn fargeyt men nit in trogn. AC

העברעיש רעדט מען, ייִדיש רעדט
זיך אַליין.

Hebrew one learns, Yiddish comes
naturally.
*Hebreyish ret men, yidish ret zikh
aleyn.* P

גיי רעד – אַז די צונג איז אין גלות!

Go talk – when the tongue is in exile!
Gey red – az di tsung iz in goles! AC

קיין צונג רעדט ניט אַזוי פיל
שלעכטס ווי די אייגענע.

No tongue speaks as much ill as one's own.
Keyn tsung ret nit azoy fil shlekhts vi di eygene. NS

„מרבה דברים, מרבה שטות" – וואָס
ווינציקער מ'רעדט, געזינטער איז.

"A lot of words, a lot of foolishness" – the less you talk, the healthier.
"Marbe dvorim, marbe shtus" – vos vintsiker m'ret, gezinter iz. IB

מיט דער צונג קען מען אַלץ מאַכן.

With the tongue anything is possible.
Mit der tsung ken men alts makhn. P

ניט גערעדט איז אויך גערעדט.

Not speaking also talks.
Nit geret iz oykh geret. P

אויף אַ מויל איז קיין שלאָס ניטאָ.

There's no lock on a mouth.
Oyf a moyl iz keyn shlos nito. AC

ווען דאָס פֿערד וואָלט געהאַט וואָס
צו זאָגן וואָלט עס גערעדט.

If the horse had anything to say, it would speak up.
Ven dos ferd volt gehat vos tsu zogn volt es geret. NS

וואָס אויף דער לונג איז אויף דער
צונג.

What's on the lung is on the tongue.
Vos oyf der lung iz oyf der tsung. P

וואָס ווייניקער מען רעדט, אַלץ
געזינטער איז.

The less said, the better.
Vos veyniker men ret, alts gezinter iz. P

STATUS

אַ קרוין איז נאָך ניט אַ רפֿואה אויף
קאָפּווייטיק.

A crown is no cure for headache.
A kroyn iz nokh nit a refu'e oyf kopveytik. AC

א שנײַדערס ווײַב איז ניט קיין
אשת איש.

A tailor's wife is not much of a wife.
[derogatory comment on the lowly status of a tailor]
A shnayders vayb iz nit keyn eyshes ish. SK

אן אויפֿגעקומענער עושר האָט פֿײַנט
אן אלטן מאַן.

A parvenu detests an old man.
[because he has a long memory]
An oyfgekumener oysher hot faynt an altn man. IB

אז מען זיצט לעבן א רבֿ מיינט נאָך
ניט אז מ׳איז א רבֿ.

Sitting next to the rabbi is no guarantee of becoming one.
Az men zitst lebn a rov meynt nokh nit az m'iz a rov. AC

בײַ „בואי בשלום״ שטייט דער
אָרעמאַן אויבן אָן.

During Sabbath prayers, when the entire congregation turns its back to the altar, the pauper standing at the back finds himself in the front row.
Bay ''bo'i basholem'' shteyt der oreman oybn on.

דעם רבֿס טאָכטער טאָר ניט וואָס
דעם בעדערס טאָכטער מעג.

The rabbi's daughter is forbidden what the bath-house attendant's daughter is allowed.
Dem rovs tokhter tor nit vos dem beders tokhter meg. NS

די פּאָד-פּאַנעס זײַנען ערגער ווי די
פּאַנעס אַליין.

The underlings are worse than the masters.
Di pod-panes zaynen erger vi di panes aleyn. NS

חתן-כּלה זאָגן ניט ווי די מחותּנים
זאָלן זיך משׂמח זײַן.

Bride and groom don't tell the in-laws how to celebrate.
Khosn-kale zogn nit vi di mekhutonim zoln zikh mesameyekh zayn. AC

ניַין רבנים קענען קיין מנין ניט
מאַכן אָבער צען שוסטערס יאָ.

Nine rabbis can't convene a minyan but ten shoemakers can.
*Nayn rabonim kenen keyn minyen nit
makhn ober tsen shusters yo.* IB

אין באָד איז די טוקערין אויך אַ
פאַרשוין.

At the baths even the attendant is
a somebody.
In bod iz di tukerin oykh a parshoyn. IB

אָרעם און ריַיך ליגן אין דער ערד
ביַידע גליַיך.

When poor or rich die, in the
earth they equally lie.
*Orem un raykh lign in der erd beyde
glaykh.* IB

רב משה מעג, מאָשקע טאָר ניט.

Mr. Moses can, little Moses can't.
Reb moyshe meg, moshke tor nit. IB

וואָס העלפט מיַין פויליש רעדן אַז
מען לאָזט אין הויף ניט אַריַין?

What's the use of speaking Polish
if they don't let you in the door?
*Vos helft mayn poylish redn az men
lozt in hoyf nit arayn?* NS

וואָס איז דער חילוק ווען דער נאַר
שלאָגט אָדער דער חכם שלאָגט –
ווייי טוט עס דאָך.

What difference if a fool or a
clever man flogs you – it hurts
just the same.
*Vos iz der khilek ven der nar shlogt ode
der khokhem shlogt – vey tut es dokh.* N

STUBBORNNESS

אַן עקשן איז די גרעסטע קרענק.

Stubbornness is the greatest ill.
An akshn iz di greste krenk. P

עֶר שטעלט זיך מיטן קאָפּ אַראָפּ און די פֿים פֿאַרקערט!

He places himself head down and feet up!
Er shtelt zikh mitn kop arop un di fis farkert! IB

פֿאַר אַן עקשן איז קיין רפֿוּאָה ניטאָ.

There's no cure for stubbornness.
Far an akshn iz keyn refu'e nito. AC

וואָם מיינסטו מיט: ניין?

What do you mean when you say: no?
Vos meynstu mit: neyn? AC

SUCCESS

נצחון פֿאַרשיכּורט אָן וויַין.

Success dizzies without wine.
Nitsokhn farshikert on vayn. NS

אַז עם פֿירט זיך גליַיך איז מען ריַיך.

When things go without a hitch, you're rich.
Az es firt zikh glaykh iz men raykh. NS

עֶר לעבט ווי גאָט אין אָדעם!

He lives like God in Odessa.
[He's living the life of Riley.]
Er lebt vi got in odes. AC

„המבדיל בין קודש לחול" – אַז עם געראָט איז טאַקע וויַיל.

"He who distinguishes the sacred from the profane" – if it succeeds it's a gain.
"Hamavdil beyn koydesh lakhol" – az es gerot iz take voyl. IB

SUITABILITY

א בחור טאָר קיין שדכן ניט זיַין און
א הונט טאָר קיין קצב ניט זיַין.

A bachelor shouldn't be a match-maker and a dog shouldn't be a butcher.
*A bokher tor keyn shatkhn nit zayn
un a hunt tor keyn katsef nit zayn.* IB

א גאַנץ יאָר שיכור און פורים
ניכטער.

The whole year full of rye and on Purim dry.
[when it's appropriate to have a drink]
A gants yor shiker un purim nikhter. P

א הון וואָס קרייט, א גוי וואָס רעדט
ייִדיש און א ייִדענע וואָס לערנט
תורה איז ניט קיין גוטע סחורה.

A crowing hen, a Goy speaking Yiddish, and a woman studying Torah are not good commodities.
*A hun vos kreyt, a goy vos ret yidish
un a yidene vos lernt toyre iz nit
keyn gute skhoyre.* AC

א כשרער פויגל שטעלט זיך ניט
אויף א טריפה׳נעם חזיר.

A kosher bird doesn't settle on a treyf pig.
*A kosherer foygl shtelt zikh nit oyf a
treyfenem khazer.* IB

א שידוך זאָל מען טאָן אין דער היים
און גנב׳נען זאָל מען אין דער
פרעמד.

Matchmaking should be done at home and robberies far away.
*A shidekh zol men ton in der heym
un ganvenen zol men in der fremd.* IB

בעסער א פאַלשער 'גוט מאָרגן'
איידער אַן אמתער 'שוואַרץ יאָר'.

Better an insincere 'good morning' than a real 'go to hell.'
*Beser a falsher 'gut morgn' eyder an
emeser 'shvarts yor.'* NS

דאָס קינד איז געבוירן צו דער צייַט
נאָר די חופה האָט מען צו שפעט
געשטעלט.

The baby was born at the right time but the wedding was held too late.
*Dos kind iz geboyrn tsu der tsayt
nor di khupe hot men tsu shpet
geshtelt.* WZ

דרײַ זאַכן טויגן ניט: אַ פּויער אַ
חרוץ, אַן אָרעמער פּריץ און אַ
רב אַן עם-האָרץ.

Three things are unsuitable: a
diligent peasant, an impoverished
nobleman, and an ignorant rabbi.
*Dray zakhn toygn nit: a poyer a
khorets, an oremer porets un a rov
an amorets.* IB

עס איז ניטאָ קיין שלעכטער בראָנפֿן
פֿאַר אַ שיכּור, קיין שלעכטע מטבע
פֿאַר אַ סוחר און קיין מיאוסע
נקבֿה פֿאַר אַ נואף.

There's no such thing as bad
whisky to a drunkard, tainted
money to a merchant, or an ugly
woman to a lecher.
*Es iz nito keyn shlekhter bronfn far
a shiker, keyn shlekhte matbeye far
a soykher un keyn mi'ese nekeyve
far a noyef.* NS

עס פּאַסט װי אַ חזיר אוירינגלעך!

It's as suitable as earrings on a pig!
Es past vi a khazer oyringlekh! IF

עס פּאַסט װי אַ פּאַטש צו גוט שבת.

It's as fitting as a slap in answer
to a greeting.
Es past vi a patsh tsu gut shabes. AC

פֿאַר אַ קוש גיט מען ניט קיין ביס און
פֿאַר אַ ביס גיט מען ניט קיין קוש.

A kiss doesn't merit a bite and a
bite doesn't merit a kiss.
*Far a kush git men nit keyn bis un
far a bis git men nit keyn kush.* NS

אויב דער שוך פּאַסט,
קענסטו אים טראָגן.

If the shoe fits, wear it.
Oyb der shukh past, kenstu im trogn. P

שׂימחת-תּורה זײַנען אַלע שיכּורים
ניכטער.

On Simkhat-Torah all drunkards
become sober.
[when it's appropriate to take a drink]
*Simkhes-toyre zaynen ale shikurim
nikhter.* P

װוּ מען דאַרף האָבן זאַלץ טויג ניט קיין
שמאַלץ.

Where salt is needed shortening
won't do.
*Vu men darf hobn zalts toyg nit keyn
shmalts.* AC

TEACHERS

אַ מלמד – אַ ייִד וואָס האַנדלט
מיט גויים.

A Hebrew teacher – a Jew who deals with goyim.
A melamed – a yid vos handlt mit goyim. AC

אַז דער מלמד קריגט זיך מיט דער
ווײַב איז אָך און וויי צו די תלמידים.

When the teacher quarrels with his wife, the pupils suffer.
Az der melamed krigt zikh mit der vayb iz okh un vey tsu di talmidim. IB

פֿאַר דרײַ האָט נאָט אָנגענגרייט
אַ באַזונדערן גן-עדן: פֿאַר רבנים,
נאמנים און מלמדים – נאָר ער שטייט
נאָך, עד היום, ליידיק.

God has prepared a special paradise for three kinds of people: rabbis, the faithful, and teachers; however, to this day it's empty.
Far dray hot got ongegreyt a bazundern gan-eydn: far rebonim, nemonim un melamdim – nor er shteyt nokh, ad hayom, leydik. NS

קיין מלמדות וואַרפֿט מען ניט אַוועק.

Tutoring is not wasted.
Keyn melamdes varft men nit avek. IB

ווען דער תלמיד האָט זיך געשמדט
איז דער רבי דער משומד.

When the pupil turns apostate, the rabbi is blamed.
Ven der talmed hot zikh geshmat iz der rebe der meshumed. NS

דער מלמד אַרבעט מיטן טײַטל
און דער גביר מיטן בײַטל.

The teacher flogs with his stick
and the rich man with his wallet.
*Der melamed arbet mitn taytl un der
g'vir mitn baytl.* IB

TEMPTATION

אַ כּפּרה די כּהונה פֿאַר אַ שיין פּנים.

To hell with the priesthood for a
pretty face!
A kapore di kahune far a sheyn ponim! IB

אַן אָפֿענע טיר וועט אָנצינדן דעם
יצר-הרע אַפֿילו בײַ אַ צדיק.

An open door will tempt even a saint.
*An ofene tir vet ontsindn dem
yeytser-hore afile bay a tsadik.* AC

דעם אָרעמאַנס יצר-הרע איז אַ
סקאָרינקע ברויט.

The pauper's temptation is a crust
of bread.
*Dem oremans yeytser-hore iz a
skorinke broyt.* NS

דעם שכנס ווײַב איז שטענדיק מער
חניוודיק.

The neighbor's wife is always
more appealing.
*Dem shokhns vayb iz shtendik mer
kheynivdik.* AC

דער יצר-הרע האָט אים
אַרײַנגענאַרט אין אַ זאַק.

The evil inclination has tricked
him into a sack.
*Der yeytser-hore hot im arayngenart
in a zak.* NS

דער יצר איז אַ מצר.

Temptation brings tribulation.
Der yeytser iz a meytser. NS

פֿון טיי, תהילים און אַ שיינע
מיידל זאָגט מען זיך ניט אָפּ.

**Don't refuse a glass of tea,
Psalms, or a pretty girl.**
*Fun tey, tilim un a sheyne meydl
zogt men zikh nit op.* AC

ווען די אויגן וואָלטן ניט געזען
וואָלטן די הענט ניט גענומען.

**If the eyes wouldn't see, the hands
wouldn't take.**
*Ven di oygn voltn nit gezen voltn di
hent nit genumen.* AC

זײַ ניט דאָס וואָס דו ביסט.

Don't be what you are.
Zay nit dos vos du bist. P

THEFT

אַ גנבֿ ניט שיינע מתנות.

A thief gives handsome presents.
A ganef git sheyne matones. NS

אַ גנבֿ האָט אַ גוט האַרץ – ער
דערבאַרעמט זיך איבער יענעמס.

**A thief has a good heart – he
takes pity on other people's
possessions.**
*A ganef hot a gut harts – er der-
baremt zikh iber yenems.* AC

אַ גנבֿ האָט איין וועג, זײַנע
נאָכיאָגערס –
זיבן.

**A thief chooses one path, his pur-
suers confront seven.**
*A ganef hot eyn veg, zayne
nokhyogers – zibn.* C

אַ גנבֿ האָט לאַנגע הענט און
קורצע קעשענעס.

**A thief has long hands and short
pockets.**
*A ganef hot lange hent un kurtse
keshenes.* NS

אַ גנבֿ נעמט מיט די אויגן.

A thief takes with his eyes.
A ganef nemt mit di oygn. NS

אַז אַ גנבֿ גייט גנבֿענען בעט ער
אויך גאָט.

Before a thief goes stealing, he
also prays to God.
*Az a ganef geyt ganvenen bet er
oykh got.* AC

אַז מען נעמט שלאָגט מען איבער די
הענט.

If you grab, you'll get slapped.
Az men nemt shlogt men iber di hent. AC

בעסער מיט אַ היימישן גנבֿ
איידער מיט אַ פֿרעמדן רבֿ.

Better with a hometown thief than
with a strange rabbi.
*Beser mit a heymishn ganef eyder
mit a fremdn rov.* NS

דער גנבֿ פֿאַרדינט שנעלער דעם
רובל ווי דער קייסער מאַכט אים.

The thief earns his money faster
than the tsar can mint it.
*Der ganef fardint shneler dem rubl
vi der keyser makht im.* NS

דער גנבֿ איז ערלעך ווען גנבֿענען
איז שווערלעך.

A thief becomes honorable when
theft is not tolerable.
*Der ganef iz erlekh ven ganvenen iz
shverlekh.* AC

די גאַנצע וועלט איז איין גנבֿ.

The whole world is one thief.
Di gantse velt iz eyn ganef. NS

ער האָט אַוועקגעגנבֿעט דעם חומש
מיטן „לא תגנבֿ".

He stole the Bible containing:
"thou shalt not steal."
*Er hot avekgeganvet dem khumesh
mitn ''loy signoyv.''* NS

ער איז ניט קיין גנבֿ, נאָר אַז עס
לאָזט זיך, נעמט ער.

He's no thief – he only takes if it
happens to be lying there.
*Er iz nit keyn ganef, nor az es lozt
zikh, nemt er.* NS

ער שטאַמט פֿון ייחוס! ער איז דעם
אַלטן גנבֿס אַן אוראייניקל.

He has a noble pedigree! He is the
illustrious old thief's great-
grandson.
*Er shtamt fun yikhes! er iz dem altn
ganefs an ureynikl.* AC

ער איז אזא גנב, אז די אויערן זײַנען
בײַ אים ניט זיכער.

He's such a thief, his own ears
aren't safe.
*Er iz aza ganef, az di oyern zaynen
bay im nit zikher.* AC

עס איז גוט א ײדן א טובה צו טאָן.

It's good to do a Jew a favor.
[and relieve him of his possessions]
Es iz gut a yidn a toyve tsu ton. AC

עס וועט פֿון אים אויסוואַקסן א
רבֿ פֿון גנבֿים!

He'll grow up to be a rabbi of a thief
[la crème de la crème!]
*Es vet fun im oysvaksn a rov fun
ganovim!* AC

פֿאַר א גנבֿ טאָר מען קײן תּליה ניט
דערמאָנען.

Don't talk of the gallows in front
of a thief.
*Far a ganef tor men keyn tli'e nit
dermonen.* NS

גנבֿענען און ראָבעווען זאָל מען און
ערלעך זאָל מען זײַן.

Thieve and rob if you must but be
honorable.
*Ganvenen un robeven zol men un
erlekh zol men zayn.* AC

געבענטשט זײַנען די הענט וואָס
נעמען זיך אַלײן.

Blessed are the hands that help
themselves.
*Gebentsht zaynen di hent vos nemen
zikh aleyn.* AC

קלײנע גנבים הענגט מען, גרױסע
שענקט מען.

Petty thieves are hanged, major thieves are pardoned.
Kleyne ganovim hengt men, groyse shenkt men. AC

מיט אַ גנבֿ איז גוט צו האַנדלען.

It's good to do business with a thief.
Mit a ganef iz gut tsu handlen. NS

אױפֿן גנבֿ ברענט דאָס היטל.

On the thief's head the hat burns.
Oyfn ganef brent dos hitl. P

אױפֿן גנבֿ מיט אַ צילינדער ברענט
ניט דאָס היטל.

When the thief wears a silk top hat, it won't burn.
[A thief with important connections has no need to worry.]
Oyfn ganef mit a tsilinder brent nit dos hitl. NS

װען אַ גנבֿ קושט זאָל מען זיך די
צײן איבערצײלן.

When a thief kisses you, count your teeth.
Ven a ganef kusht zol men zikh di tseyn ibertseyln. AC

װען מען דאַרף האָבן אַ גנבֿ נעמט
מען אים פֿון דער תליה אַראָפּ.

When a thief is needed, he's taken even from the gallows.
Ven men darf hobn a ganef nemt men im fun der tli'e arop. IB

װעסטו גנבֿענען – װעסטו האָבן.

If you steal – you'll have.
Vestu ganvenen – vestu hobn. NS

װאָס איז קלענער פֿון אַ מױז מעג
מען עס טראָגן אַרױס.

What is smaller than a mouse may be carried from the house.
Vos iz klener fun a moyz meg men es trogn aroys. NS

THREATS

אַז מען קען ניט בײַסן זאָל מען ניט
װײַזן די צײן.

If you can't bite, don't show your teeth.
Az men ken nit baysn zol men nit vayzn di tseyn. NS

EXAMPLES

איך וועל אים דערלאַנגען אַז ער
וועט ניט וויסן ווי אַלט ער איז!

I'll give him so that he won't
remember how old he is!
*Ikh vel im derlangen az er vet nit
visn vi alt er iz!* AC

איך וועל אים געבן אַז ער וועט דערזען
די עלטער באָבע פאַר די אויגן.

I'll give him so that he'll see his
great-grandmother before his eyes!
*Ikh vel im gebn az er vet derzen di
elter bobe far di oygn!* AC

איך וועל אים באַגראָבן אין דער ערד
ווי אַן אוצר!

I'll bury him in the ground like a
treasure!
*Ikh vel im bagrobn in der erd vi an
oytser!* MS

איך וועל אים געבן פון אַ שטיין
די וייכע.

I'll give him the soft center of a stone
*Ikh vel im gebn fun a shteyn di
veykhe!* NS

איך וועל אים געבן קדחת מיט כשרן
פאָדעם!

I'll give him convulsions with
kosher thread!
*Ikh vel im gebn kadokhes mit
koshern fodem!* NS

TIME

אַ שעה פאַר שבת איז נאָך אַלץ
ניט שבת.

An hour before Sabbath isn't yet
Sabbath.
*A sho far shabes iz nokh alts nit
shabes.* IB

אַ זייגער מאַכער איז אַ גנב.

A watchmaker is a thief.
A zeyger makher iz a ganef. NS

אַן איבערגעוואַקסענע מויד איז ווי
אַ פאַראַיאָריקער לוח.

A girl past her prime is like an
outdated calendar.
*An ibergevaksene moyd iz vi a
farayoriker lu'ekh.* NS

אַלץ איז גוט נאָר אין דער צײַט.

Everything is good in its time.
Alts iz gut nor in der tsayt. P

ביז מען דערלעבט די נחמה קען
אַרויס די נשמה.

**Before comfort comes, the soul
succumbs.**
*Biz men derlebt di nekhome ken
aroys di neshome.* AC

דעם ייִדן פֿעלט תּמיד אַ טאָג צו
דער וואָך.

**A Jew is always short a day in the
week.**
*Dem yidn felt tomed a tog tsu der
vokh.* AC

די צײַט איז דער בעסטער רופֿא.

Time is the best healer.
Di tsayt iz der bester royfe. AC

עס וועט אויסהאַלטן פֿון
אסתּר-תּענית ביז פּורים.

**It will last from the Fast of Esther
to the onset of Purim.**
[not very long]
*Es vet oys'haltn fun ester-tones biz
purim.* P

ניט אַלע קלוגע זײַנען גלײַך: איינער
איז קלוג פֿאַר דער צײַט, אַ
צווייטער נאָך דער צײַט און אַ
דריטער – צו דער צײַט.

**Not all smart people are equal:
some are smart too soon, some too
late, and some – at the right time.**
*Nit ale kluge zaynen glaykh: eyner iz
klug far der tsayt, a tsveyter nokh
der tsayt un a driter – tsu der tsayt.* AC

CHANGING TIME

אַ נײַער מלך מיט נײַע גזרות, אַ נײַ
יאָר מיט נײַע עבֿירות.

**A new ruler with decrees anew, a
new year with new sins to do.**
*A nayer meylekh mit naye gezeyres,
a nay yor mit naye aveyres.* NS

אַנדערע צײַטן, אַנדערע לײַטן.

Other times, other people.
Andere tsaytn, andere laytn. NS

די צײַט קען אַלץ איבערמאַכן.

Time alters everything.
Di tsayt ken alts ibermakhn. AC

צייטן בייטן זיך.

Times change.
Tsaytn baytn zikh. AC

DELAYED TIME

מען פֿאַרשפּעטיקט ניט חתונה
האָבן און שטאַרבן.

It's never too late for marrying or
dying.
*Men farshpetikt nit khasene hobn un
shtarbn.* NS

אָפּלייגן איז נאָר גוט קעז.

Delay is only good for making cheese.
Opleygn iz nor gut kez. IB

FUTURE TIME

ביי טאָג וואָלט מען געוואָלט אַז עס
זאָל זיין נאַכט און ביי נאַכט – אַז
עס זאָל זיין מאָרגן.

If it's day, people want it to be
night; if it's night, they want it to
be tomorrow.
*Bay tog volt men gevolt az es zol
zayn nakht un bay nakht – az es zol
zayn morgn.* AC

איטלעכער מאָרגן ברענגט זיינע
זאָרגן.

Every morrow brings its sorrow.
Itlekher morgn brengt zayne zorgn. NS

PASSAGE

אַ גרויסער טאָג – און גייט אויך
אַוועק.

A great day – and it also ends.
A groyser tog – un geyt oykh avek. AC

דאָס גוטע און דאָס שלעכטע איז
ניט אויף אייביק.

Neither the good nor the bad lasts
for ever.
*Dos gute un dos shlekhte iz nit oyf
eybik.* AC

היינט רויט, מאָרגן טויט.

Today red, tomorrow dead.
Haynt royt, morgn toyt. AC

ניטאָ קיין אייביקע זאַך אויף דער
וועלט.

Nothing lasts for ever.
Nito keyn eybike zakh oyf der velt. AC

PAST TIME

א טאָג מיט א נאַכט א מעת-לעת
פֿאַרבראַכט.

A night and a day and twenty-four
hours went away.
A tog mit a nakht a mesles
farbrakht. NS

אַמאָל איז געווען און היַינט איז
ניטאָ.

Once it was, today no more.
Amol iz geven un haynt iz nito. P

אַז מען קומט ניט צו דער ציַיט מוז
מען עסן וואָס איבעריק בליַיבט.

If you don't come on time, what
you eat won't be prime.
Az men kumt nit tsu der tsayt muz
men esn vos iberik blaybt. NS

אַז מען קומט נאָך עלינו שפּיַיט
מען אויס און מען גייט אַהיים.

If you come after the prayer, you
go home with a stomach that's
bare.
Az men kumt nokh aleynu shpayt
men oys un men geyt aheym. AC

דער מענטש איז וואָס ער איז אָבער
ניט וואָס ער איז געווען.

A person is what he is but no
longer what he used to be.
Der mentsh iz vos er iz ober nit vos
er iz geven. NS

פֿאַרלאָרענע יאָרן איז ערגער ווי
פֿאַרלאָרענע געלט.

Lost years are worse than lost money.
Farlorene yorn iz erger vi farlorene
gelt.

PRESENT TIME

באַק ווי לאַנג דער אויוון באַקט.

Bake as long as the oven is hot.
Bak vi lang der oyvn bakt. NS

בעסער היַינט אַן איי איידער מאָרגן
אַ האָן.

Better an egg today than a hen
tomorrow.
Beser haynt an ey eyder morgn a
hon. NS

ניס בוימל אויפֿן לאָמפ אַזוי לאַנג
ווי ער ברענט נאָך.

Pour oil on the wick as long as it
burns.
*Gis boyml oyfn lomp azoy lang vi er
brent nokh.* NS

שמיד, קלאַפ דאָס אײַזן כּל־זמן
ס׳איז הייס.

Blacksmith, strike while the iron is
hot.
*Shmid, klap dos ayzn kolzman s'iz
heys.* NS

TORAH

בעסער לערנען אַ בלאַט גמרא איידער
צו זײַן פֿאַר פֿאָניע די כּפרה.

Studying Talmud is better by far
than serving in the army of the
tsar.
*Beser lernen a blat gemore eyder tsu
zayn far fonye di kapore.* AC

די תּורה לײַכט, די תּורה ברענט,
אָבער וואַרעמען וואַרעמט דאָס
קערבל.

The Torah lights, the Torah
shines, but only money warms.
*Di toyre laykht, di toyre brent, ober
varemen varemt dos kerbl.* NS

אין דער הייליקער תּורה געפֿינט מען
אַלץ, אפֿילו אַ דאַרע וואַנץ.

In the holy Torah you can find
everything, even a skinny insect.
*In der heyliker toyre gefint men alts,
afile a dare vants.* NS

מיט תּורה ווערט מען אין ערגעץ
ניט פֿאַרפֿאַלן.

With Torah you don't get lost.
*Mit toyre vert men in ergets nit
farfaln.* NS

רש״י מאַכט און מאַכט און מען גייט
פֿאָרט נאַקעט און באָרוועס.

Rashi discourses and discourses
and still we go around naked and
barefoot.
*Rashi makht un makht un men geyt
fort naket un borves.* AC

תּורה איז די בעסטע סחורה.

Torah-wise is the best merchandise.
Toyre iz di beste skhoyre. P

ווו תורה דאָרט איז חכמה.

In Torah is wisdom.
Vu toyre dort iz khokhme. IB

TRAVEL

אַז דער שטיין לינט אויף איין אָרט
ווערט ער אויך באַוואָקסן מיט גראָז.

When the stone remains in one spot, it also gets covered with moss.
Az der shteyn ligt oyf eyn ort vert er oykh bavaksn mit groz. NS

אַז מען האָט ניט קיין סום גייט מען
צו פוס.

If you have no horse, you walk, of course.
Az men hot nit keyn sus geyt men tsu fus. IB

אַז מען קומט איבער די פּלאַנקן קריגט
מען אַנדערע געדאַנקען.

When you've climbed the fence, other thoughts commence.
Az men kumt iber di plankn krigt men andere gedanken. NS

אַז מען זיצט אין דער היים צעריַיסט
מען ניט קיין שיך (שטיוול).

If you stay at home you don't wear out your shoes (boots).
Az men zitst in der heym tserayst men nit keyn shikh (shtivl). P

דער שענסטער שפּאַציר איז פאַר
דיַין אייגענער טיר.

The nicest tour is in front of your own door.
Der shenster shpatsir iz far dayn eygener tir. N

דאָרט איז גוט וווּ מיר זײַנען ניטאָ.

Where we aren't, it's good to be.
Dort iz gut vu mir zaynen nito. NS

אײדער אַזוי צו פאָרן איז שוין
בעסער צו גיין צו פום.

Rather than ride like that [in a hearse], it's better to walk.
Eyder azoy tsu forn iz shoyn beser tsu geyn tsu fus. P

אָװע-טאָװע, פון נסיעות האָט מען
מעשיות.

No matter where you roam, you always bring a story home.
Ove-tove, fun nesi'es hot men mayses. AC

אויף ניט גיין און ניט פאָרן זאָל מען
קיין חרטה ניט האָבן.

Don't regret not travelling.
Oyf nit geyn un nit forn zol men keyn kharote nit hobn. NS

ווען מען פאָרט אַרויס ווייסט מען, ווען
מען קומט צוריק ווייסט מען ניט.

We know when we start a trip, we don't know when we'll return.
Ven men fort aroys veyst men, ven men kumt tsurik veyst men nit. NS

וווּ מען פאָרט אַרײַן, דאָרט מוז מען
בלײַבן.

Wherever you stray, that's where you stay.
Vu men fort arayn, dort muz men blaybn. NS

זיצטו גיט, טאָ ריק זיך ניט.

If you're well situated, don't move.
Zitstu git, to rik zikh nit. NS

TROUBLES

אַ פֿרעמדע צרה איז קיין ציבעלע
ניט ווערט.

Someone else's troubles aren't worth even an onion.
A fremde tsore iz keyn tsibele nit vert. AC

אַ צעריסן געמיט איז שווער צו היילן.

It's hard to heal a broken spirit.
A tserisn gemit iz shver tsu heyln. AC

א גאנץ יאר האַדעוועט מען די כפרה
און ערב יום-כיפור פליט זי אַוועק.

The whole year one fattens the sacrificial bird and on the eve of Yom Kippur it flies away.
[Refers to traditional ritual observed prior to commencement of High Holy Days.]
A gants yor hodevet men di kapore un erev yomkiper flit zi avek. IB

אַז עס איז אַזוי גוט פּאַרװאָס איז
אַזוי שלעכט?

If things are so good, how come they're so bad?
Az es iz azoy gut farvos iz azoy shlekht? AC

אַז עס קומט פּורים פאַרנעמסט מען
אַלע יסורים.

When Purim starts, we forget all our smarts.
Az es kumt purim fargest men ale yesurim. AC

אַז מען געװײנט זיך צו צו צרות
לעבט מען מיט זיי אין פֿריידן.

If you're accustomed to troubles, you live with them happily.
Az men geveynt zikh tsu tsu tsores lebt men mit zey in freydn. AC

אַז מען זאָל אויפֿהענגען אױף דער
װאַנט אַלע פּעקלעך צרות װאָלט זיך
איטלעכער געכאפט זײַן אייגנס.

If you could hang on the wall all the world's packs of troubles, everyone would grab for his own.
Az men zol oyfhengen oyf der vant ale peklekh tsores volt zikh itlekher gekhapt zayn eygns. P

בעסער צען קלײנע דאנות איידער
אײן גרוויסע.

Better ten small worries than one big one.
Beser tsen kleyne dayges eyder eyn groyse. IB

די גרעסטע צרה – אַ וויַיב אַ כלבֿטע.

The worst misery – a wife a bitch!
Di greste tsore – a vayb a klafte! AC

דער בראָך זאָל זיַין פֿאַר אַלע בראָך!

This disaster should make up for all disasters!
Der brokh zol zayn far ale brekh! IB

דער מענטש האָט צוויי ברירות:
אָדער קריעה רײַסן אָדער
פֿאַרשװאַרצט װערן.

A person has two choices: either
tear one's clothing in mourning or
be miserable.

*Der mentsh hot tsvey breyres: oder
kri'e raysn oder farshvartst vern.* IB

ער האָט צו זינגען און צו זאָגן!

He's got a lot to sing and say!

[He's got no end of troubles. 'To sing and say'
derives from the Middle Ages when troubadours
sang and recited stories and poems.]

Er hot tsu zingen un tsu zogn! P

עס דאַכט זיך אַז בײַ יענעם לאַכט
זיך, קומסט צו דער טיר ערגער װי
בײַ מיר.

Others are happier it seems to me,
but up close they're worse off than
me.

*Es dakht zikh az bay yenem lakht
zikh, kumst tsu der tir erger vi bay
mir.* SK

עס גייט מיר װי אַ צדיק אויף דער
װעלט!

I'm doing well – like a saint in
this world!

Es geyt mir vi a tsadik oyf der velt! P

עס איז אַזוי לאַנג װי דער
ייִדישער גלות.

It's as long as the Jewish exile!

Es iz azoy lang vi der yidisher goles! ℞

עס איז װייך געבעט אָבער האַרט
צו שלאָפֿן.

The bed is soft but it's hard to sleep

Es iz veykh gebet ober hart tsu shlofn.

אײנע קלאָגט װאָס די פֿערל זײַנען
שיטער, די צװייטע קלאָגט װאָס
דאָס לעבן איז ביטער.

One complains that her pearls are
few, another complains that her
life is a bitter brew.

*Eyne klogt vos di perl zaynen shiter,
di tsveyte klogt vos dos lebn iz biter.* ℞

פֿרעמדע צרות קען מען
אַריבערטראָגן.

Other people's troubles are bearable

Fremde tsores ken men aribertrogn. ℞

איבערגעקומענע צרות איז גוט צו
דערצײלן.

Past troubles are good to narrate.

*Ibergekumene tsores iz gut tsu dert-
seyln.* AC

געהאַקטע לעבער איז בעסער ווי
געהאַקטע צרות.

Lots of food is better than lots of troubles.
Gehakte leber iz beser vi gehakte tsores. P

קיינער ווייסט ניט וועמען דער שוך
דריקט.

No one knows whom the shoe pinches.
Keyner veyst nit venem der shukh drikt. AC

מען דאַרף נאָר בעטן אויף יאָרן,
צרות וועלן שוין ניט פֿעלן.

Just pray for years, there'll be no lack of troubles.
Men darf nor betn oyf yorn, tsores veln shoyn nit feln. AC

מען לאָזט ניט לעבן!

They don't let you live!
Men lozt nit lebn! P

מען וואָלט געקענט לעבן נאָר מען
לאָזט ניט!

We could live if only they'd let us!
Men volt gekent lebn nor men lozt nit! AC

נייע וועלטן – נייע קרענקן!

New worlds – new troubles!
Naye veltn – naye krenkn! IF

אויף אַ פּאַרכעוואַטן פֿערד
שטעלן זיך אַלע פֿליגן.

On a scabby horse all the flies congregate.
Oyf a parkhevatn ferd shteln zikh ale flign. AC

אויף מאָרגן זאָל גאָט זאָרגן!

For tomorrow let God worry!
Oyf morgn zol got zorgn! P

שלאָף, וועסטו די צרות פֿאַרגעסן!

Sleep, so you can forget your troubles!
Shlof, vestu di tsores fargesn! IB

שׂימחת דאַרף מען מאַכן, צרות קומען
אַליין אין הויז אַריַין.

Celebrations have to be made, troubles come by themselves.
Simkhes darf men makhn, tsores kumen aleyn in hoyz arayn. AC

צרות זײַנען פֿאַר מענטשן ווי
זשאַווער צו אײַזן.

Troubles are to people like rust to iron.
Tsores zaynen far mentshn vi zhaver tsu ayzn. NS

צרות מיט יויך איז גרינגער צו
פֿאַרטראָגן ווי צרות אָן יויך.

Troubles with soup are easier to bear than troubles without soup.
Tsores mit yoykh iz gringer tsu far-trogn vi tsores on yoykh. NS

צרות טויגן אויף כּפּרות.

Troubles suffice for sacrifice.
Tsores toygn oyf kapores. IB

צום שטיין זאָל מען קלאָגן נאָר ניט
בײַ זיך אַליין זאָל מען טראָגן.

Tell your troubles to a stone, don't keep them to yourself alone.
Tsum shteyn zol men klogn nor nit bay zikh aleyn zol men trogn. NS

ווען ניט די רפֿואה וואָלט ניט געווען
די קרענק.

If not for the remedy, we wouldn't have the problem.
Ven nit di refu'e volt nit geven di krenk. AC

ווערעם עסן טויטערהייט און דאגות
עסן לעבעדיקערהייט.

Worms gnaw the dead and worries gnaw at the living.
Verem esn toyterheyt un dayges esn lebedikerheyt. NS

ווײ צו אַזאַ לעבן וואָס טרײסט מיטן
טויט!

Woe to such a life that is
comforted by death!
Vey tsu aza lebn vos treyst mitn toyt! NS

יעדער מענטש האָט זײַן פּעקל.

Every person has his own load to
carry.
Yeder mentsh hot zayn pekl. P

יעדער מאָרגן ברענגט זיך זאָרגן.

Every morrow brings its sorrow.
Yeder morgn brengt zikh zorgn. P

יענעמס מכּה איז ניט מײַן רפֿואה.

Someone else's ailment isn't my cure.
Yenems make iz nit mayn refu'e. P

TRUTH

אַ האַלבער אמת איז אַ גאַנצער ליגן.

A half-truth is a whole lie.
A halber emes iz a gantser lign. NS

אַ ליגן טאָר מען ניט זאָגן, דעם אמת
איז מען ניט מחויב צו זאָגן.

A lie you must not tell, the whole
truth you're not obliged to tell.
*A lign tor men nit zogn, dem emes iz
men nit mekhu'yev tsu zogn.* AC

אַז מען זאָגט דעם אמת פֿאַרשפּאָרט
מען צו שווערן.

If you tell the truth you don't
have to swear.
*Az men zogt dem emes farshport
men tsu shvern.* NS

דער שפּיגל זאָגט אויס דעם אמת.

The mirror reveals the truth.
Der shpigl zogt oys dem emes. NS

דער אמת האָט אלע מעלות אָבער
ער איז אַ שעמעוודיקער.

The truth has virtues but it's shy.
*Der emes hot ale mayles ober er iz
a shemevdiker.* NS

דער אמת האָט פֿיס – איז ער אַנטלאָפֿן,
דער שקר האָט קיין פֿיס ניט – איז
ער געבליבן.

The truth has legs and runs away,
the lie has no legs and must stay.
*Der emes hot fis iz er antlofn, der
sheker hot keyn fis nit iz er geblibn.* NS

דער אמת קומט אַרויס ווי בּוימל
אויפֿן וואַסער.

Truth surfaces like oil on water.
*Der emes kumt aroys vi boyml oyfn
vaser.* P

דער שפֿיץ קומט אַרויס הײַנט
אָדער מאָרגן.

The point will surface either today
or tomorrow.
*Der shpits kumt aroys haynt oder
morgn.* AC

דער רמז שלאָנט שטאַרקער ווי דער
אמת.

Insinuation hits harder than the
plain truth.
*Der remez shlogt shtarker vi der
emes.* NS

די טייג איז זיכער ניט גער.טן אַז
דער בעקער גיט עס צו.

The dough must really be bad if
the baker admits it.
*Di teyg iz zikher nit gerotn az der
beker git es tsu.* AC

אמת איז נאָר בּײַ גאָט און בּײַ מיר
אַ בּיסל.

The truth is known only to God
and to me, a little.
*Emes iz nor bay got un bay mir a
bisl.* NS

הימל און ערד האָבּן געשוווירן אַז
קיין זאַך זאָל ניט זײַן פֿאַרלוירן.

Heaven and earth have assured
that the truth will not be
obscured.
*Himl un erd hobn geshvoyrn az keyn
zakh zol nit zayn farloyrn.* IB

אָט דאָ ליגט דער הונט בּאַנראָבּן!

Right here is where the dog lies
buried!
Ot do ligt der hunt bagrobn! P

אויף אַן אמת איז גוט עדות צו זאָגן.

It's good to be a witness to the
truth.
Oyf an emes iz gut eydes tsu zogn. IB

ווייניקער אַ וואָרט אַבּי דעם אמת.

A word less, as long as it's the
truth.
Veyniker a vort abi dem emes. AC

VALUE

א גרױסער עולם און ניטאָ קײן
מענטש.

A big crowd and not one notable.
*A groyser oylem un nito keyn
mentsh.* NS

אלע מעלות בײַ איינעם איז ניטאָ
בײַ קײנעם.

Perfection anywhere is very rare.
*Ale mayles bay eynem iz nito bay
keynem.* NS

אַז עס רײַסט זיך אָפּ אַ צװײַגל װײנט
מען, אַז עס פֿאַלט אַ בױם
שװײַגט מען.

When a branch snaps, we cry;
when a tree falls, we remain
silent.
*Az es rayst zikh op a tsvaygl veynt
men, az es falt a boym shvaygt men.* IB

דאָס מאָגערע פֿון די פֿעטע איז
אױך גוט.

The lean of the fat is also good.
Dos mogere fun di fete iz oykh gut. NS

עס האָט אַזאַ װערט װי אַן
אָפּגעשלאָגענע הושענא.

It's worth as much as a frayed
branch.
*Es hot aza vert vi an opgeshlogene
heshayne.* IB

עס האָט מײן באָבעם טעם!

It's got my grandmother's taste!
[It's tasteless.]
Es hot mayn bobes tam! P

עם איז ווערט אַ זעץ אין דר'ערד!

It's worth a stomp on the ground!
Es iz vert a zets in dr'erd! P

עם איז ווערט דער באָבעס ירושה!

It's worth grandma's legacy.
[It's worthless.]
Es iz vert der bobes yerushe. P

עם איז ווערט חי קאַק (פּאָלעווינע)!

It's worthless (by half)!
['Kak' is an acronym for katarinen kronen, a
gold coin in the Austro-Hungarian empire,
later devalued.]
Es iz vert khay kak (polevine)! P

פֿון אַ חזיר אַ האָר איז אויך גוט.

A hair from a pig also has value.
Fun a khazer a hor iz oykh gut. IB

מײַן נשמה איז אויך אויף דעם באַרג
סיני געשטאַנען.

My soul also stood at Mount Sinai!
*Mayn neshome iz oykh oyf dem barg
sinay geshtanen!* IB

מען קען אים אין אַ פֿינגער
אַרײַנוויקלען.

You can wrap him up in a finger.
Men ken im in a finger araynviklen. IB

אומזיסט קריגט מען נאָר מיסט.

There's no charge for garbage.
Umzist krigt men nor mist. NS

WEALTH

אַ גאָלדענע פֿען איז ניט קיין
פֿאַרזיכערונג אויף שיין
שרײַבן.

A golden pen is no guarantee for good writing.
A goldene pen iz nit keyn farzikherung oyf sheyn shraybn. NS

אַ נגידס טאָכטער איז תמיד שיין.

A rich man's daughter is, of course, beautiful.
A nogeds tokhter iz tomed sheyn. NS

אַ ייִד אַ גבֿיר צאַצקעט זיך מיט זײַן געשוויר.

A rich man can afford to fuss over every pimple.
A yid a gvir tsatsket zikh mit zayn geshvir. AC

אַרום אַ פֿעטן טאָפּ איז זיך גוט צו רײַבן.

Near a full pot it's good to stay.
Arum a fetn top iz zikh gut tsu raybn. IB

אַז מען גנבֿעט אַ סך אייער קען מען אויך ווערן אַ נגיד.

If you steal enough eggs, you can also become rich.
Az men ganvet a sakh eyer ken men oykh vern a noged. NS

אַז מען האָט אַ נײַ קלייד אויף דער וואַנט איז דאָס אַלטע קלייד קיין שאַנד.

With a new dress on the wall the old is no disgrace at all.
Az men hot a nay kleyd oyf der vant iz dos alte kleyd keyn shand. NS

אַז מען זיצט אין אַ הייסער וואַנע
מיינט מען אַז די גאַנצע שטאָט
איז וואַרעם.

If you sit in a hot bath, you think the whole town is warm.
Az men zitst in a heyser vane meynt men az di gantse shtot iz varem. NS

אַז מען איז אפֿשר רײַך איז מען
געוויס קלוג.

If you are even suspected of being rich, you are, of course, assumed to be clever.
Az men iz efsher raykh iz men gevis klug. NS

בײַ אַ שווערן וואָגן איז גרינג צו
פֿוס צו גיין.

It's easy to walk alongside a loaded wagon.
Bay a shvern vogn iz gring tsu fus tsu geyn. AC

בעסער אַ רײַכן שכן אײדער אַן
אָרעמען בעל־הבית.

Better a rich neighbor than a poor landlord.
Beser a raykhn shokhn eyder an oremen balebos. NS

דער אָרעמאַן האָט ווייניק פֿײַנט,
דער רײַכער האָט ווייניק פֿרײַנד.

The pauper has few enemies, the rich man few friends.
Der oreman hot veynik faynt, der raykher hot veynik fraynd. NS

דעם נגיד פֿאַסט אַלץ.

The rich can get away with anything.
Dem noged past alts. AC

דער עושר בלאָזט זיך און דער
אָרעמאַן ווערט געשוואָלן.

The rich bloat from plenty, the
poor from hunger.
*Der oysher blozt zikh un der oreman
vert geshvoln.* NS

דער עושר האָט קיין יושר.

The rich man's way is without fair
play.
Der oysher hot keyn yoysher. P

דאָס לעצטע העמד זאָל מען פאַרזעצן
אַבי אַ גביר צו זײַן.

Pawn the shirt off your back if it
will make you a millionaire.
*Dos letste hemd zol men farzetsn abi
a gvir tsu zayn.* AC

ער איז אַ גביר – ער פאַרמאָגט אַ
גאַנץ קעפל קרויט!

He's rich – he owns a whole head
of cabbage!
*Er iz a gvir – er farmogt a gants
kepl kroyt!* AC

עס איז גוט צו זײַן אַ גביר – דער
רב אַליין מאַכט דעם הספד.

It's good to be rich – the rabbi
himself delivers your eulogy.
*Es iz gut tsu zayn a gvir – der rov
aleyn makht dem hesped.* AC

פֿון נגידים קומען אַרויס קליינע
נגידימלעך.

The rich breed more rich.
*Fun negidim kumen aroys kleyne
negidimlekh.* AC

מען זאָגט אָרעמעלײַט ווײַל די רײַכע
זײַנען גאָר קיין לײַט ניט.

One says: 'poor people' because
the rich aren't even people.
*Men zogt oremelayt vayl di raykhe
zaynen gor keyn layt nit.* AC

ניט דער רײַכער צאָלט, דער
ערלעכער צאָלט.

The rich don't necessarily pay, the
honest do.
Nit der raykher tsolt, der erlekher tsolt. NS

תכריכים מאַכט מען אָן קעשענעם.

Shrouds are made without pockets.
Takhrikhim makht men on keshenes. P

ווען עס גייט גלײַך ווערט מען רײַך.

When things go without a hitch,
you get rich.
Ven es geyt glaykh vert men raykh. NS

ווען מען דאַרף ניט עסן וואָלטן אלע
געווען רײַך.

If we didn't need food, we'd all be
rich.

*Ven men darf nit esn voltn ale geven
raykh.* NS

וואָס קומט אַרױס פֿון זילבערנעם
בעכער אַז ער איז פֿול מיט
טרערן?

What use is a silver cup if it's full
of tears?

*Vos kumt aroys fun zilbernem bekher
az er iz ful mit trern?* IB

ווו פֿלייש און פֿיש איז אַ
פֿריילעכער טיש.

Lots of food creates a good mood.

Vu fleysh un fish iz a freylekher tish. NS

יידישע עשירות איז וי וי שניי אין
מאַרץ.

Jewish wealth is like snow in
March.

Yidishe ashires iz vi shney in marts. NS

WICKEDNESS

אַ געוואָרענער איז ערגער ווי אַ
געבוירענער.

Wicked by choice is worse than
wicked by birth.

A gevorener iz erger vi a geborener. AC

אַ משומד איז ערגער פֿאַר אַ גוי.

An apostate is worse than a Goy.

A meshumed iz erger far a goy. NS

אַז דער רשע קוקט אין וואַסער
פּגרן די פֿיש.

When an evil-doer looks in the
water, the fish die.

*Az der roshe kukt in vaser peygern
di fish.* NS

דער טאַטע דײַנער איז אַ גוטער
מענטש נאָר דער זון זײַנער איז
אַ פּאַסקודניאַק.

Your father is a fine person but
his son is a scoundrel.

*Der tate dayner iz a guter mentsh
nor der zun zayner iz a paskudni'ak.* AC

ער איז אַ דימאַנט: מען קען מיט
אים גלאָז שנײַדן!

He's a diamond: you can cut glass
with him!

*Er iz a dimant: men ken mit im gloz
shnaydn!* P

ווער עס גראָבט אַ גרוב פֿאַר יענעם
פֿאַלט אַליין אַרײַן.

Whoever digs a pit for others falls
into it himself.
*Ver es grobt a grub far yenem falt
aleyn arayn.* NS

ער איז אַ גוטער: ער שלאָגט זיך ניט!

He's a good person: he doesn't
fight with himself.
Er iz a guter: er shlogt zikh nit! NS

עס קען האַרט ווערן דער קאָפּ
פֿון זײַנע טובֿות.

Your head can get hardened from
his favors.
*Es ken hart vern der kop fun zayne
toyves.* P

איך קום פֿריער, דערנאָך און
שפּעטער אויך!

I come first, last, and always!
*Ikh kum fri'er, dernokh un shpeter
oykh!* IB

אויף אַ שלאַנג טאָר מען קיין
רחמנות ניט האָבן.

Don't take pity on a snake.
*Oyf a shlang tor men keyn
rakhmones nit hobn.* IB

WISDOM

אַ קלוגער ווייסט וואָס ער זאָגט, אַ
נאַר זאָגט וואָס ער ווייסט.

A wise person knows what he
says, a fool says what he knows.
*A kluger veyst vos er zogt, a nar
zogt vos er veyst.* AC

אַ קינדערשער שׂכל איז אויך אַ שׂכל.

A child's wisdom is also wisdom.
A kindersher seykhl iz oykh a seykhl. AC

בעסער אַ גאַנצער נאַר איידער אַ
האַלבער חכם.

Better a complete fool than half a
sage.
*Beser a gantser nar eyder a halber
khokhem.* NS

דער קלינסטער מענטש באַנאַרישט
זיך.

The wisest person can commit folly.
Der kligster mentsh banarisht zikh. P

דער שׂכל פאָרט אויף אָקסן.

Wisdom travels by oxen. [slowly]
Der seykhl fort oyf oksn. NS

דער תלמיד-חכם וייסט וואָס עם
פעלט אים נאָך צו וויסן.

A learned person knows that he
lacks knowledge.
*Der talmed-khokhem veyst vos es felt
im nokh tsu visn.* AC

די קלוגע גייען צופוס און די
נאַראָנים פאָרן.

Wise people go on foot and fools
ride. [A comment on the success of fools.]
*Di kluge geyen tsu fus un di
naronim forn.* IB

איטלעכער איז קלוג אין די אייגענע
אויגן.

Everyone is wise in his own eyes.
Itlekher iz klug in di eygene oygn. NS

קאָפ, גיב שׂכל!

Head, give wisdom!
Kop, gib seykhl! AC

ניט פאַר קלוגע איז געלט, ניט פאַר
שיינע איז קליידער.

Not all the wise have money nor
all the beautiful nice clothes.
*Nit far kluge iz gelt, nit far sheyne
iz kleyder.* NS

שׂכל קריגט מען ניט אויף דער בערזע.

Wisdom can't be bought at the
exchange.
Seykhl krigt men nit oyf der berzhe. NS

שׂכל און חרטה קומען צו שפעט.

Wisdom and regret come too late.
Seykhl un kharote kumen tsu shpet. IB

WITNESSES

אַ בלעכער און אַ קוימען קערער נעמט
מען ניט פֿאַר קיין עדות.

Don't use a tinsmith or a chimney-
sweep as witnesses.
*A blekher un a koymen kerer nemt
men nit far keyn eydes.* NS

אַז דער מענטש פֿאַלט, זאָגט אַפֿילו
די שפֿין אויף דער וואַנט עדות
קעגן אים.

When a person stumbles, even a
spider on the wall will testify
against him.
*Az der mentsh falt, zogt afile di
shpin oyf der vant eydes kegn im.* IB

פֿאַר אַ שטומען (בלינדן) עדות
לויפֿן גנבֿים ניט אַוועק.

From a mute (blind) witness
thieves don't run.
*Far a shtumen (blindn) eydes loyfn
ganovim nit avek.* NS

גאָט איז איינער, וואָס ער טוט זעט
קיינער.

God is one and always was, none
can witness what He does.
Got iz eyner, vos er tut zet keyner. NS

אויף אַן אמת איז גוט עדות צו זאָגן.

It's easy to be a witness to the
truth.
Oyf an emes iz gut eydes tsu zogn. IB

ווער עס עסט אויף דער גאַס קען
קיין עדות ניט זאָגן.

If you eat in the street, you can't
bear witness.
*Ver es est oyf der gas ken keyn
eydes nit zogn.* NS

WOMEN

אַ פֿרוי ברענגט אַרויס מער אין אַ
קרעכץ איידער אַ מאַנספּאַרשוין
אין אַ גאַנצן „על חטא".

A woman conveys more in a sign
than a man in an entire prayer of
atonement.
*A froy brengt aroys mer in a krekhts
eyder a mansparshoyn in a gantsn
"al khet."* NS

אַ פֿרױ איז װי אַן איבערזעצונג –
נישט שײן װען געטרײַ און נישט
געטרײַ װען שײן.

**A woman is like a translation –
not beautiful when faithful and not
faithful when beautiful.**

*A froy iz vi an iberzetsung – nisht
sheyn ven getray un nisht getray ven
sheyn.* AC

אַ פֿרױ זאָגט ליגן אַפֿילו װען זי
שװײַגט.

A woman lies even when she is silent.

A froy zogt lign afile ven zi shvaygt. AC

אַ געמאַכטע מכשפֿה איז ערגער װי
אַ געבױרענע.

**A woman turned witch is worse
than a born one.**

*A gemakhte makhsheyfe iz erger vi
a geboyrene.* C

אַ קלײן װײַבעלע קען אױך האָבן אַ
גרױס מױל.

**A little woman can also have a big
mouth.**

*A kleyn vaybele ken oykh hobn a
groys moyl.* AC

אַ מײדל איז װי אַ זײַדן טיכל –
אַז עס װערט נאָר אַ פֿלעק קען מען
עס מיט זיבן זײפֿן ניט אױסװאַשן.

**A girl is like a silk cloth – if
there's a spot, seven soapings
won't wash it out.**

*A meydl iz vi a zaydn tikhl – az es
vert nor a flek ken men es mit zibn
zeyfn nit oysvashn.* NS

אַ מײדל איז װי סאַמעט – אַדרבא,
גיב אַ גלעט.

**A girl is like velvet – by all means,
caress her.**

*A meydl is vi samet – aderabe, gib a
glet.* NS

אַ שװענגערדיקע פֿרױ פֿאַרגלוסט
זיך עסן אױפֿגעפֿרישטע שנײ.

**A pregnant woman craves toasted
snow.**

*A shvengerdike froy farglust zikh esn
oyfgefrishte shney.* AC

אַלע װײַבער האָבן ירושה פֿון זײער
מוטער חוה.

All women are heirs to Mother Eve.

*Ale vayber hobn yerushe fun zeyer
muter khave.* AC

די פֿרױ האָט די יסורים און דער מאַן
מאַכט דעם ברית.

The wife suffers the labour pains
and the husband celebrates the bris.
*Di froy hot di yesirim un der man
makht dem bris.* NS

די צונג בײַ די ווײַבער איז אַזוי ווי אַ
שווערד און זיי גיבן אַכטונג אַז עס
זאָל ניט פֿאַרזשאַווערט ווערן.

Women's tongues are like swords
and they're careful not to let them
rust.
*Di tsung bay di vayber iz azoy vi a
shverd un zey gibn akhtung az es zol
nit farzhavert vern.* AC

גיי פֿאַרשטיי אַ מיידל – זי וואַרט
אויף דער חתונה און וויינט צו
דער חופה.

Try to understand a girl – she
yearns for the wedding and weeps
on her way to the bridal canopy.
*Gey farshtey a meydl – zi vart oyf
der khasene un veynt tsu der khupe.* NS

מען טאָר ניט גלייבן דעם פֿערד אין
וועג און דער ווײַב אין דער היים.

Don't trust a horse on the road or
a wife at home.
*Men tor nit gleybn dem ferd in veg
un der vayb in der heym.* IB

מיידלעך געדענקען דעם טאָג ווען
זיי זײַנען געבוירן און פֿאַרגעסן
דעם יאָר.

Girls remember the day of their
birth but forget the year.
*Meydlekh gedenken dem tog ven zey
zaynen geboyrn un fargesn dem yor.* AC

שטיף און לאַך און היט אָפּ די זאַך!

Laugh and jest but be careful is
best!
Shtif un lakh un hit op di zakh! NS

ווײַבער האָבן נײַן מאָס רייד.

Women have nine measures of
speech.
Vayber hobn nayn mos reyd. NS

וויינען און לאַכן זײַנען בײַ ווײַבער
לײַכטע זאַכן.

Laughing and crying come to
women without half trying.
*Veynen un lakhn zaynen bay vayber
laykhte zakhn.* NS

זי איז אַ ייִדענע מיט אַן אוירינגל.

She's a dame with an earring!
[formidable]
Zi iz a yidene mit an oyringl! P

– ווײַבער רעדן אַלע אין איינעם
זיי ווייסן פֿריִער אַז ס'איז ניטאָ
וואָס צו הערן.

Women all talk at the same time –
they know beforehand there's
nothing worth listening to.
*Vayber redn ale in eynem – zey
veysn fri'er az s'iz nito vos tsu hern.* NS

WORDS

אַ גוט וואָרט איז קאַראַנטער ווי אַ
נדבֿה.

A kind word is better than alms.
A gut vort iz karanter vi a nedove. NS

אַ גוטער אויסדרוק מאַכט אַ גוטן
אײַנדרוק.

A fitting expression makes a good
impression.
A guter oysdruk makht a gutn ayndruk.

אַ פּאַטש פֿאַרהיילט זיך, אַ וואָרט
געדענקט זיך.

A blow will heal but words you feel.
*A patsh farheylt zikh, a vort gedenkt
zikh.* NS

אַ פֿען שיסט ערגער פֿון אַ פֿײַל.

The pen is more deadly than an
arrow.
A pen shist erger fun a fayl. NS

אַ ווייך וואָרט ברעכט אַ ביין.

A gentle word can even break a bone
A veykh vort brekht a beyn. NS

אַן איבעריק וואָרט האָט קיין אָרט.

A superfluous word has no place.
[A superfluous word should not be heard.]
An iberik vort hot keyn ort. NS

פֿון אַ וואָרט ווערט אַ קוואָרט.

One word becomes a herd.
Fun a vort vert a kvort. NS

מאַך עס קײַלעכדיק און שפּיציק!

Make it round and to the point!
[Come to the point!]
Makh es kaylekhdik un shpitsik. AC

אַ װאָרט איז װי אַ פֿײַל – בײַדע | A word and an arrow are the
האָבן גרױסע אײַל. | same – both deliver with speedy
aim.
*A vort iz vi a fayl – beyde hobn
groyse ayl.* NS

װערטער זאָל מען װעגן און ניט צײלן. | Words should be weighed and not
counted.
Verter zol men vegn un nit tseyln. P

יעדעם װאָרט אױף זײַן אָרט. | Every word in its place.
Yedes vort oyf zayn ort. P

WORK

אַן אָפּגעשײלט אײ פֿאַלט אױך | Even a peeled egg doesn't fall into
ניט אַלײן אין מױל אַרײַן. | one's mouth all by itself.
*An opgesheylt ey falt oykh nit aleyn
in moyl arayn.* AC

אַרבעט איז קײן שאַנד. | Work is no disgrace.
Arbet iz keyn shand. NS

אַז מען לײגט אַרײַן נעמט מען אַרױס. | If you put in you can take out.
Az men leygt arayn nemt men aroys. P

די הענט ליגן ניט אין קימפּעט. | The hands are not busy with
childbirth alone.
Di hent lign nit in kimpet. AC

דינג דיר אַ משרת און טו עס דיר
אַליין.

Hire a servant and do it yourself.
Ding dir a meshores un tu es dir aleyn. AC

די שווערסטע מלאָכה איז ליידיק
צו גיין.

The hardest work is to be idle.
Di shverste melokhe iz leydik tsu geyn. P

גרינג קומט קיין זאַך ניט אָן.

Nothing comes easy.
Gring kumt keyn zakh nit on. P

מיט פֿרעמדע הענט איז גוט פֿײַער
צו שאַרן.

It's good to stoke the fire with someone else's hands.
Mit fremde hent iz gut fayer tsu sharn. P

רעד ווייניקער און טו מער!

Talk less and do more!
Red veyniker un tu mer! P

WORLD

אַ שיינע וועלט, אַ ליכטיקע וועלט,
נאָר ווי פֿאַר וועמען?

A beautiful world, a radiant world, but oh, for whom?
A sheyne velt, a likhtike velt, nor vi far vemen? NS

די גאַנצע וועלט איז נאָך ניט משוגע.

The entire world hasn't yet gone crazy.
Di gantse velt iz nokh nit meshuge. P

די וועלט איז אַ גרויסע און ס'איז
ניטאָ זיך ווו אַהינצוטאָן.

The world is huge and there's no
place to turn.
*Di velt iz a groyse un s'iz nito zikh
vu ahintsuton.* AC

די וועלט איז אַ קליינע, אַלע
באַגעגענען זיך.

The world is small and brings
together all.
*Di velt iz a kleyne, ale bagegenen
zikh.* NS

די וועלט איז אַ רעדל און עם דרייט
זיך.

The world is a wheel and it turns.
Di velt iz a redl un es dreyt zikh. NS

די וועלט רוקט זיך ביז זי ווערט
פֿאַררוקט.

The world goes, until it goes
crazy.
Di velt rukt zikh biz zi vert farukt. NS

„הבֿל הבֿלים", די גאַנצע וועלט
איז אַ חלום.

"Vanity of vanities," the whole
world is a dream.
*"Hevel hevolim," di gantse velt iz a
kholem.* NS

„עולם כמינהגו נוהג"– דעריבער זעט
טאַקע די וועלט אוים אַזוי.

"The world goes its usual way" –
that's why it looks the way it does.
*"Oylem keminhogoy noyheg" –
deriber zet take di velt oys azoy.* NS

YOUTH

שיינע מיידלך און געפגרטע
פיש האלטן ניט לאַנג.

**Pretty girls and dead fish don't
keep.**
*Sheyne meydlekh un gepeygerte fish
haltn nit lang.* AC

„שיכור ולא מיין" – אַזוי איז דער
מענטש ווען ער איז יונג.

**"Drunk but not from wine" – that
is a person in his youth.**
*"Shiker velo meyayin" – azoy iz der
mentsh ven er iz yung.* AC

וואָס די אַלטע קײַען טוען די יונגע
שפּײַען.

**What the old chew, the young
spew.**
*Vos di alte kayen tu'en di yunge
shpayen.* NS

וואָס מען מאַכט קאַליע אין דער יוגנט
קען מען אויף דער עלטער ניט
פֿאַרריכטן.

**What one spoils in youth cannot
be repaired by age.**
*Vos men makht kalye in der yugnt
ken men oyf der elter nit far'rikhtn.* NS

יונג בלוט טוט זעלטן גוט.

Young blood seldom does good.
Yung blut tut zeltn gut. NS

יונגע יאָרן, נאַרישע יאָרן.

Youthful years, foolish years.
Yunge yorn, narishe yarn. NS

GLOSSARY

Bagel A hard, doughnut-shaped roll, first boiled, then baked.

Bar Mitsvah Ceremony marking initiation of a Jewish male, at age thirteen, into the religious community.

Blintz Cheese, groats, or berries rolled in thin sheets of dough, then fried.

Borsht Soup, usually made of beets, cabbage, or sorrel, served hot or cold.

Bris The act and ceremony of circumcision performed on Jewish males on the eighth day of life.

Cantor Trained professional singer who assists in religious services by singing portions of the liturgy. He was subject to scrutiny and comment; his mistakes and gaffes were discussed and enlarged upon.

Challah The braided bread made of white flour, used for Sabbath and holidays.

Channukah Eight-day celebration commencing on 25th day of Kislev (November-December), commemorating victory of Judah Maccabee over Syrian king Antiochus, and subsequent rededication of Temple. Called the Festival of Lights.

Charoseth Mixture of ground nuts, apples, cinnamon, and wine on the Seder plate symbolizing mortar used in building the pyramids.

Chelm Name of a real town which folklore has immortalized as the home of amiable simpletons known as 'The Wise Men of Chelm.'

Cholent A hot dish, usually consisting of beans and meat, prepared on Friday and simmered overnight for the noonday Sabbath meal.

Chutspeh Boldness, effrontery, impudence, insolence, nerve, unmitigated gall.

Goy(im) (From the Hebrew, literally 'nation.') Gentile(s), non-Jew(s). Also refers to Jews ignorant of Jewish traditions and observances.

Haggadah The book of the Passover home service which, through narrative and song, recounts the tale of Jewish slavery in Egypt and the liberation. It is read the first two nights of Passover (one night in Israel).

Haman An official in the court of the King of Persia. An implacable enemy of the Jews whom he planned to exterminate. His plans were foiled by Mordechai and Queen Esther and he was subsequently hanged. The triumph of the Jews over their enemies is celebrated in the holiday of Purim.

Hassid(im) A follower of significant and extensive religious movement (Hassidism) founded in the eighteenth century in Eastern Europe, emphasizing ecstasy, mass enthusiasm, close-knit group cohesion, and charismatic leadership. At its height, this movement embraced nearly one half the Jews of Eastern Europe.

Hazzan(im) Trained professional singer(s) who assist(s) in religious services by singing portions of the liturgy (same as cantor).

Kohen, Kohanim A descendant of the priestly class, holding special status to this day. They are the first to be called to the reading of the Torah in the synagogue, they may not marry divorcees, and they are not allowed into the cemeteries except for the burial of closest kin.

Korakh A Jew who became Pharaoh's treasurer in Egypt. He amassed so much wealth that three hundred mules were required to carry the keys to his treasures. His pride in his wealth brought about his subsequent downfall.

Kosher Food that is fit for consumption according to Jewish dietary laws; also used to mean someone or something that is proper, suitable, and acceptable.

Latkehs Potato pancakes, traditionally served at Channukah.

Litvak(s) Jew(s) from Lithuania, traditionally thought of as being more reserved and scholarly than Jew(s) from other regions. Having a reputation for being dry and humorless.

Mamzer Bastard. Term often used affectionately to describe a clever, ingenious person.

Matzah Unleavened bread prescribed for all Passover meals to commemorate the bread eaten by the Children of Israel during the Exodus from Egypt.

Mazel-tov Congratulations! (Literally, good luck!)

Megillah Scroll. Chiefly, the Book of Esther, read aloud in the synagogue on Purim.

Mezuzah A rolled piece of parchment, containing Biblical quotations, encased in a small box and affixed to the doorposts of Jewish homes and synagogues.

Minyan Quorum of ten adult males, the minimum requirement for synagogue services.

Mordechai Consultant to the Queen of Persia. Together with Queen Esther, he was instrumental in averting the extermination of the Jewish People, as planned by Haman.

Passover The eight-day festival commencing the 15th day of Nisan (March-April), which commemorates the deliverance of the Jews from Egyptian bondage.

Purim Celebrates the Feast of Lots in memory of the triumph over Haman, who had selected the 14th day of Adar (March) for the extermination of the Jewish People. It is a holiday noted for its gaiety, masquerades, and festive meal.

Rabbi Religious leader of the Jewish community.

Rashi The great commentator of the Bible and Talmud (1040–1105) whose notes traditionally accompanied the text.

Rosh Hashanah The Jewish New Year, celebrated the first and second days of Tishrei (September-October). Together with Yom Kippur, considered the most solemn days of the Jewish year.

Seder Home service observed on the first two nights of Passover (one night in Israel), when the Haggadah is recited.

Shalom Literally, peace. Also a man's name.

Shalom Aleichem Peace to you! Greeting to which the response is the reverse: aleichem sholem.

Shevuoth Feast of Weeks, celebrated on the 6th and 7th days of Sivan (May-June), seven weeks after Passover. Commemorates the giving of the Torah to Moses on Mount Sinai.

Shiveh Observance of seven days of intensive mourning after the death of close kin (parent, spouse, child, sibling).

Shlemiel An incompetent, inept person; a clumsy bungler.

Shlimazl A consistently luckless person.

Shofar Ram's horn, blown several times during the Rosh Hashanah service and once at the conclusion of Yom Kippur.

Shtetl Jewish small-town community of Eastern Europe.

Simkhat Torah Holiday marking completion and renewal of annual cycle of reading the Torah in the synagogue. It is marked by singing, dancing, and levity. A drink of liquor after reading a portion is usual if not obligatory.

Succah Wooden hut or booth with thatched roof used for the observance of the Succoth holiday.

Succoth The Feast of Tabernacles; eight-day celebration commencing the

15th day of Tishrei (October). It commemorates the Jews' having lived in huts or booths during their wanderings in the desert.

Talmud The body of written Jewish law and tradition.

Tisheh B'av The 9th day of the month of Av. Fast day commemorating the final destruction of the Temple in the year 70.

Torah The five books of Moses, often used as a synonym for the whole complex of Jewish learning.

Treyf(eh) Forbidden, unfit according to Jewish dietary laws.

Yom Kippur The Day of Atonement. The holiest, most solemn day in the Jewish year. A fast day spent in prayer, atonement, and confession of sins by the individual in direct communion with God. Takes place on the 10th day of Tishrei (September-October), eight days after Rosh Hashanah.

BIBLIOGRAPHY

YIDDISH

Bal Makhshoves *Geklibene shriftn*. Vilna, 1910

Bernstein, Ignaz *Yidishe shprikhverter un redensarten*. 2nd edition. Warsaw, 1908

Dubnow, Shimon *Yidishe geshikhte*. Farlag Shklarski, New York, 1941

Furman, Israel *Yidishe shprikhverter un redensarten*. Hamenoreh Press, Tel Aviv, 1968

Katz, Sholem *Fun folks moyl*. Farlag 'Toronto,' Toronto, 1940

Miller, Sholem *Funem yidishn kval*. Farlag 'Dos yidishe vort,' Winnipeg, 1937

Olsvanger, Immanuel *Royte Pomerantsen*. Schocken Books, New York, 1965 (transcription)

Shtutshkof, Nokhem *Der oytser fun der yidisher shprakh*. Yiddish Scientific Institute-YIVO, New York, 1950

Steinberg, Israel *Khokhme fun yidishn kval*. Tel Aviv, 1962

Yehoash-Spivak *Verterbukh*, New York, 1911

ENGLISH

Alcalay, Reuben *The Complete Hebrew-English Dictionary*. Masada Publishing, Tel Aviv, 1970

- *Words of the Wise*. Anthology of Proverbs and Practical Axioms. Massada Press, Jerusalem, 1973

Ausubel, Nathan, ed. *A Treasury of Jewish Folklore*. Crown Publishers, New York, 1948

- *A Treasury of Jewish Humour*. Doubleday and Company, New York, 1951

Avidan, Moshe 'Poland.' Pages 790-89 in *Encyclopedia Judaica*, vol. 13. Macmillan Company, New York, 1972

Ayalti, Hanan J., ed. *Yiddish Proverbs*. Schocken Books, New York, 1963

Baron, Joseph L. *A Treasury of Jewish Quotations*. Crown Publishers, New York, 1956

Baron, Salo *Modern Nationalism and Religion*. Meridian Books, New York 1960

Birnbaum, Solomon A. *Yiddish – A Survey and Grammar.* University of Toronto Press, Toronto and Buffalo, 1979

Dubnow, Simon *Nationalism and History.* Meridian Books, New York, 1961

Feinsilver, Lillian Mermin *The Taste of Yiddish.* A.S. Barnes and Company, New York, 1980

Harkavy, Aleksander *English-Yiddish, Yiddish-English Dictionary. Hebrew Publishing Company, New York,* 1898

Heschel, Abraham Joshua *The Earth is the Lord's.* Farrar, Straus, Giroux, New York, 1978

Howe, Irving and Greenberg, Eliezer, eds. *A Treasury of Yiddish Stories,* 'Introduction,' pages 1-71. Viking Press, New York, 1954

Kogos, Fred *1001 Yiddish Proverbs.* Castle Books, New York, 1970

Noy, Dov 'Folklore.' Pages 1374-1410 in *Encyclopedia Judaica,* vol. 6. Macmillan Company, New York, 1972

Rosenbaum, Samuel *A Yiddish Word Book for English-Speaking People.* Van Nostrand Reinhold Company, New York, 1978.

Roskies, Diane K., and David G. *The Shtetl Book.* Ktav Publishing House, USA, 1975

Rosten, Leo *Treasury of Jewish Quotations.* McGraw Hill, New York, 1972

– *The Joys of Yiddish.* McGraw Hill, New York, 1968

Rubin, Ruth *Voices of a People.* Thomas Yoseloff, New York, 1963

Samuel, Maurice *In Praise of Yiddish.* Cowles Book Company, New York, 1971

Silverman-Weinreich, Beatrice 'Towards a Structural Analysis of Yiddish Proverbs.' Pages 1-20 in *YIVO Annual XVII,* New York, 1978

Shmeruk, Chone *Yiddish Literature.'* Pages 798-833 in *Encyclopedia Judaica,* vol. 16. Macmillan Company, New York, 1972

Shwartzbaum, Chaim *Studies in Jewish and World Folklore.* Berlin, 1968, Pages 417-24.

Weinreich, Max *History of the Yiddish Language.* University of Chicago Press, Chicago, 1980

Weinreich, Uriel *College Yiddish.* Yiddish Scientific Institute-YIVO, New York, 1949

– *Modern English-Yiddish, Yiddish English Dictionary.* YIVO Institute for Jewish Research, McGraw Hill Book Company, New York, 1968

– 'Yiddish Language.' Pages 790-8 in *Encyclopedia Judaica,* vol. 16. Macmillan Company, New York, 1972

Weltman and Zukerman *Yiddish Sayings Mama Never Taught You.* Perivale Press, California, 1975

Zborowski, Mark and Herzog, Elizabeth *Life Is with People.* International Universities Press, New York, 1952

HEBREW

Even-Shoshan, Avraham *Hamilon Hekhadash.* Kiryat Sefer, Jerusalem. 1969.